Korean Traditional
Landscape Architecture

Korean Traditional Landscape Architecture

The Korean Institute of Traditional Landscape Architecture

 Hollym

Korean Traditional Landscape Architecture

by The Korean Institute of Traditional Landscape Architecture

The Korea Foundation has provided financial assistance
for the undertaking of this publication project.

First published in 2007
Third printing, 2015
by Hollym International Corp., USA
Phone 908 353 1655   **Fax** 908 353 0255
http://www.hollym.com   **e-Mail** contact@hollym.com

 Hollym

Published simultaneously in Korea
by Hollym Corp., Publishers, Seoul, Korea
Phone +82 2 734 5087   **Fax** +82 2 730 5149
http://www.hollym.co.kr   **e-Mail** info@hollym.co.kr

ISBN: 978-1-56591-252-6
Library of Congress Catalog Card Number: 2007940527

Printed in Korea

Preface and Acknowledgements

Often referred to as the Land of the Morning Calm, Korea, a nation with a 5,000-year-old history, boasts its own unique garden culture, along with other traditional developments, such as Hangeul (Korean writing system), *hanbok* (Korean traditional clothing), *hanok* (Korean traditional houses), and *hansik* (Korean food). Unfortunately, these developments have been largely unknown in the world.

There is also evidence that Korea, a small country in East Asia, has been observed closely in the past by certain foreign intellectuals. Rabindranath Tagore (1861-1941), an Indian poet and thinker who received the Nobel Prize in 1913, gave high praise to Korea during a trip to Japan, in his poem, "The Lamp of the East."

In the golden age of Asia

Korea was one of its lamp-bearers

And that lamp is waiting to be lighted once again

For illumination in the East.

The renowned German philosopher Martin Heidegger (1889-1976) also claimed that Korea was the source of Eastern civilization, and said that he most respected Korea, the suzerain state of Eastern thought. In particular, he credited the "Dangun state" with peacefully ruling Asia for over two thousand years. Virgil Gheorghiu (1916-1992), the Romanian writer of *The 25th Hour*, also wrote: "In the *25th Hour*, I said that the light comes from the East and that place is Korea. The spirit that can save humankind is that of *hongik ingan* and *ihwa segye* (widely benefiting all of humanity and righteously governing the world)."

Though Korea and Koreans are a proud country and people, they are still largely unknown in the world. It is the task of contemporary scholars to make Korea better known to the world, based on the country's strong economy. Though bookshops in other countries frequently carry a number of books on China and Japan, including books on gardens or traditional landscape architecture, the sad reality is that virtually nothing has been published in regards to the culture of Korean traditional landscape architecture or Korean gardens.

When I served as the president (2004-2005) of the Korean Institute of Traditional Landscape Architecture (KITLA), which was founded in December 1980 with an aim to preserve and develop the traditional landscape architecture of Korea, I promised to publish this book in various languages in order to make traditional landscape architecture known to the world. At long last, I am finally able to publish this book in English, along with the Chinese and Japanese versions. At the same time, books on traditional Chinese and Japanese landscape architecture have been translated into Korean, making comparative studies possible.

Though it is a small accomplishment, I would like to acknowledge all the help I have received. I would first like to thank the authors who took the time to write the articles despite their busy schedules, Kang Choong-seo who traveled up and down the country to take the photographs that were included in this volume, and our financial supporters in the landscape architecture industry who provided help despite the difficult circumstances, especially Lee

Kwang-sung (CEO, Ahsan Landscape Architecture), Jeong Jong-hyun (CEO, Shinhan Green Tech), Lee Young-bok (CEO, Youngsan Landscaping Co.), and Yoon Jung-seo (CEO, Taesung Afforestation Industry). I would also like to thank the Korea Foundation, which supports the publication of books on Korea in order to promote Korean culture overseas, Park Chan-soo of Hollym Corporation, who manages the publication of this book, Park Sang-yeon and Yi Jeong-hyeon for translation, and Sora Kim-Russell for proofreading.

Finally, I would like to extend my thanks to Dr. Roh Song-ho (SH Corporation), Secretary-General of KITLA, and Secretary Kim Soo-jin (Ph.D Candidate, Korea University) at the Institute for taking care of all the difficulties related to the publication. I sincerely hope that this small book will act as an impetus to introduce the culture of Korean traditional landscape architecture to the world. I also hope that with active publication of more specialty books in each field, the entire world will be able to share in Korean culture and that we will be able to do our part towards improving the quality of human life everywhere.

December, 2007

Sim Woo-kyung
Editor-in-chief / Coauthor

Contents

Chapter 1

Background of Korean Traditional Landscape Architecture

I. Introduction

Traditional culture is the result of human wisdom accumulated over years of countless trial and error. It is therefore the most familiar, natural, and comfortable culture for a given group of people. Traditional landscape architecture in particular is valuable as it is a unique record of an era and place, a comprehensive rather than partial expression of culture, and a vessel that contains various elements of traditional cultures, including clothing, food and housing.

Traditional landscape architecture is all the more important as it embodies people's definitions of utopia, and because the philosophy and symbolism of a particular ethnic group are embedded within it. Also, it is valuable as it has both direct and indirect influence on people's minds and bodies. With the advent of the 21st century, "biodiversity" and "cultural diversity" have emerged as important issues around the world, and the key to solving them can be found in traditional landscape architecture, which has been developing in each country. The traditional landscape architecture of a given country is a culmination of influences from the natural environment, religious thought, the spirit of the time, and national identity. Therefore, it has a very distinct identity and has developed uniquely in each country. In the modern era, however, due to the indiscriminate spread of the powerful Western cultures, the cultures of the world are becoming more and more uniform.

This chapter will look at the background and characteristics of Korean traditional landscape architecture by examining the natural environment and the philosophical background that greatly influenced its development.

II. Background of the Natural Environment

The traditional culture of each country reflects the wisdom of adapting to nature and varies based on the unique development of each region. Traditional landscape architecture can be classified broadly into Western and Eastern. Within these broad sets of influences, each country developed its own traditional style based on its natural environment, religion, Zeitgeist, and national identity.

1. Location and Topography

The Korean peninsula is located between 34 and 43 degrees north latitude and between 124 and 133 degrees east longitude. It has an area of 220,000km and a length of 737km. Approximately 65 percent of its territory is mountainous, with higher peaks in the north than in the south. With Mt. Baekdusan (2,794m above sea level) at the apex, 13 mountain ranges form the skeletal structure of the peninsula. The average altitude reaches 482m, which is higher by 300m than in Europe but lower than the average altitude of 825m of the Earth. These mountain ranges include Baekdudaegan, which extends from Mt. Baekdusan in the north, to Mt. Taebaeksan, and Mt. Jirisan in the south.

Regarding the coastline, the east coast is rugged and sharp as it borders on Baekdudaegan and has few scenic features. In contrast, the south and west coast have low mountains and a strongly indented coastline. They contain much beautiful scenery, including many small islands, and are mostly protected as national parks.

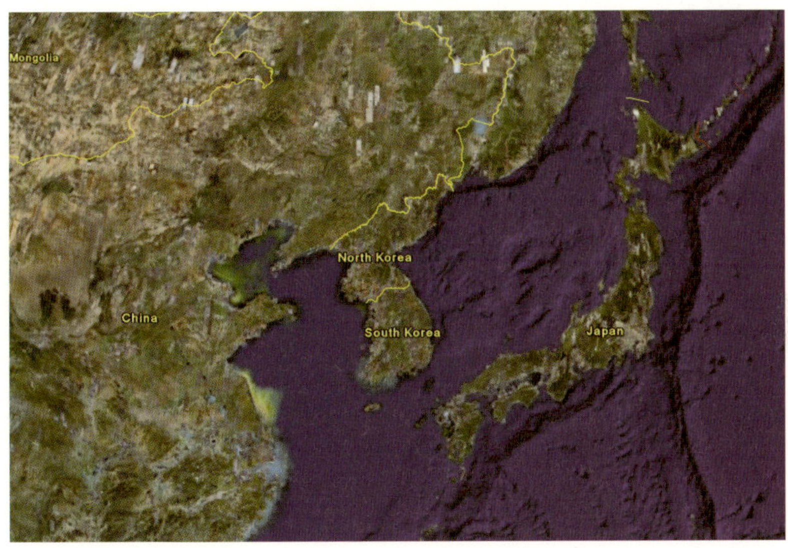

Figure 1. Satellite-view of Korea (Source: Google Earth)

2. Climate

Apart from the central mountainous regions, the average annual temperature is 10-16℃. The hottest month of August rises to 23-27℃, while May measures 16-19℃ and October 11-19℃. January, the coldest month, drops to between -6 and -7℃. The annual rainfall in the central region is recorded at 1,100-1,400mm, the southern region at 1,000-1,800mm, and the Jeju area at 1,450-1,850mm, with 50 to 60 percent of rain falling in summer. Northwest winds in winter and southwest winds in summer are strong and frequent. Wind systems are distinct each season: Though September and October have relatively weak winds, coastal regions are much influenced by the sea breeze. Humidity is high in July and August at 80 percent throughout the country, falling to approximately 70 percent in September and October. The rainy season begins in Jeju region from the second half of mid-June and gradually reaches the central region in the first half of late June, lasting about 30 days. Approximately 28 typhoons occur in the western North Pacific of which two or three directly or indirectly influence Korea.

Geographically, Korea is located within the middle latitude temperate zone and has four distinct seasons. Winter is cold and dry due to the continental high pressure system, while summer is influenced by the North Pacific high pressure system that brings high temperatures and humidity. Spring and autumn have mostly clear and dry days due to migratory anticyclone activity.

3. Vegetation and Animal Life

Korea has very diverse natural vegetation. Coniferous forests are developed in the areas between 1,500 and 2,500m above sea level in the north, and a combination of coniferous and broadleaf forests are found in some regions in the north and in central areas. Deciduous broadleaf trees, which represent Korea's natural forest vegetation, are distributed mostly in the central region. Evergreen broadleaf forests grow in the south and along the east and west coast, Carpinus laxiflora are found on the slopes of granite and granite gneiss mountain valleys, and evergreen forests of warm temperate zones grow in the extreme south and in the southern archipelago. There are 4,577 species, which include 201 families, 1,102 genera and 3,347 species, of vegetation that are currently growing in Korea. Compared to 1,500 species in Denmark and 2,000 in Great Britain, the amount of vegetation is quite high in Korea.

Diverse animal species also inhabit the Korean peninsula with 1,463 species of vertebrates, 905 species of fish, 41 species of amphibian and reptile, 417 species of birds, 100 species of mammals and 11,853 species of insects.

4. Landscape

A peninsula with both a continental and marine climate, Korea's main landscape is formed by mountains high and low. Clear water flows in abundance in the valleys and four distinct seasons help create a beautiful landscape that merits the expression *geumsu gangsan*, "a land of picturesque rivers and mountains as if embroidered on silk."

Poet Jo Ji-hun (1920-1968) summarized Korea's natural environment as follows: First, its geographical location in the east of the eastern hemisphere as a peninsula protruding from the Asian continent with various islands allows both a continental and oceanic climate. Therefore, "the bright and lovely island scenery and calm and solitary continental scenery are well matched, and the marine environment is beautiful." Second, though it is located in a temperate zone according to its latitude, subtropical, warm and cold zones alternate to create the cycle of four distinct seasons. Therefore, Korea's climate is characterized as both mild and bracing. Third, the cold and warm currents along the coast support abundant marine resources, the land is rich in mineral resources, and the soil is also of good quality. With the addition of appropriate rainfall, Korea is also favorable from a zoological perspective.

In this context, the ancestors of Korea, with an over 5,000-year-long history of landscape architecture, chose to adapt to nature and were satisfied with

Figure 2. Korean landscape, called *geumsu gangsan*

Figure 3. Beautiful Korean landscape, Dodam Sambong

Figure 4. Borrowing the scenery of distant mountains

enjoying the surrounding scenery by building simple pavilions in natural locations or borrowing the mountain scenery within their gardens. The reason a more elaborate visual landscape architecture was not developed may be because they avoided artificial landscape architecture as much as possible.

III. Philosophical and Religious Background

The main influences on different styles of traditional landscape architecture are views of nature and the pursuit of the ideal world. Views of nature are generally formed under religious influences, while the pursuit of the ideal world is greatly influenced by the natural environment. Fundamentally, however, both elements originate from the natural environment. Western landscape architecture is characterized by a geometric approach centering on human beings and mastery of nature. The desire for an environment that supports survival with ample shade, water, grain, and trees formed the basis of the physical landscape architecture. On the other hand, Eastern landscape architecture developed based on metaphysics, including the desire for harmony

Figure 5. Village guardian tree

Figure 6. Ritual offering to the village guardian deity

with nature, worship of nature, and the quest for eternal youth. These different approaches to landscape architecture developed according to the differing ideologies in each part of the world.

Though one cannot deny the influence the foreign religions of Confucianism, Buddhism and Taoism had on Korean traditional culture, one should not disregard the influence indigenous beliefs and views of nature had on Korean tradition before the transmission of foreign religions. Despite the fact that indigenous beliefs were themselves trivialized or ignored, as they were not systematized or organized, it is evident that they were deeply influential as a form of grassroots culture. The true aspect of a country's traditional culture can only be understood when the deepest layers of its philosophical system are recognized.

1. Dangun Myth

Many nations have foundation myths that confirm their identities and form a sense of shared belonging for their people. Myth is regarded as the prototype of human discovery, including politics, society, science, literature and history. In order to understand the roots of the Korean people, it is necessary to examine the fundamental, indigenous elements of Korean culture, rather than only foreign elements, such as Confucianism, Buddhism and Taoism. In other words, understanding and analyzing Korea's ancient and mythical elements should take precedence over other endeavors. According to the foundation myth of Korea, Hwanin, "the Lord of Heaven," put his many sons in charge of governing the stars. He then gave Three Heavenly Treasures (*cheonbuin*) to Hwanung, the son of Hwanin, who sought to govern the human world. Hwanung thus descended with three thousand followers to a spot under the tree by the Holy Altar at the top of Mt. Taebaeksan, and he called this place Sinsi, or "City of God." Among the three thousand followers were included the Earl of Wind (*pungbaek*), the Master of Rain (*usa*), and the Master of Clouds (*unsa*). He took charge of some three hundred and sixty areas of responsibility, including agriculture, life expectancy, illness, and good and evil in order to found a country that would widely benefit all of humanity and righteously govern the world.

Here, a bear and a tiger came to ask Hwanung to turn them into human beings. Hwanung told them the conditions they would have to meet. When the bear overcame the ordeal and became a woman, Hwanung transformed into a human and fathered a child with the bear-woman. This boy became Dangun Wanggeom, the founder of Old Joseon.

In other words, by understanding Dangun, the founder of the Korean people, as a man-god and by establishing his importance, the Korean people determined their own identity as a union of human and divine. Based on this legend, Koreans have taken pride in their identity as the descendents of Heaven.

There are many examples in Western literature that mention the Dangun myth. Constant Virgil Gheorghiu (1916-1992), the Romanian writer of *The 25th Hour*, said: 'I said that the light comes from the East in the *25th Hour*, and that place is Korea. The spirit that can save humankind is that of "widely benefiting all of humanity and righteously governing the world" (*hongik ingan* and *ihwa segye*) of Korea.' In *La Presse Française* (April 18, 1986), he went on to say, "*Hongik ingan*, the ruling ideology of Dangun, is the most powerful philosophy and the most perfect law in the world." The renowned German philosopher Martin Heidegger (1889-1976) also mentioned that the basis of his philosophical thought was the Eastern concept of shamanism, that the origin of the Eastern civilization is Korea, and that he most respected Korea, the suzerain state of Eastern thought. He credited the "Dangun state" with peacefully ruling Asia for over two thousand years, and studied *Cheonbugyeong*, Korea's ancient scripture.

Rabindranath Tagore (1861-1941), an Indian poet and thinker who received the Nobel Literary Prize in 1913, also praised Korea in his article, "The Lamp of the East," published in the *DongA Ilbo* on April 2, 1929: "In the golden age of Asia / Korea was one of its lamp-bearers / And that lamp is waiting to be lighted once again / For illumination in the East." It cannot be a coincidence that these thinkers, who never even visited Korea, all praised it so highly.

2. Indigenous Beliefs

In the early stages of human history, human beings were in awe of nature and maintained organic relationship with it. Indigenous Korean beliefs include a variety of deities, such as earth god, water god, wood god, Maitreya, and tutelary deities. These deities were believed to give blessings and chase away misfortune.

Household beliefs include *jowangsin* (kitchen god), *seongjusin* (god of the hearth, who represents all house deities), *cheukgansin* (toilet god), *soeguyeongsin* (god of the stable), *josangsin* (family ancestors), *umulsin* (god of the well), and *chilseongsin* (god of the seven stars, who controls the fortune of humans), to name a few. Koreans have lived with these various household deities while wishing for the peace and welfare of the family.

On the other hand, village beliefs that wish for the prosperity and peace of the community have been transmitted in more diverse natures, functions, and types than household beliefs. As the fundamental belief system of the Korean people, village beliefs have maintained the worldview of the "unity of God and humans" through the heavenly god, mountain spirit, earth mother, god of grains, founder spirits, and the spirits of the deceased. Overcoming the hardships of reality and human limits, villagers tried to understand and affirm the realization of a new and abundant life from a spiritual perspective.

Village beliefs are like a mirror that reflects the image of our past and our present. Sincere prayers for others' blessings, humility before the divine, acceptance of human existence, and the earnest yearning to solve the difficulties of the invisible world together are clearly displayed in village beliefs.

Figure 7. Performance of farmer's music after the ritual for the village guardian deity

Figure 8. Making prayers to the sacred tree

There are many examples of village beliefs: village shrines for guardian dieties on the east coast; genital worship, including *sugumagi* and *golmaegi* that are built following *fengshui* (K.: *pungsu*) principles and the *bibo* method to complement deficient elements; a shrine for the sacred horse ridden by the mountain spirit or village guardian deity; a stone pagoda (pointed pagodas are called *doltap* while rounded ones are called *dolmudeom*) or rock that is worshipped as a sacred object; the worship of a deified person; *sotdae*, a pole with a wooden bird or stone pillar erected at the village entrance during a village rite calling for peace, protection, and a bountiful harvest; *jangseung*, tutelary posts that chase away evil spirits and protect the village from misfortune; a sacred tree spirit regarded as the origin of the village beliefs; and a mountain spirit. They have been passed down through the generations and established as a grassroots culture in Korea. In Korean folk belief, shamanism, animism and totemism have combined to produce a pantheistic culture.

3. Mountain Spirit Belief

As Korea is a mountainous country, belief in a mountain spirit is still largely maintained along with mountain worship. In particular, the mountain spirit is venerated in relation to Dangun, the founder of Korea, with the belief that Dangun went into Asadal at the age of 1908 and became a mountain spirit. Also, Korean Buddhism absorbed this belief in a mountain spirit, making it even more actively revered.

Presently, it is estimated that there are approximately 3,000 large and small Buddhist temples in Korea. Ninety-five percent of these temples have either a mountain spirit shrine or a Buddhist painting of a mountain spirit. This amounts to approximately 2,400 paintings of the mountain spirit. There are two reasons why mountain spirits, which are unrelated to Buddhism, are worshipped in temples.

First, Buddhist temples were built in the same locations where indigenous worship of the mountain spirit had taken place, incorporating the mountain spirit into Buddhism. Second, the construction of Sansingak (Mountain Spirit Shrine) on the most auspicious site within the temple grounds reflected the monks' wish to receive the help of the mountain spirit in their training.

Though the mountain spirit is generally categorized as a shamanic spirit, shamanism in Korea is but one of many religious traditions that have developed in relation to the mountain spirit. Therefore, the existence of the mountain spirit can be seen as partially independent from all religious traditions.

Figure 9. Mountain Spirit Shrine

4. Seondo or Pungnyudo

The primitive religion in Korea was Seondo (仙道). As this religion became deeply rooted in people's minds, Odumido (early name of Taoism) was welcomed and embraced even following the introduction of Confucianism and Buddhism from China. This phenomenon is well described in the preface of the *Nallangbi* (Inscription on the Monument of Knight Nan) written by Choe Chi-won (857-?), a scholar from the Unified Silla era:

> "There is a profound and mysterious Way in the country, called *pungnyu*. The origin of *pungnyu* is detailed in *Seonsa*. It embraces the three teachings [Confucianism, Buddhism and Taoism] and enlightens people. Confucius of Lu Dynasty taught that one should be filial to one's parents and loyal to one's sovereign; Laozi of Zhou Dynasty believed that one should practice non-action and conduct wordless teaching; and it is the teaching of Sakyamuni of India that one should avoid evil and do good deeds."

As such, the Korean traditional Way (*do*) was called *pungnyu,* and the national Way that was sublimated into the *hwarang* system was Pungnyudo, which included the tenets of the three religions, namely Confucianism, Buddhism and Taoism. The aim was to enlighten all people and teach them to be respected and true human beings.

The term *pungnyu* means "the flow of the wind" or "the flow of *gi*" (Ch.: *qi* 氣, life force or energy). Pungnyudo signifies enjoying this flow of *gi*, while Pungnyuseondo means attaining truth by grasping the flow of *gi* and becoming a *sinseon,* or immortal. Therefore, the spirit of Pungnyuseondo has been flowing within Korean culture for thousands of years.

The training process of *hwarang* explains most clearly the religious meaning of *pungnyu*. For example, enjoying the mountains and rivers is not simply about enjoying nature but about having a religious interaction with spirits in nature. The word *pung* (風, wind) also means "spirits" in the Chinese classics.

Practicing traditional *pungnyu* and capturing the flow of *gi* while praising love and dancing for joy is called Pungnyuseondo. This is mentioned in the "Biographies of the Eastern Barbarians" in *Houhanshu* (Book of Later Han Dynasty) as follows: 'Dongi tribes who live in eastern areas were native people who enjoyed drinking, singing and dancing. They sometimes wore ceremonial dresses, hats and silk clothing, and used ritual vessels in everyday life. There was a saying, "When the Middle Kingdom [China] has lost the rites, seek them among the Four Barbarians."' In the chapter on Buyeo, it is also recorded that "In eating and drinking they all use ritual vessels. In their meetings they make ceremonial toasts and wash the goblets. Bowing and deferring, they ascend and descend. They sacrifice to heaven using the correct month, the twelfth lunar month. When there is a great assembly in the state, they eat and drink, dance and sing for days on end. Such occasions are called *yeonggo*. At this time, they decide criminal cases and release prisoners. In the event of military action, they also offer sacrifices to heaven. They kill an ox and read its hoof to divine good or bad fortune. The singing and humming of the people passing in the streets continued day and night."

According to the chapter "Wangzhi" of *Liji* (Book of Rites), the East is called *i* (夷), which means "the root that forms the base." That is, all things are rooted in the earth. As the people were gentle in nature, it was called "the country of

Figure 10. Pavilions, a place for enjoying *pungnyu* (Uisangdae)

Figure 11. Culture of spirited play

gentlemen that was easy to govern with law" or "the country that never dies." In other words, it was a country of immortals. In *Shanhaijing* (The Classic of Mountains and Rivers), it is said that "in the country of gentlemen, people are fully dressed and wear knives. They hunt and eat animals and keep two tigers on their side." This latter image probably refers to the tigers that are always depicted sitting next to the mountain spirit in paintings.

5. Immortality and Taoist Thought

The first record on *sinseon* (神仙) appears in Chinese *Shiji* (The Records of the Grand Historian) written by Sima Qian (c. 145-90 BC) where it is stated, "From the times of Emperor Wei of the Qi Dynasty and Emperor Zhao of the Yan Dynasty, people were sent to the sea, and as a result, Penglaishan, Fangzhangshan and Yingzhoushan were found. These three divine mountains for immortals to live are said to belong to Bohai [Balhae]… Various immortals and the elixir of life are all here." In this document, *sinseon* are described as immortals or divine human beings who live in the three divine mountains. Qin Shi Huang, the first emperor of Qin Dynasty, searched for immortals to try to achieve eternal life, believing that they lived forever and possessed the elixir of life.

The Taoist ideology of the pursuit of immortality, or *sinseon sasang*, is generally accepted as having originated in China around the emergence of full-scale Taoism, a combination of indigenous Chinese religion and Laozi's Taoism. The *Samguk sagi* (Historical Record of the Three Kingdoms) then records that Chinese Taoism was first introduced to Korea in the 7th year of King Yeongnyu's reign (624) of Goguryeo. However, a mural painting found in

Goguryeo tombs, built two to three centuries earlier, suggests an already elaborate form of *sinseon*. This implies that Taoism was either introduced to Korea long before the official records were created, or as parts of Balhae Bay, the origin of Taoism, were competing against Old Joseon politically and culturally around 300-400 BC, it is possible that Korean Taoism developed spontaneously in Korea, on a parallel with China.

Also, the Gilt-bronze Incense Burner of Baekje (Korean National Treasure No. 287) found inside the tomb in Neungsan-ri, Buyeo-gun in 1993 was created in the early 7th century based on the ideology of immortality. Roof tiles with landscape and phoenix patterns (Treasure No. 343) found at the temple site at Oe-ri, Gyuam-myeon, Buyeo-gun also clearly express the world of immortals. These examples show that ideology of immortality was widely spread in Korea even before Taoism was introduced.

The first record of the use of *sinseon* in Korean landscape architecture can be found in An Jeong-bok's *Dongsa gangmok* (Annotated Account of Korean History): In the 35th year of King Mu's reign (634), "a pond was dug in the south of the palace and water was drawn in from twenty or so *li* away. Willow trees were planted around the pond, and an island that resembled Mt. Bangjangsan (Ch.: Penglaishan), where immortals were said to live, was built at the center of the pond." The exact location of this pond is debatable but is thought to be Gungnamji of Buyeo City, Chungcheongnam-do.

The ideology of immortality was used as a primary motif at Anapji in Gyeongju City, Gyeongsangbuk-do, where three divine mountains were constructed at the center of the pond. The Chinese mountain Wushan with twelve peaks, known in Taoism as a world of immortals, was also constructed, clearly reflecting the desire for the world of immortals. The Gwanghallu garden at Namwon City, Jeollabuk-do also expresses realistic aspects of the world of immortals. Though Confucianism was the national religion during Joseon Dynasty, many of the gardens belonging to noble families as well as palace gardens reflected the ideology of immortality, confirming its status as an important basis of traditional landscape architecture in Korea.

Laozi, the founder of Taoism, wrote his most famous work, the *Daodejing*. The book is a short text of around 5,000 Chinese characters in 81 chapters or sections, of which 37 are called "Daojing" and 44 are "Dejing." Despite its small size, it is the most influential book in Chinese and Asian culture. Based on the concept of *wuwei*, or non-action, Laozi suggests in the Chapter 25 that "Humans are modeled on the earth. The earth is modeled on heaven. Heaven is

Figure 12. Landscape architecture that dreams of the world of immortals (Myeongokheon)

modeled on the *tao*. The *tao* is modeled on nature." In other words, he saw that it was most ideal for human beings to follow the law of nature, and though landscapes were created by men, it was best to make it look as though they were created by nature itself. In Chapter 8, the comparison of the *tao* to the humility of water, which benefits all things in the universe but always stays at a lower place, directly contributed to the use of water in traditional landscape architecture.

6. *Fengshui* Theory

Fengshui (K.: *pungsu*), or traditional geomancy, is undoubtedly one of the most fundamental concepts that form the root of Korean culture. In a mountainous country such as Korea, mountains have been highly revered. When choosing auspicious sites, *fengshui* was used, and its techniques were thus developed and passed on to today. Rather than evaluating it as merely a perspective on geography that is unique to the East, the idea of *fengshui* should be regarded as an ancient science used by all human beings who sought to live in harmony with nature. In the West, where religion is predominantly monotheistic and a climate of scientific rationality developed, geomancy was denounced as unscientific and was thus discarded. However, recent excavations have shown that geomancy was used when choosing sites of importance in the West before the time of Christ, which confirmed the universal idea of nature. In the East, Confucianism, Buddhism, Taoism and indigenous beliefs embraced the idea of *fengshui*, and integrated the idea of *yin* and *yang*, the Five Elements, and the traditional concept of the four deities who guard the four directions.

Continuous theoretical research, publications, and influential practices by professional geomancers formed a layer of traditional culture.

Though Doseon (827-898), a Seon (Zen) monk at the end of Silla, is known as the founder of Korean traditional geomancy, it is clear that the concept of *fengshui* had already spread through the Korean peninsula before his time. Thus, *fengshui* can be considered a traditional geographical science, and Seon monks must have used it as a means to enlighten the people. Doseon's theories on territory and space can be called *biboseol*, which is a theory of preparing an auspicious site by making up for lacking elements and minimizing strong elements. He invented *bibo satapseol*, a method of supplementing geographical energies through the building of Buddhist pagodas on particular sites. The *bibo* theory dominated some five hundred years of Goryeo Dynasty and greatly influenced the Joseon Dynasty as a principle of location and arrangement in geographical landscapes.

In the Goryeo era, Buddhism, *fengshui* theory, and *docham* theory which was used to predict the fortune of a nation or an individual, were the main ideologies that led society. In "Ten Injunctions," King Taejo defined the concept of *fengshui*. Based on Doseon's *bibo* theory, the Sancheon Bibo Dogam office was established in the first year of King Sinjong's reign (1197). In terms of how *bibo* theory was applied in Korea, earthen mounds, stone tombs, and groves were used to complement the energy of the earth. This is still found in a number of villages in Korea.

During the Joseon era, village folk religion and *bibo* theory were combined. In this process *jangseung*, *sotdae*, groves, village guardian trees and stone pagodas were used to complement the earthly energy of a village. In Hanyang, the capital of Joseon Dynasty, pine trees were planted in the mountains around the palace in order to preserve and strengthen earthly energy, and forest preservation policies were implemented, much like today's greenbelt policy. Botoso was constructed at present-day Bugak Tunnel, which was an important spot between Mt. Samgaksan and Mt. Baegaksan. It was managed by the Chongyungcheong office. Mounds were raised on each side of the mouth of the Cheonggyecheon stream, through which the life force of the capital escaped, in order to amass this force. A *haetae* (mythical unicorn-lion) sculpture was built on Gwanghwamun, while Namji pond was dug in front of Namdaemun to control the "fire element" of Mt. Gwanaksan according to *fengshui*.

The method for choosing auspicious sites for building houses developed into the method of structural arrangement for achieving balance and harmony between buildings and their natural surroundings. The latter method, which creates pleasant environments rich in *gi* (life force or vital energy) by emphasizing minimal changes to the landscape rather than aggressive development, has become the foundation of Korean landscape architecture.

Though the original topography of the land should be preserved as much as possible by selecting proper locations and developing them in an environmentally friendly way, the current method of development, which only considers economic aspect and constructs man-made cities on fertile farmland, is devastating the entire land, making it difficult to apply the *bibo* method. Therefore, now it is urgently necessary to apply the *bibo*. Yi Jung-hwan (1690-1752) emphasized in *Taengniji* (Ecological Guide to Korean Geography): "In general, for the selection for human settlement, the geographical advantage of the site should be considered fist, then its physiological and economic condition, followed by the traits of the villagers' mind and human nature, and finally its

Figure 13. Location of the village following the *fengshui* principles (Oeam-ri)

Figure 14. Royal tomb located at the auspicious site, a front mountain, and a far front mountain

Figure 15. Locaton of the village in harmony with nature (Hahoe Village)

natural scenery of mountains and rivers. If the site falls short on one of these important factors, it will not be a favorable place to live." His suggestion may seem to only apply to agricultural society, but it is important to heed his remark that one must be prudent in deciding where to live, taking everything into consideration. During the Joseon era, *fengshui* was widely used to select sites for ancestral graves in keeping with Confucian ancestor worship, but it was later denounced as a form of magic that deluded the people. However, *fengshui* was an age-old view of geography for choosing ideal living spaces; thus, the *fengshui* used for houses or buildings should be researched further.

7. *Yin-Yang* and Five Elements Thought

The theory of *yin-yang* and the Five Elements is a combination of the *yin* and *yang* theory, which explains all universal and human phenomenon through the principles of *yin* (receptive, feminine, dark, passive force) and *yang* (creative, masculine, bright, active force), and the Five Elements which, under the influence of the former, explains the coming into being and extinction of all things through changes in wood, fire, earth, metal and water. It is difficult to find clear evidence regarding the origin of this thought, but many scholars believe that the theory of *yin* and *yang* emerged after the mid-Warring States period, while the theory of the Five Elements appeared later. The concept of *yin* and *yang* also appears in the ancient history of Korea: Heavenly King Hwanung is said to symbolize *yang* while the bear and tiger that live on earth symbolize *yin*. The birth of Dangun, the founder of Old Joseon, represents the union of Hwanung (*yang*) and the bear (*yin*).

The theory of *yin* and *yang* is rooted in numbers, and number three in particular is of profound importance in Korean culture. This is based on the principle of Samjae, which means the three essential elements: heaven, earth, and man. The theory of *yin-yang* and the Five Elements is also shared in common by Confucianism, Buddhism and Taoism, and is thus embedded in various aspects of East Asian culture. In traditional landscape architecture, a round island at the center of a square pond (*bangji wondo*) was constructed based on the *yin-yang* theory, and planting was determined by the five directions, as based on the theory of the Five Elements.

8. Confucian Thought

Though Confucian thought is often confused with Confucianism, the latter is a political and religious ideology developed by Confucius and the former is a philosophy. This philosophy was created by Confucius (551-479 BC), whose name was Kong Qiu. He was born in the State of Lu during the Spring and Autumn period. The main theories he developed included the concepts of *li*, saying "if lords act like lords, then subjects will act like subjects, and, in turn, fathers will behave as fathers should, and sons will then act like sons," *ren*, "loving others," and *zhongyong*, taking a middle path and avoiding extremes. Also, in his statement on the Mandate of Heaven, he says, "life and death are destined, and wealth and honor are determined by Heaven," which means that though the Mandate of Heaven is unknown and unchangeable, people can still reach a very high stage through learning and cultivation of their moral life.

Confucius was not only a great philosopher but also a great educator. He emphasized the importance of "enjoying learning with a modest mind" and "learning the old in order to see the new." He asked, "Is it not pleasant to learn with constant perseverance and application?" He connected socio-politics to individual cultivation of the mind and based his principal philosophy on the saying, "To put the world in order, we must first put the nation in order; to put the nation in order, we must put the family in order; to put the family in order, we must cultivate our personal life." His *Analects* include profound philosophical thoughts on society, life, education and learning, and also universal insights that transcend time and space. Thus, this Confucian scripture contains a wealth of spiritual insight for all people and can continue to enlighten future generations.

After Confucius died, his philosophy was passed on and spread by his disciples, among which the most influential was Mencius (372-289 BC). He advocated *xingshan* theory, which argues that humans are basically good in nature, and *renzheng* theory, or benevolent governance theory, which stated, "People should be greater, empire less important, and rulers even less." Both theories had great influence on later generations and became the orthodox view during the feudal era of ancient China. His book, *Mencius,* is an important Confucian scripture. Xunzi (325-238 BC) also contributed greatly to the development of Confucian thought. He believed that humans are basically evil in nature, asserting that "human nature is evil and to say it is good is a lie." He argued that when individual desire develops freely, it is followed by inevitable conflict between people, which will give rise to social disorder. Therefore, good and evil should be corrected through propriety in order to avoid social confusion. He also took a leap from Confucius and Mencius's idea of "leaving destiny to Heaven" and asserted that "destiny can be overcome by human efforts."

There are varying views as to when such Confucian thoughts were introduced to Korea. However, Taehak, or National Confucian Academy, was established in the second year of King Sosurim's reign (372) of Goguryeo and became the first systematic form of education. During the reigns of Baekje's King Geunchogo (346-375) and King Geunsugu (375-384), Ajikgi and Wangin were sent to Japan to disseminate Confucian thought and eliminate illiteracy. This shows that Confucian studies were widespread by the beginning of the Three Kingdoms era. Though Confucianism waned temporarily when the Goryeo Dynasty adopted Buddhism as the state religion, King Seongjong (r. 981-997) established a national university called Gukjagam to educate the elites.

In the 15th year of King Chungnyeol's reign (1289), An Hyang (1243-1306) brought back *Zhuzi quanshu* (The Complete Works of Zhu Xi) from China. He went on to promote Confucianism by rebuilding the National Academy (Gukhak) and repairing the Confucian Shrine.

In early Joseon Dynasty, Jeong Do-jeon (1342-1398) led the criticism of Buddhism, which had been the state religion during Goryeo, saying it was a metaphysical religion that negated reality and selfish thought system that pursued only empty theory. Thus, in order to control national problems and social conflicts at the end of Goryeo, Joseon accepted Neo-Confucianism, which was based on *Zhouli* (Rites of Zhu Xi), as a state religion. Social contradictions were seen as the intensification of mutual hatred between human beings and the degradation of ethics. As the solution to these social problems, Neo-Confucianism, which is based on the "three bonds and five moral disciplines" in human relations, was adopted as a state religion.

Confucianism developed greatly during the Joseon era with scholars such as Yi Hwang (1501-1570) and Yi I (1536-1584), the most respected Neo-Confucian scholars of the Joseon era. They developed profound logical arguments based on the theory of *i-gi*, which asserted that the essence of the universe sprang from two elements, namely *i* (principle) and *gi* (material force). However, the social confusion caused by the Gimyo Sahwa (Purge of the Literati of 1519) forced a number of Confucian scholars to renounce the world and retreat into the mountains to live as hermits; as a result, pavilions and *byeolseo* gardens, i.e. retreat gardens, were built in beautiful landscapes far from residential areas, which was a development to Korea. In particular, Confucian scholars of the Joseon era admired Zhu Xi (1130-1200) of China, who built his Wuyi Academy in Wuyi Mountains to teach junior scholars. They hung the landscape painting of Wuyi Mountains in their room and enjoyed a similar lifestyle by building pavilions in mountain valleys. They were also enchanted by "Ailianshuo" (On Loving Lotuses), written by Zhou Dunyi (1017-1073), wherein the author compares a lotus flower to a gentleman. Consequently, planting and admiring lotuses in ponds became very popular. In this regard, the inclusion of lotuses in landscaping is a result of Confucian rather than Buddhist influence.

During the Joseon era (1392-1910) when Neo-Confucianism was the ruling ideology, *hyanggyo*, local schools managed by the state, and *seowon*, private academies, were responsible for education. *Seowon* in particular were built on auspicious sites with beautiful scenery and served as ritual spaces where the spirit tablets of the ancient sages who were respected academically or spiritually were kept and where rituals were performed. They were also learning spaces where students pursued a Neo-Confucian education. *Seowon* architecture thus became public landscape architecture. As scholar-officials, who sought to cultivate themselves and govern others, revered the image of a gentleman (*gunja*), various gardening elements, for example the "four gentlemen" plants (bamboo, orchid, chrysanthemum, and plum), stones, water, etc., were placed throughout *seowon* gardens. This in turn had the effect of further educating the students in Confucian values.

Confucian ideology, which emphasized hierarchy and ancestor worship, influenced the style of landscape architecture. At commoners' houses, separate courtyards were arranged for the servants' quarters, the men's quarters, the women's quarters, the back garden, the ancestral shrine, and the separate house. The style of landscaping varied according to the location of the courtyard. In the case of palaces, the landscape depended on the location of the "three gates and three courts." Following the Confucian segregation of men and women,

Figure 16. Retreat garden decorated with symbolic elements (Seoseokji)

Figure 17. Living area of a spacious back garden

Figure 18. Various usages of the courtyard (traditional wedding)

Figure 19. Scene of rituals held at the Royal Ancestral Shrine

the back garden was built for women. Terraced flowerbeds built on a slope were a special feature of the back garden where flower trees served a decorative purpose while fruit trees and herbs had a more practical function.

9. Buddhist Thought

Buddhism was introduced to Korea via China in the second year of King Sosurim's reign (327) during Goguryeo. Initially, temples were built within the capital under the protection of the royal family. However, as Seon Buddhism spread widely, temples sought the quiet mountains rather than crowded city centers that hindered ascetic practices. Enlightened monks not only found auspicious sites but also acquired temple sites by taking over indigenous religious sites.

Following its first precept of abstaining from harming living beings, Buddhism provides spaces where all living beings can co-exist. By applying the ideal of Buddhism to the positioning of temples, Buddhism has represented the Pure Land of Perfect Bliss and created elaborate temple arrangements. During the Goryeo era in particular, Buddhism had a great influence on society in general as the state religion and introduced the monk examination system. This system guaranteed the social success of monks, causing them to abuse their power and thus bringing about the collapse of the dynasty. At the same time, due to the high social status of monk artisans, a number of cultural heritage sites, many of which are now national treasures, including temple buildings and *dancheong* (five-color painting), stone architecture (pagoda, lantern, funerary stupa, etc.), bridges and retaining walls still remain to this day. However, with the Joseon era policy of suppressing Buddhism and upholding Confucianism, Buddhism was oppressed and its powers weakened greatly. However, as some members of the royal family preferred Buddhism, it did not disappear completely despite such oppression.

Though Buddhism is a foreign religion that entered Korea via China, it took root in Korean soil and was reborn as Korean Buddhism, playing an important role in sustaining Korean traditional culture. Considering that seventy percent of Korea's national treasures are Buddhist cultural property, Buddhist influence on Korean culture is indeed great.

As temples were built in auspicious locations, the beauty of the surrounding scenery did not require any artificial landscaping except for the planting of the

Figure 20. Temple landscape architecture as a place for *seon* practice (Buseoksa temple)

symbolic five trees and six flowers mentioned in Buddhist scriptures. Unlike landscape architecture in layman's homes, which pursued visual beauty, temple landscapes were environments of abstinence and places for *seon* meditation.

As polytheism forms the backdrop of Korean culture, it has developed into a culture that is distinctly different from monotheistic Western culture, and a comprehensive knowledge of all of its cultural layers is needed to understand Korea's traditional landscape architecture.

IV. Conclusion

Ever since Dangun founded Korea on the ideals of "widely benefiting all of humanity and righteously governing the world" some 5,000 years ago, Korea has strongly defended its territory against various foreign invasions, and has developed a culture that best suits its land. The fact that its traditional landscape architecture has also continued and developed distinctly from that of China and Japan makes it all the more important. With the opening of ports, foreign cultures have spread without an appropriate filtering process, and Koreans now live in an era of confusion and are in danger of losing their national identity. It is therefore vitally important that we retrieve what is ours and protect the uniqueness of Korean culture.

Chinese artificial landscape architecture consisted of the palace landscape architecture of northern China, which was constructed on a super-human scale, and the family gardens of southern China, which combined various scenes in one location. Japan developed landscape architecture by using natural scenery in miniature, as it was an island that faced the constant threat of natural disasters such as typhoons and earthquakes. Unlike the landscape architecture of these two countries, Korean landscape architecture first selected ideal sites that were appropriate for use, the existing environment was respected, and the sites were cultivated using *bibo* theory. By using materials that have symbolic value, Korean landscape architecture seeks to realize an ideal and respect the natural surroundings, creating an environmentally friendly culture where human beings co-exist with all other living beings.

References

Choe, Chang-jo. 1984. *Hanguk-ui pungsu sasang* (Korean traditional Geomancy). Minumsa.

Choi, Won-seok. 2000. "Yeongnam jibang-ui bibo" (Cultural Geography of the *Bibo* in Yeongnam Region). Ph.D. diss., Korea University.

Chung, Dong-o. 1986. *Hanguk-ui jeongwon* (Korean Gardens). Minumsa.

Francis, M., and R. T. Hester. 1991. *The Meanings of the Garden*. MIT Press.

Hanguk Dogyo Munhwa Hakhoe (Korean Academy of Taoism and Culture), ed. 2000. *Hanguk-ui sinseon sasang* (Ideology of Immortality in Korea). D.K.S.

Jo, Ji-hun. 1997. *Hanguk munhwasa seoseol* (Introduction to the History of Korean Culture). Nanam.

Joo, Kang-hyun, and Jang Jeong-ryong. 1993. *Joseonttang maeul jikimi* (Village Guardians of Korea). Youlhwadang.

Kim, Seong-gu, trans. 1996. *Jungjuk jeongsa joseon yeolgukjeon* (Korea in the Chinese Dynastic Histories). Dongmoonsun.

Lee, Jeong-sik, and Yoon Pyung-sub. 1997. *Jasaeng singmulhak* (A Study of Native Plants). Seoil.

Lee, Sang-hae. 2002. *Seowon* (Private Academies). Youlhwadang.

Mason, D. A. 2003. *Sansin–Hanguk-ui sansin-gwa sanak sungbae-ui jeontong*, translated by Sin Dong-uk. Seoul: Hollym. Originally published as *Sprit of the Mountains: Korea's San-Shin and Traditions of Mountain Worship* (1999, Hollym).

Min, Kyung-hyun. 1991. *Hanguk jeongwon munhwa–siwon-gwa byeoncheonnon* (Korean Garden Culture–On the Origin and Changes). Yekyong.

Min, Yong-hyon. 2004. *Seon saengmyeong johwa-hanguk cheolhak-gwa munhwa-ui jeongsin segye* (Seon, Life, and Harmony–Spiritual World of Korean Philosophy and Culture).

Mosineun Saramdeul.

Pennick, N. 1979. *The Ancient Science of Geomancy*. T & H.

Shim, Jae-ryong. 2002. "Hangugin-ui jayeon-gwan" (Koreans' Views of Nature). Cheolhak *sasang* (Philosophical Thought) 15.1: 109-127.

Sim, Woo-kyung. 1988. "Jogyeong-eseo saengtaehak-gwa pungsu sasang-ui gwallyeonseong" (Relationship between Ecology and *Fengshui* in Landscape Architecture)." *Hanguk jeongwon hakhoeji* (Journal of Korean Institute of Traditional Landscape Architecture) 6.1: 1-25.

Yi, Jung-hwan. 1989. *Taengniji* (Ecological Guide to Korea), translated by Yi Ik-seong. Eul Yoo.

Yi, Neung-hwa. 1986. *Joseon dogyosa* (History of Taoism in Korea), translated by Yi Jong-eun. Boseong Munhwasa.

Author

Sim Woo-kyung

(Landscape Architecture Program, Korea University)

Sim Woo-kyung is a professor in the Landscape Architecture Program at Korea University. He received his Ph.D. from Korea University in 1984. He served as President of the Korean Institute of Traditional Landscape Architecture (2004-2005) and Korean Society for Plants, People and Environment (1998-2002). He was also a visiting professor in the Department of Landscape Architecture, GSD Harvard University in 2004. His main publications include *Design Theory on Planting for Landscape Architecture* (1990, co-author) and *History of Landscape Architecture in the West* (2005, co-author). E-mail: wksim@korea.ac.kr

Chapter 2

Landscape Architecture of the Royal Palace

I. Introduction

The royal palace was the home of the king who stood at the center of all major affairs within the monarchy. Accordingly, the palace was the symbolic, spiritual, and geographic center of the country, in addition to serving as a functional complex where national rites, governance, and the private activities of the royal family were carried out. It is thus a valuable cultural property with unique cultural traits. Though Korea prides itself on the magnificent history and culture of the royal palace, drastic changes over the past century have greatly damaged the original form of the royal palace, and the aesthetics and methods of garden construction particular to the palace have been lost. Today, academic research is needed to understand, preserve, and utilize the traditional landscape architecture of Korea's royal palaces in order to make it internationally known. Thus, this chapter presents a chronological study of the royal palace gardens, which are considered the finest in Korea, centering on existing records of landscape architecture of the royal palaces and spanning the Old Joseon, Three Kingdoms, Unified Silla, Goryeo and Joseon eras.

II. Characteristics of the Era

1. Old Joseon

The leaders of Old Joseon built a state civilization where they governed relatively small territories. Mud walls and wooden fences were built on low hills so they could defend themselves and govern the farmers who worked in the outer fields. This type of walled town was the very first state to appear on the Korean Peninsula. Among the walled town states, Old Joseon, which was located near the Liaohe and Daedonggang rivers, was the most advanced. Old Joseon, with Asadal as the capital, was ruled by Dangun Wanggeom, who is thought to have had both a political and religious function. Remains of the Old Joseon royal palace have not yet been found, but the *Samguk yusa* (Memorabilia of the Three Kingdoms) records the foundation myth, which states that Dangun descended to a spot under a tree by the Holy Altar at the top of Mt. Taebaeksan and established Sinsi (City of God). With the increasing importance of agriculture, the harvest thanksgiving festival became the most important religious ritual. Therefore, religious and political function were separated and the master of ritual presided over a separate town called *sodo*. It is said that a large tree was erected in the *sodo*, and bells and drums were hung from it for use in religious ceremonies. Based on ancient nature worship, these sacred trees came from the capital and were thereafter sanctified as "village guardian trees."

In this record, it is stated that King Noeul of Dangun Joseon created *yu*, which was a type of hill where birds and other animals were raised free-range. This is considered to be the beginning of landscape architecture in Korea.

According to the *Daedong sagang*, a history of Korea written by Kim Gwang in 1929, Cheongnyugak was built in the rear garden during King Uiyang's reign, where the king held grand banquets with his officials. It is written that in the 10th year of King Jese's reign, peach and plum flowers were in full bloom just a few days after the winter solstice. This was thirty years before Emperor Wu of Han Dynasty in China began constructing Shanglinyuan.

2. Three Kingdoms Era

Goguryeo was founded in the north as a result of continuous resistance by indigenous powers against Chinese rule. Meanwhile, in the southern part of the peninsula, Baekje and Silla were working to suppress neighboring states and establish states of their own, giving rise to the Three Kingdoms era. Landscape architecture was most advanced in Baekje. The people of Baekje were highly artistic and surpassed Goguryeo and Silla at one point in the formative arts. They also strongly influenced the culture of the Asuka era of Japan. According to the *Nihon shoki* (The Chronicles of Japan), Nojagong, a garden designer who had migrated from Baekje, constructed Mt. Sumeru and a bridge in the south garden of the royal palace in 612. This suggests that there might have been a number of such gardeners in Baekje at the time. Though no Baekje gardens remain today, according to the Annals of the Baekje Kingdom of the *Samguk sagi* (Historical Record of the Three Kingdoms), at least three magnificent gardens were created.

The first was the royal garden of King Jinsa (385-392), the 16th king of Baekje; the second, that of King Dongseong (479-501), the 24th king; and the third, that of King Mu (610-641), the 30th king. King Jinsa's royal garden had a pond surrounded by natural scenery and an artificial mountain where rare flowers were grown and animals were raised. Magnificent pavilions were constructed in King Dongseong's garden, and in King Mu's garden, water was drawn in from as far as 20 *li*, or 8 km, away to make a pond in which artificial islands were created. Willows were planted around the pond, and the royal family held feasts on a boat in the pond, the bow of which was carved to resemble a dragon head.

Among these gardens, Gungnamji found at Gunsu-ri in Buyeo, Chungcheongnam-do province, is the only remaining relic of ancient landscape architecture. This pond was part of the royal villa where the mother of King Mu (634) used to reside. It was originally 99,000 m² in size, but only 31,350 m² remain today (See Figure 1). The fact that the island, which represented Mt. Bangjangsan (Ch.: Fangzhangshan), was built in the pond south of the palace suggests that the landscaping method was based on the ideology of immortality, which emphasizes eternal life. It also shows how simple gardens began to take on symbolic and religious meanings over time.

Early in the 35th year of King Wideok's reign in Baekje (589), Wangheungsa temple, which was built on the shore of Baengmagang river to disseminate Buddhism, was completed. To celebrate the completion, a canal was dug from

Figure 1. View of Gungnamji, Buyeo

Baengmagang river, which was 20 *li* away, to the front of the palace. Willows, forsythia, peony and other rare plants and flowers were planted on the banks of the canal. Small man-made islands named Bongnaesan (Ch.: Penglaishan) and Bangjangsan were built along the river. Considering Baekje's strength at the time, the creation of this canal shows how advanced Baekje's landscape architecture was and how such techniques were used to create Gungnamji pond.

By serving as a northern buffer against mainland invasions, Goguryeo aided in the founding of the Baekje and Silla kingdoms and took the lead in establishing the foundation of Korea's ancient culture. However, after the Silla kingdom allied with the Tang and burnt down the Goguryeo palace, all that was left were relics and limited records. In the *Dongsa gangmok* (Annotated Account of Korean History) it is stated that while Yuri (AD 3), the second king of Goguryeo, was gone on a hunt for five days, Hyeopbu, the king's advisor, advised him to return. However, the king did not like this advice and demoted the advisor to manager of the royal garden. Disheartened, the former advisor left for a neighboring country in the south. This passage demonstrates that in the early Goguryeo period there was an official position that was responsible for the royal garden, and that royal landscape architecture had already reached a high level. Also, relics have been found at the site of Janganseong and Anhakgung palace, which were built during the reign of King Yangwon (427), the 24th king of Goguryeo, which seem to indicate the existence of a great garden. In particular, a garden for an attached building west of the South Palace consists of a naturally curved pond and an artificial mountain. There are also three divine islands in the pond. This shows that the garden was made using an atypical natural scenery method. The *Samguk sagi* records that branches of pear trees in the royal city crisscrossed each other in the early second lunar month of the second year of King Yangwon's reign (546), which tells us that the palace garden was full of pear flowers during Goguryeo.

Though Silla was the first state to be founded, the state foundation was only established in the early fourth century. It is recorded that the founder of Silla was born in a sacred forest called Gyerim. Silla initially chose Geumseong for its capital before expanding gradually into the neighboring areas with the construction of Wolseong Palace. Wolseong Palace, of which traces remain even today, is located on a small hill on the southern shore of Namcheon stream. This palace is also called Banwolseong because it is shaped like a half moon. It is approximately 78 meters in width and 220 meters in length. Walls were built to the east, west, and north, and Namcheon stream surrounds the wall, which functions as a natural moat.

Due to the geographical conditions, landscape architecture also began later than in Baekje or Goguryeo. However, with the recognition of Buddhism in the mid-fifth century, a number of temples, including Heungnyunsa, Hwangnyongsa, Sacheonwangsa and Bulguksa, were built one after the other. Gupumyeonji pond, located in front of the Cheongungyo and Baegungyo bridges at Bulguksa temple, was an oval, man-made pond, around which pavilions, stone pagodas, Jahamun gate, Cheongungyo and Baegungyo bridges were built so that their shadows would fall on its surface, which were meant to induce religious inspiration. In this sense, it was a holy pond that represented the Buddhist paradise and served as a boundary to demarcate the sacred and the profane. Gupumyeonji represents the essence of Buddhist art along with Dabotap and Seokgatap pagodas.

Guryongji pond, located at Tongdosa temple, which was founded by Monk Jajang during the reign of Queen Seondeok (646), the 27th queen of Silla, is said to have been so big when the temple was built that one could float a boat on it. Today, however, it is an oval pond of 15㎡ crossed by a stone bridge.

The records from Goguryeo, Baekje and Silla similarly state that frost fell in the 7th lunar month, followed by plum blossoms in the 8th lunar month, and peach and plum blossoms in the 10th lunar month. This suggests that when the weather officer made his observations, the fruit trees in the royal garden were used as criteria for recording the change of seasons.

3. Unified Silla Era

Silla developed significantly from about the 6th century and unified the peninsula by conquering Baekje in 660 and Goguryeo in 668. This also resulted in ethnic, cultural and linguistic unification. Though Silla adopted the culture of the Tang Dynasty and was influenced by the advanced cultures of Baekje and Goguryeo, a prominent culture of its own came into being after unification. Examples from this new culture include the landscape architecture of Imhaejeon and Poseokjeong. Imhaejeon was constructed by King Munmu (661-681), who unified the three states.

According to the *Samguk sagi*, King Munmu ordered his subjects to dig a pond, build an artificial mountain, plant flowers, and raise rare birds and other animals in the garden of the royal palace in the second lunar month. The garden was vast in size, spanning 180 meters east and west and 200 meters north and south for a total area of almost 4 hectares. The water surface of the garden took up 1.7 hectares, which was over forty percent of the entire area. Along the straight edge of the pond, several adjunct buildings stood, including

Imhaejeon hall. Along the curved shore, a man-made mountain suggested the scenic beauty of Mt. Wushan in China, with its twelve summits and rocky precipices. This landscaping method of boldly harmonizing the straight lines with the curves of the topography is a unique feature of the Imhaejeon landscape (See Figure 2).

An outstanding landscape techique was achieved by stacking stones two meters higher on the straight shore than on the curved shore, creating the effect of looking down into the garden from the buildings. In addition, the stone water tank was very well-equipped for filtering out sand silt when water was poured into the pond.

Figure 3. View of Poseokjeong, Gyeongju

Three islands, two large and one small, were built inside the pond. The man-made mountain that stretched from north to east on the shore and the three islands may have been constructed based on the ideology of immortality. They were meant to be viewed from Imhaejeon or while boating on the pond.

As the name of the building, Imhaejeon (臨海殿), clearly shows, the pond was built by hardening the ground with lime and laying pebbles over it in order to symbolize the sea where immortals were thought to live.

It is presumed that there was a pavilion on the site of Poseokjeong which was located at the western base of Mt. Namsan in Gyeongju. However, only a curving ditch, in the shape of abalone and made of granite, remains today (See Figure 3). Modeled on the U-shaped water channel of the Orchid Pavilion where Wang Xizhi relaxed while composing poems, Posekjeong was used for *goksuyeon*, in which the king and other noblemen would float wine cups on the water while composing poems. This has been clearly proven in recent experiments where cups were floated on the water. This skill at making a water channel from freely wrought granite while preserving the dynamic characteristics of water produced the effect of heightening the dramatic effect of poetry readings, demonstrating an artistic visual aesthetic that is found in neither China nor Japan.

From the records on King Heongang (875-886) and King Gyeongae (924-927), it appears that while Imhaejeon was used for official events or to receive foreign guests, Poseokjeong was a place of entertainment for the royal family.

4. Goryeo Dynasty

Wang Geon, who was based in Songak in 918, actively helped Gungye during the time of upheaval in the late Silla but ousted the latter at the end and acceded to the throne. He named his kingdom Goryeo to signify that it succeeded Goguryeo and chose Gaegyeong as the capital. Architecture at this time was heavily influenced by *fengshui* (K.: *pungsu*), a theory of divining propitious sites for houses or graves based on the theory of *yin-yang* and the Five Elements, and *docham* theory, which was used to predict the fortune of a nation or an individual. Therefore, the royal capital of Goryeo was built in an auspicious site according to these theories. After the foundation of Goryeo, a magnificent palace was immediately constructed in the capital, Buddhism was appointed the state religion, and ten temples were built within the capital. Goryeo thus assumed the dignified appearance of a cultural state but also underwent a number of hardships, including a military revolt, a Khitan invasion, and transition to a tributary state under Mongol aggression. However, it continued to flourish in culture and art: It made the most significant achievement in Korean art with the development of the world's first movable metal type and Goryeo celadon, as well as marvelous developments in landscape architecture.

The garden culture of Goryeo blossomed during the reign of King Uijong (1146-1170), the 18th king of Goryeo. While gardens were built in the private homes of the royal family and men of power, retired high officials, literati, and scholars retreated to quiet riverside or lakeside villages or into the mountains to build villas or cottages. They used the natural landscape as architecture. This had a strong influence later on Joseon Dynasty and became an important element of Korean landscape architecture that could not be found elsewhere. Yeongyeonggung, the main palace throughout the 500 years of Goryeo Dynasty, was located on a hill at the foot of Mt. Songaksan in the north. Unlike royal palaces built on flat land, the main buildings of the Manwoldae palace were centered on a garden located on the main axis, but other buildings were freely arranged according to the topography and landscape. The royal garden was located behind the main hall. It was surrounded by pine trees, and various pavilions such as Sangchunjeong, Sanhojeong, Wangchokjeong, and Saru were built with peony and other flower trees planted in between. The records state that a feast was held to celebrate the beauty of the flowers, and *goksuyeon*, a form of recreation in which the king and other noblemen would float wine cups on water while composing poetry, took place here, which suggests the construction of stone channels.

At this time, there were frequent exchanges with the Song Dynasty of China. Due to the introduction of a number of plants that were originally from China, imported plant materials were commonly used in landscape architecture at the time. A typical example was peony (L. Paeonia Suffruticcosa Andr.), which came from Gansu Province and Jiaxi Province in China and had spread rapidly throughout the peninsula since its introduction during the reign of King Jinpyeong (579-632), the 26th king of Silla. There are many records stating that a prize for poetry written in Chinese characters was presented at Sanhojeong pavilion in the 4th lunar month of the 24th year of King Munjong (1069). Hwasihoe, an event held to celebrate the peony tree planted by the king himself, was held in the 7th year of King Yejong (1111). Yangseongjeong pavilion was beautifully decorated with uniquely shaped rocks and flower trees in the 11th year of King Uijong (1156). Considering these records, the Goryeo era gardens were mainly flower gardens that centered on flower trees and plants chosen for their aesthetic value. The kings were so active in decorating their gardens that they moved flowering plants from commoners' houses and bought additional flowers from Song merchants. The gardens were intended to merge with the natural landscape. Goryeo gardens were thus distinct from not only Chinese gardens but also from Japanese gardens.

What is noteworthy about Goryeo's landscape architecture is that flowering plants are mentioned in almost all records, which shows that they were considered the most important. Rather than simple flowers, sumptuous flowers such as peonies, pomegranates, azaleas, lotuses and chrysanthemums were preferred.

5. Joseon Dynasty

Yi Seong-gye, who overthrew Goryeo and acceded to the throne in 1392, moved the capital from Gaegyeong to Hanyang. With Confucianism as the state religion, the Joseon Dynasty enjoyed unprecedented prosperity in the 15th century. Its unique culture flourished despite the Japanese and Chinese invasions dating from the 16th century. The, *fengshui* theory, based on the theory of *yin-yang* and the Five Elements, and *docham* theory greatly influenced the construction of the royal palace in the capital. Concerning the arrangement of the palace in particular, Jongmyo (Royal Ancestral Shrine) was placed to the left, Sajikdan, an altar for the god of earth and the god of crops, to the right, and the government office at the front of the main palace, Gyeongbokgung. It also followed the arrangement principle of "three gates, three courts." That is, the royal palace was built following a specific pattern in order to embody central power. First, the arrangement of Gyeongbokgung palace along a north-south axis was similar to the planning principle for palaces and fortresses recorded in the Kaogongji section of *Zhouli* (Rites of Zhou). Second, Changdeokgung and Changgyeonggung palaces were built along an east-west axis as based on the concept of the "Palace of East," signifying the queen mother. The king's palace was placed in the west, while the queen mother's palace was placed in the east. This became an important principle that influenced the spatial structure inside the royal palace.

Gyeongbokgung, the main palace, and Changdeokgung and Changgyeonggung, the royal separate palaces, were then landscaped. Gyeongbokgung was the first main palace to be constructed in Hanyang after King Taejo founded Joseon. Still standing today are the Gyeonghoeru pond and

Figure 4. View of Gyeonghoeru, Gyeongbokgung palace

garden that were constructed during King Taejong's reign, along with Amisan garden, the Jagyeongjeon wall, and the Hyangwonji pond and Hyangwonjeong pavilion, all of which were built during the reign of King Gojong. The Gyeonghoeru pond and garden are centered on a large, square pond, which is close to the northwest side of Geunjeongjeon hall, and Gyeonghoeru pavilion (See Figure 4). Gyeonghoeru was used to receive foreign visitors or as a banquet hall for the king's subjects since the early Joseon. It was sometimes also used as a venue for the state examination, which the king himself conducted. The Gyeonghoeru pond and garden consist of a square-shaped pond, 130 by 110 meters, and three square islands. A pavilion was constructed on the biggest island, which was connected to the shore of the pond by three stone bridges with stone railings. Gyeonghoeru was an ideal location for hosting official events as far as defense was concerned, and one could view Mt. Inwangsan and

Figure 5. Amisan garden, Gyeongbokgung palace

Figure 6. Jagyeongjeon wall, Gyeongbokgung palace

Mt. Bukhansan from west to north as well as the pond and garden below. Also, the elegant buildings and pine trees in Mansesan, an artificial mountain that was built at the center of the pond, were reflected on the surface of the water, adding to the visual splendor.

Terraced flowerbeds adjoining the northeast side of Gyeonghoeru were called Amisan garden, and they were built in the back garden of Gyotaejeon, the queen's bedchamber. This garden was built for the queen's walks and recreation. The mud that was dug while creating the pond at Gyeonghoeru was used to create this artificial flowerbed, which reached approximately 55 meters in width and 30 meters in length. Four terraces, which were each about three meters high, were decorated with gravel, oddly-shaped stones, and decorative chimneys. Plum, peony, cherry, pear, pine, and azalea trees were beautifully planted to represent Amisan as the world of immortals (See Figure 5).

Behind the terraced flowerbed in Amisan, tall trees such as zelkova or elm were planted as a backdrop, rather than building a wall, as it harmonized with the naturl grove.

Jagyeongjeon, the queen mother's sleeping quarters, is situated to the east of Gyotaejeon and is surrounded by a beautiful wall decorated with flower and plant patterns. The brick wall is beautifully decorated with flowers including peonies, plum, peach and pomegranate blossoms, and chrysanthemums, and designs of the ten symbols of longevity such as the sun, mountains, clouds, rocks, pine trees, herbs of eternal youth, turtles, deer, and cranes (See Figure 6). As it was difficult to decorate flowerbeds just like Amisan in these small spaces, efforts were made to beautify the walls instead. This wall also symbolized filial piety and wishes for the queen mother's longevity.

Hyangwonji pond, which was situated on the north side of Gyeongbokgung

Figure 7. Hyangwonji pond and Hyangwonjeong pavilion, Gyeongbokgung palace

and to the south of Geoncheonggung, King Gojong's bedchamber, was an almost square-shaped pond, 76 meters in width and 70 meters in length (See Figure 7). King Gojong enjoyed walks in this garden every morning and evening. Hyangwonjeong, a two-story hexagonal pavilion, stood on a round island at the center of the pond, and the surrounding trees and flowers enhanced the beauty of the pavilion. Flowers and trees were planted around the square pond. It must have been a comfortable place for the royal family when they came here to admire the lotus flowers on the surface of the pond. Currently, however, a number of old trees and flowers have been removed from the area, giving it a certain feeling of emptiness.

The most typical example of Joseon landscape architecture is the back garden of Changdeokgung palace. Constructed by King Taejong (1405), the third king of Joseon, Changdeokgung had a back garden approximately $198,000\,m^2$ in size on the northeast side of the palace where the royal family came for rest and recreation. It was originally called Huwon (Back Garden), Bugwon (North Garden), or Geumwon (Prohibited Garden) but is now commonly called Biwon (Secret Garden). This garden underwent several constructions and renovations through the generations of kings since the early Joseon, finally becoming the spacious garden that exists today. Following the spatial characteristics of gardens, built according to geographical features, Huwon can be divided into four areas called Buyongji, Aeryeonji, Bandoji, and Ongnyucheon.

Located at the center, Buyongji was filled with buildings, such as Buyongjeong, Juhamnu, Yeonghwadang, Sajeonggi Bigak, Seohyanggak, Huiujeong, and Jewol Gwangpunggwan. It was also closest to the entrance of

Figure 8. Buyongji pond, Changdeokgung (Seoul)

Huwon. Buyongji is a square pond 34.5 meters in width and 28.4 meters in length with a round island at the center of which a pine tree was planted. The square pond and round island were based on the theory of *yin-yang* and the Five Elements, which states that the sky is round and the earth square. Buyongjeong pavilion stands with two of its pillars planted underwater on the southern shore of the pond, Sajeonggi Bigak, the building that houses the monument on which the records of four springs are engraved, is on the western shore of the pond, Yeonghwadang stands to the east on a platform called Chundangdae, and Juhamnu is located at the top of a five-tier terraced flowerbed on the northern side. These buildings vary not only in size and shape but also in height so that the buildings and their surroundings provide very diverse visual changes when viewed from different locations (See Figure 8).

Figure 9. Juhamnu, Changdeokgung palace

While admiring the space, it is also important to appreciate the meaning that is inherent within it. Juhamnu is located nearest the palace at the highest point when coming down the hill, and Yeonghwadang stands below. Upon reaching the latter, Buyongjeong and Sajeonggi Bigak unfold before one's eyes (See Figure 9).

Juhamnu was the king's private library but was also used for small banquets. Yeonghwadang held state examinations, which the king attended, and was also a place where people came to enjoy the surrounding flowers. Sajeonggi Bigak describes the four springs in the garden and Buyongjeong represents a person looking up at the sky with his or her feet planted on the ground.

Though it was used for the king's enjoyment, the garden was also a quiet, solemn place where the king's responsibilities fell heavily. That is, he had to

Figure 10. Aeryeonjeong, Changdeokgung palace

Figure 11. Banwolji, Changdeokgung palace

read as many books as possible in order to execute the affairs of the state properly, to wisely select men of talent and hope for the wisdom of the prince who would succeed him, and to cultivate his character so as to execute all these duties without the slightest mistake.

Turning north with Buyongji on the left leads to Bullomun, the gate of eternal youth, next to which is the square-shaped Aeryeonji pond. On the northern shore stands the single-story Aeryeonjeong pavilion. The size of the pond is approximately 30 meters east to west and 26 meters north to south, and the hill to the north is covered with deciduous trees. Just like Buyongjeong, Aeryeonjeong has two pillars under water. The reflection of the pavilion surrounded by the forest reminds the viewer of a true landscape painting (See Figure 10). When the royal family strolled through the royal garden, Aeryeonjeong must have made a perfect place to stop and rest with its view over the walls of Gioheon and Uidugak, the crown prince's reading rooms. King Sukjong's "Account of Aeryeonjeong" and King Jeongjo's "Aeryeonjeong Poem" describe how pleasant Aeryeonjeong was all year long.

Going around the foot of the hill to the north, one comes across the naturally-curved Banwolji pond on the left. Its overall shape and its pavilion are unprecedented for Korean traditional gardens. Banwolji is divided into an upper part where Jondeokjeong is located and a lower part where the fan-shaped Gwallamjeong is found. *Donggwoldo* (Illustration of the Palaces of Joseon Dynasty) shows that it was originally made of two square ponds. Banwolji is surrounded by forest, and its secluded and cozy atmosphere makes it a suitable place to enjoy swimming and fishing. It is a good place for thinking and meditation (See Figure 11).

Figure 12. Ongnyucheon, Changdeokgung palace

Figure 13. Terraced flowerbeds at Nakseonjae, Changdeokgung palace

Upon leaving Banwolji, a path going over the hill to the north and through a forest leads to a hollow where various pavilions are located with Ongnyucheon stream at the center (See Figure 12).

What is special here is *goksugeo*, a curved water channel for floating wine cups, and an artificial waterfall located in front of Soyojeong. Cheonguijeong is found further inside. King Injo (1636) wrote the word "Ongnyucheon" (玉流川) on the Soyoam rock, and a poem by King Sukjong is also carved on the rock. A channel is dug in the shape of a letter C in front of this rock. From Soyojeong, one can view a 1.6-high waterfall that passes through the channel from Ongnyucheon. In a poem he wrote in 1670, King Sukjong said that the waterfall is 300 *ja* (about 90 meters) in height and looks like it is falling from the Milky Way. He also said it looks as though a white rainbow arches over it, and that it sounds like thunder resounding in a valley. The poem displays both generosity of expression and great learning in its description of the miniature landscape by evoking the mountain range from a single hill and rivers and lakes from a single cup of water.

Cheonguijeong, which was built at the northwest end of the hollow, is the only building with a round, thatched roof. However, the bright *dancheong* just below the roof makes an odd contrast with its very detailed design and high quality. Though the pond was sometimes used for raising fish, the straw thatching of the roof was also designed to remind people of the importance of rice agriculture even during times of recreation. As Ongnyucheon was farthest away from the palace and its surroundings were quiet and secluded, it is reminiscent of a rural retreat garden (*byeolseo jeongwon*) where artificiality was kept to a minimum with the use of a natural stream.

To the east of Changdeokgung palace is the back garden of Nakseonjae. It is a four-level terraced flowerbed with various plants, oddly-shaped rocks, and chimneys (See Figure 13). The two-story pavilion built at the top, which appears after the garden, provides an overall view of the area.

Using a high-north-low-south configuration, the back garden was built as a flowerbed and filled with flowers and decorative objects. Though the space was small, the high-low orientation enhanced the visual aesthetics. This form of landscape architecture kept women in mind, as they had few opportunities to go out. From the closed space, one can exit through the back door, climb to the pavilion, and look out over not only the neighboring roofs but also the distant landscape. It was a perfect place to shake off the oppressiveness of a confined space and enjoy a cool breeze in the summer. This type of arrangement and sentiment can only be found in Korean gardens (See Figure 14).

Figure 14. Sangnyangjeong, Changdeokgung palace

As such, the back garden of Changdeokgung had well-arranged ponds and pavilions. Trees, shrubs, and other plants were placed to harmonize with the surrounding scenery, and flowerbeds were built on hillsides with shrubs and flowering plants. In particular, broadleaf trees that distinctly marked the change in season were selected for the garden. These trees reflected the effort to maintain the principle of harmonizing gardens with nature and each distinct season. Also, one should not forget that the back garden of Changdeokgung was not simply a space for rest and recreation, but also a healing place where the king could gain wisdom and restore his energy through moral training based on meditation, reading, and writing of poetry in order to focus on the affairs of the state.

III. Conclusion

As seen above, the origin of the traditional landscape architecture of the royal palace in Korea can be traced to various activities. It may have originated with the practical usage of trees stemming from an agricultural lifestyle, the transplanting of flower and fruit trees for aesthetic purposes, or the creation of sacred forests based on the belief in the sanctity of forests and trees. As a community-based lifestyle became more consolidated, the king's palace and recreational areas were decorated to transmit ideology and culture and to represent the yearning for eternal life as embodied by the ideology of immortality. This trend continued after the Joseon era and had a great influence on the unique landscaping of the royal palace with its square ponds and round islands, the back gardens preferred by scholar-officials, and the construction of rural retreat gardens that maintained the natural landscape.

Finally, the Korean perspective on nature that is reflected in traditional landscape architecture as represented by the royal garden is embedded with *fengshui* theory, which views nature as the source of life, the concept of immortality, the aim of which is to escape suffering through harmony with nature, and the idea of "Unity of Heaven and Man" (*cheonin habil*), which pursues enlightenment by learning from nature. These concepts have been translated into design elements, such as naturalness, free-spiritedness, and simplicity, all of which are connected to the harmony between form and object and formation of spirituality in the structural elements and techniques of the garden, that is, the harmony of relationships. By providing a view of nature with visual adornments, the Korean traditional garden has a greater value in that it displays people's thoughts about nature.

References

Byun, Woo-hyuk. 1987. "Ijo sidae jeongwon-ui sumok-gwa baesik" (Planting of Trees in Joseon Dynasty Gardens). *Hwangyeong-gwa jogyeong* (Environment and Landscape Architecture) 16: 79-87.

Chung, Dong-o. 1986. *Hanguk-ui jeongwon* (Korean Gardens). Mineumsa.

___________. 1987. "Jeontong jeongwon-eseoui singmul-ui sangjingseong" (The Symbolism of Plants in Traditional Gardens). *Hwangyeong-gwa jogyeong* (Environment and Landscape Architecture) 18: 74-79.

Chung, Jae-hun. "Hanguk jogyeong-ui siksu baesik" (Plant Cultivation in Korean Landscape Architecture). *Munhwaje* (Cultural Properties) 13: 57-73.

Hong, Sa-jung. 1982. *Hangugin-ui miuisik* (Koreans' Aesthetic Concept of Beauty). Jeonyewon.

IFLA Korean Organizing Committee, ed. 1992. *Hanguk jeontong jogyeong* (Korean traditional Landscape Architecture). Doseo Chulpan Jogyeong.

Joo, Nam-chull. 1990. *Biwon* (Secret Garden). Bitkkalinneun Chaek-deul Series 35. Daewonsa.

Lee, Ki-baik. 1990. *Hanguksa sillon* (A New History of Korea). Rev. ed. Ilchogak.

Yoo, Byung-rim, Hwang Gi-won, and Park Chong-hwa. 1989. *Joseonjo jeongwon-ui wonhyeong* (The Archetype of Gardens in the Joseon Dynasty). Graduate School of Environment, Seoul National University.

Authors

Kim Yong-ki

(Department of Landscape Architecture, Sungkyunkwan University)

Kim Yong-ki is a professor in the Department of Landscape Architecture at Sungkyunkwan University. He received his Ph.D. from Kyushu University in 1980. He is currently a member of the Gyeonggi-do Cultural Properties Committee. He wrote many books, including *Design Theory on Planting for Landscape Architecture* (1990), *Planning and Designing of the Garden* (1993), and *History of Landscape Architecture in the East* (1996). E-mail:kyk4401@skku.ac.kr

Choi Jong-hee

(Division of Horticulture and Environmental Design, Pai Chai University)

Choi Jong-hee is a professor in the Division of Horticulture and Environmental Design at Pai Chai University. He received his Ph.D. from Sungkyunkwan University in 2000 and D.S. from University of Genoa in 2001. He is currently a member of the Gyeonggi-do Cultural Properties Committee. His main publications include *The Ideal World of Islam* (2003), *History of Landscape Architecture in the West* (2005), and *The Politics of Eden, God's Garden: Aesthetics of British Gardens* (2005). E-mail: jhchoi2000@pcu.ac.kr

Chapter 3

RESIDENTIAL LANDSCAPE ARCHITECTURE

I. Introduction

With Korea's four distinct seasons and beautiful natural scenery of mountains, rivers, trees and stones, the ancestors of Korea created cultural spaces where nature and artificiality were organically assimilated by choosing the appropriate locations based on the principle of integration with nature rather than its development or modification.

Yi Jung-hwan (1690-1752) of the Joseon era, who systematically proposed a theory of environmental space, wrote in *Taengniji* (Ecological Guide to Korea) about the importance of geographical advantages, economic conditions, traits of the villager's mind and human nature, and the natural scenery in selecting a site for a human settlement. In other words, he said that the best location for a residence would be one that ensured environmental, economic and social soundness. In this regard, the layout of a Korean traditional village was based on a land usage system that divides the land into such categories as residential area, surrounding area and land under cultivation. Facing south at the foot of the mountain, the village has a wide field and a low hill crossed by a stream, reflecting the principles of *baesan imsu* (mountain in back, river in front) and *jangpung deuksu* (protection from wind, access to water). Village paths and water channels that connect houses are closely related to the topography and thus display a gradual rise and rhythm.

Housing styles were determined by a variety of factors, including the natural environmental conditions, religion, ideology, politics and social status. Inner and outer spaces were divided according to status and position, and hierarchy determined living areas. In particular, the spatial structure of the traditional house was based on practicality by combining the basic unit of a building and a

Figure 1. Hahoe Village in Andong, Gyeongsangbuk-do province, known as the best village site

Figure 2. Oeam Village in Asan, facing south with Mt. Seolhwasan in back and farmland in front

courtyard called *madang*. The wide, open space of the *madang* was used to hold important ceremonies, including the coming of age ceremony, marriages, funerals, and ancestral worship. As the hub of household activity, it was the place from which household affairs were managed, and it was also used for gardening, where various plants, vegetables and herbs were grown.

II. Spatial Structure and Principles of Construction in Traditional Residential Areas

1. Locationality and Spatial Structure of the Traditional Village

Villages were chosen following a method for selecting locations with fertile land and protection against natural disasters. At times, a community space used for leisure and education was mutually built and managed with neighbors.

Villages were built with a mountain to the rear of people's homes. This mountain served as shelter from the wind while providing beautiful scenery, and was also used for gravesites and folk religion. It further served a practical purpose, providing living materials, firewood, and water to villagers. Homes were typically located on a gentle slope with an unobstructed view. They thus received cool breezes in the summer and were protected from the cold northern winds of winter. Though the houses all had a view of the outside, privacy was highly regarded. The farmlands to the front were crossed by a stream, dividing the inner and outer field. Dry fields were cultivated in the inner field while wet fields, such as rice paddies, were cultivated in the outer field.

Figure 3. Center of Hahoe Village, a lineage village belonging to the Pungsan Ryu clan

Figure 4. Spring in Oeam Village, a lineage village belonging to the Yean Yi clan

Figure 5. Supplementary grove as a boundary between the inner and outer village to give ecological soundness and mental security according to *fengshui* theory

Village paths were divided into outer, entrance, inner, and side paths based on hierarchy and the gradual rise of the topography. The outer path separated the space of the village from the outside, while the entrance path was a dividing space that led to the village entrance. The inner path was exclusive to the village, where central facilities such as pavilions or rest areas were built. The side path was an intermediate space that led to such places as the communal well, washing area, or communal workplace, functioning as a link between houses.

In particular, facilities for religious rituals (shrines for tutelary deities, tutelary posts, village guardian poles, stone monuments for filial sons and virtuous women, graves, etc.), educational buildings (local schools, private academies, etc.), leisure facilities (pavilions, ponds, etc.) and facilities used in everyday life (wells, washing areas, bathing areas, village squares, etc.) were built as the structures of the village community.

2. Spatial Structure of the Traditional House

The natural environment was regarded as an organic entity, and views of nature, religion and ideology were used in determining the location of the village and in building houses. The location and size of the house were restricted according to socio-political status, and houses were differentiated among the upper class, the middle class and the lower class.

In particular, *fengshui* theory (K.: *pungsu*), or traditional geomancy, was used in the location of the village, village roads, buildings, courtyards, fences, and trees. As sloping land was terraced to create foundations for buildings, back gardens and flowerbeds were built between this slope and the mountain in back, and ponds were dug at the front of houses. Comfortable homes were created through the methods of supplementing (*bibo*) and suppressing (*yeopseung*).

Due to the influence of Confucianism, ancestor worship, gender segregation, proper order between the old and the young, and hierarchical relationships were taken into account in establishing residential areas. Shrines that housed the spirit tablets of ancestors were located high to the northeast of the house, while living areas for men and women were strictly divided into east and west. Men used the *sarangchae* (men's quarters) while women used the *anchae* (women's quarters), further dividing the household into outer and inner areas.

Laozi and Zhuanzi thought taught adaptation to nature and the Taoist principle of seclusion greatly influenced the creation of *byeoldang* (separate house) and *byeolseo* (cottage or villa), which became idealized gardens in nature. The importance of Samjae—a concept based on *yin* and *yang* that explains the mutually dependent relationship among the heaven, the earth and humans—was reflected in the symbolic positioning of trees, plants, rocks and ponds inside gardens.

The estate and building sizes of traditional houses were restricted according to status. They were also divided into upper, middle and lower class houses according to hierarchy: *yangban* lived in upper-class houses, which followed strict gender and status segregation, and the distinction between inner/outer and high-superior/low-inferior was clearly reflected in the use of land. In other words, the *sarangchae* building and *sarang madang* courtyard was one unit, located to the east and used by the husband of the household. The ancestral shrine, which symbolized the highest rank in the household hierarchy, was positioned to the northeast. The wife's house and courtyard, *anchae* and *an madang*, were another unit located to the west, and the servants' quarters, consisting of *haengnangchae* and *haengnang madang*, were placed in a transitional space along with other buildings and courtyards.

A typical upper-class house consisted of six buildings, including *haeng-nangchae* (servants' quarters and warehouse), *sarangchae* (men's quarters), *anchae* (women's quarters), *gobangchae* (storage house for grains and goods), *sadang* (shrine where ancestral tablets were kept) and *byeoldang* (separate house built for the family head or the elderly). Each *chae* (building) had its own *madang* (courtyard), and all six of these units comprised one house.

With a mountain in back and water in front, houses were built facing south based on a combination of practical and ideological approaches to nature,

Figure 6. Panoramic view of men's quarters at Unjoru, Gurye, known as the most auspicious location (18th century)

Figure 7. Old plan of Unjoru (18th century) which reflects the characteristics of upper-class houses

including *fengshui*, and the existing socio-political system. The direction of each building and courtyard was chosen according to hierarchy and importance. Parts of the house and courtyard used by men or for extra-household functions were positioned to the east to receive the first rays of the rising sun, while buildings and courtyards used by women or for intra-household functions faced west to receive the rays of the setting sun.

3. Construction of the External Space of the Traditional House

The exterior of a traditional house is divided by a wall or a building. Courtyards are named according to the buildings (*chae*) to which they are attached: *an madang, sarang madang, haengnang madang,* or *sadang madang* Depending on their position, these courtyards can also be called *bakkat* (outer) *madang* or *dwit* (back) *madang*. These courtyards are arranged either horizontally from east to west or vertically from north to south.

1) Courtyard of the Women's Quarters (*An Madang*)

An madang was the courtyard of the women's quarters. As it is located in the innermost part of the house, it represents both centrality and closedness. The courtyard was built in the shape of a square, and its surface was leveled smooth. It served multiple functions as a hub for household activity, a site for wedding ceremonies, and a place to dry grains.

In particular, the *an madang* functioned as a quasi-inner space surrounded by buildings and walls. It was a private space of comfort where the depth of the space could be felt. As it was not very large, the space was left open rather than

Figure 8. Old house of Yun Jeung, in Nonsan, which includes *an madang*, *sarang madang*, *haengnang madang*, *sadang madang*, *bakkat madang*, *dwit madang*, and square pond

having large trees. According to *fengshui* theory, planting large trees in the courtyard blocked daylight and air circulation and marred the environment.

2) Courtyard of the Men's Quarters (*Sarang Madang*)

Sarang madang was both the courtyard of the men's quarters and a reception area. This position connoted openness as it was connected to either the *bakkat madang* or *haengnang madang*. It was relatively wide and well decorated. Flower gardens or flowerbeds were built, and auspicious trees such as pomegranate and peony were planted. Plum trees, chrysanthemums, or orchids were planted according to aesthetics and taste. Sometimes a small, stone lotus pond was built to enhance self-cultivation.

The *sarang madang* was larger than the *an madang*, and the decorative objects or plants in this yard became elegant elements of scenery that could be enjoyed from the wood-floored veranda of the *sarangchae*. If the space was wide enough, either a man-made mountain or a square pond with round islands was created. If the courtyard was small, a flowerbed was built using long carved stones. Deciduous trees with symbolic significance were planted to reflect the changing seasons and the beauty of an imagined landscape.

3) Courtyard of the Shrine (*Sadang Madang*)

Sadang madang was the courtyard of the shrine, where ancestral tablets were kept and rituals were performed. It was usually located to the east of the *sarangchae* and was surrounded by a wall. No gardens were added, but Chinese juniper trees were planted for incense, along with plants that symbolized fidelity, such as pine, bamboo, plum trees and chrysanthemum.

4) Courtyard of the Servants' Quarters (*Haengnang Madang*)

Haengnang madang, located in front of the servants' quarters, was used by servants or as a storage space. No particular gardening method was applied. However, following the *fengshui* theory that pagoda, zelkova, nettle, or gingko trees planted in front of the middle gate would bring wealth to the next three generations, two or three such trees were planted near this gate.

5) Courtyard of the Separate House (*Byeoldang Madang*)

Byeoldang madang, the courtyard of the *byeoldang*, was divided into the "inner *byeoldang*" (for the children or grandmother) inside the wall and the "outer *byeoldang*" (for the elderly family head) outside the wall. The courtyard of the inner *byeoldang* was a wide, simple space without a garden. The courtyard of the outer *byeoldang*, however, usually included garden features such as ponds and pavilions. The latter was used as a space where one could enjoy studying, admiring nature, or simply resting.

6) Outer Courtyard (*Bakkat Madang*)

The *bakkat madang* courtyard outside the main gate was a wide, open area used for various purposes such as waste disposal, grain storage, and vegetable gardening. It was also used for water channels or ponds. Other times, it was simply left empty. Ponds were used for the combined purposes of drainage of rainwater or sewage, fire prevention, fish breeding, enjoyment of scenery, and microclimate control.

Figure 9. General view of Hwallaejeong, the outer *byeoldang* at Seongyojang, Gangneung, and a square pond with square islands

7) Back Courtyard (*Dwit Madang*) or Back Garden

Dwit madang was located on sloping ground behind the *anchae* (women's quarters) and was used for practical purposes as a vegetable garden or orchard. If the slope was steep, terraced flowerbeds were built to increase the usable area. Flowering trees (cherries, apricot blossoms, royal azaleas, azaleas, etc.) were planted, and oddly-shaped stones or rocks carved with the characters of the mind control stone (洗心石), earthenware jars for soy sauce and seasoning pastes, and chimneys were placed in the back garden.

A well was also built in the back garden. Gardening was restricted so that the space would naturally harmonize with the forested hill to the rear. This created an intermediary space where human life and nature came into contact.

III. Landscape Techniques of the Traditional House

1. Planting Techniques

In the "Bokgeo" of *Sallim gyeongje* (Farm Management), written by Hong Manseon (1643-1715) during the Joseon era, Hong wrote: "Build houses on land surrounded by mountains where the forest is thick; plant Rose of Sharon (*mugunghwa*) to create a hedgerow; build an angular pavilion where the scenery is beautiful; and plant bamboo trees around one *myo* (100 m²) in size to protect the house, flower and fruit trees around another, and cucumbers and other vegetables around another. This will ensure comfort in old age." This gives an outline of the land use and planting style of traditional houses.

The techniques that were applied to traditional houses were taken into consideration: the limited planting, the vested symbolism, planting methods, locations, and directions.

1) Limited Planting and Vested Symbolism

Inner qualities, aesthetics, function, ecology, and symbolism were all considered in the selection of plants. Pine, plum, and bamboo trees, chrysanthemum, orchid, and lotus flowers were chosen based on the principle of *fengshui*, the idea of immortality, the concept of *yin* and *yang*, and Confucian ethics. Chrysanthemum flowers and willow and peach trees symbolized the life philosophy of "contentment in poverty and pleasure in

Figure 10. Lotus flowers which were greatly admired by Confucian scholars as they bloomed in muddy water and symbolized gentlemen

Figure 11. Bamboo trees which symbolized tenacity, fidelity and integrity

Figure 12. Plum trees which were widely used as they were the first to bloom and reflected the symbolic ethics of Confucian scholars

honesty" and paulownia and bamboo trees reflected seclusion and the desire for peace. In particular, plants were vested with the symbolic values of grace, wealth, integrity, fidelity, loyalty and elegance. They were also personified as guests and friends. As such, plants were selected according to a metaphysical value system, and their presence in the house emphasized the richness of spiritual world and implied ethical views.

Deciduous, broadleaf trees that changed with the seasons were preferred over evergreens. Elegantly curving branches were valued over straight branches, and trees that grew in an oval shape were very popular. Also popular were fruit (peaches, pears, Japanese apricots, plums, jujubes, apples, pomegranates, etc.) and flower trees; in particular, yellow, which symbolized the center of the universe, was preferred.

Figure 13. Gyeongjeong and Seoseokji (constructed in 1613) in Yeongyang. Plants and stones were imbued with symbolism.

2) Planting Types

Most plants were placed in the ground with the occasional use of potted plants, lattice fences, dwarf plants and cut flowers in containers. When fruit or flower trees were planted, various types of flowerbeds, mounds and terraces were created.

Hwagye were terraced flowerbeds built on a slope in the back garden. They functioned both as a flowerbed and as a retaining wall. Oddly-shaped stones, a stone pond for lotuses, and plants and flowers were harmonized in this space.

Pots were used for small gardens and plants that were vulnerable to the cold. Fruit and flower trees, as well as dwarf pines, were placed to enhance the beauty of the surrounding area. Plants that are vulnerable to the cold such as gardenias, evergreen shrubs, camellias, and pomegranates were preferred and cut peonies were kept in vases.

Fences were used to mark boundaries, shield the view, prevent animals from trespassing, and add to the depth of the space. Using various trees such as flowering trees, bamboo, juniper, yew, Oriental arborvitae, and spindle, the branches were woven into a lattice fence or screen called *chwibyeong*. *Wonjang* was a hedgerow, approximately two meters long, made using well-trimmed jujube, trifoliate orange, Rose of Sharon, or bamboo trees, or chrysanthemum flowers.

3) Planting Methods and Locations

Tree planting methods included *gunsik*, for creating dense forest, *jeomsik*, for creating visual focus with a rare tree, *sansik*, for the use of various flowering trees, and *yeolsik*, for creating a fence or boundary marker. Pine and bamboo trees were primarily planted in the back garden following the *gunsik*

Figure 14. Seobaekdang at Yangdong village, where terraced flowerbeds were built at the men's quarters and the courtyard of the shrine

Figure 15. *Maehwa seookdo* (Painting of the House Surrounded by Plum Trees), Jo Hui-ryong (1789-1866), Gansong Art Museum

method. *Jeomsik* and *sansik*, the most common methods, were used in the courtyard for the men's quarters (*sarang madang*), flower terraces and mounds, and around ponds, where a single tree or small groups of trees were planted to draw in the eye or create a sense of space. The *yeolsik* method was used for hedgerows. Rose of Sharon, trifoliate orange, and spindle trees were used functionally to mark boundaries, provide privacy, and prevent animals from trespassing.

Planting big trees in the courtyard for women's quarters (*an madang*) was avoided, and pine and bamboo trees were planted around the house. Though a belief in animism made it difficult to cut down or harm large old trees, planting of such trees was limited as they could cause damage to the house, block light and air circulation, and spread disease. For the same reason, no more than two trees or evergreens could be planted in a small yard. Instead, plants with beautiful fruits and flowers were planted in abundance.

A pagoda tree or two jujube trees planted at the gate were the most auspicious, pomegranate trees in the yard meant many descendents, and a willow tree planted outside to the east of the main gate meant wealth in animals. Therefore, a limited number and type of trees were planted at significant locations, such as in front of the gate, inside the courtyard, and next to the wall.

4) Planting Directions

In addition to location, direction was considered when using plants in house gardens. Hong Man-seon's *Sallim gyeongje* (Farm Management) recommended planting willow and peach trees in the east; plum and jujube trees in the south; gardenia and elm trees in the west; and apricot and apple trees in the north.

This method was intended to create a pleasant living environment based on *fengshui* theory and to improve upon the limits of the geographical conditions while considering the ecological characteristics.

In particular, trees such as willows, Chinese parasols, plums and chrysan-themums were to be planted in the east; trees with large leaves that provided shade such as paulownias, elms, gardenias and bamboos were to be placed in the west; peaches, plum trees and jujube trees were to be in the south; and cherries, azaleas, apricots and apples were to be planted in the north. This method was used to control the micro-climate by considering the ecological characteristics and functions of the plants.

Camellias, azaleas, gardenias and pomegranates were not planted in the northern regions, as these trees could not survive in winter. And as large trees blocked the summer wind, they were not planted in the southwest. However, large trees were preferred in the northwest, as they helped to block cold winds in winter and the hot rays of the sun in summer.

2. Waterscape Techniques

Water, which symbolizes primitiveness, vitality, and eternity, has the quality of provoking all five senses. It was therefore widely used as an element in house gardens. Ponds and water channels were created for symbolic meanings or aesthetic and practical purposes within the limits of natural geographical features. Small waterscapes using stone mortars or stone ponds for lotuses were built in the courtyard of the men's quarters or in the back garden.

Figure 16. Plum trees, lotus flowers, pine trees and bamboos were preferred in upper-class houses as they were thought to symbolize Confucian values.

Figure 17. Peony, plum, peach, and silk trees were planted in abundance according to their symbolic and practical value.

Figure 18. Irises, crape myrtles, pomegranates, and day lilies were planted based on their individual beauty and ecological characteristics.

1) Ponds

Ponds, a common water feature found in gardens and reservoirs, were built in wide, open areas, such as the *bakkat madang*, or the courtyard outside the main gate, the courtyard of the men's quarters and the courtyard of the separate house (*byeoldang*), to create beautiful water scenery. In *Imwon gyeongjeji*, Seo Yu-gu (1764-1845) said that one could "breed fish, admire scenery, provide water to rice paddies and fields, and purify people's hearts" with a pond in the garden. In this regard, it is easy to see that ponds were not only built for their practical and aesthetic values but also to cultivate people's bodies and minds.

Pond shapes varied from square to round to irregular, and small islands were sometimes placed in the middle. Usually, square ponds with round islands were built. A round island in a square pond symbolized the sky and the earth respectively. This pond design represented a sincere desire for the prosperity of the family based on the principle of the universe according to which all things were produced from the combination of *yin* and *yang*. The island symbolized the *samsinsan*, or "three divine mountains" for immortals to live.

The pond in particular expressed the ideal of quiet appreciation, which was well reflected in the restricted and abstract composition of elements, including the simple, square pond and round island, one or two trees planted on the island (such as pine, crape myrtle, bamboo or willow), and oddly-shaped stones.

The banks of the pond were neatly built using natural or artificial stones, while clay and pebbles were layered at the bottom to seal the pond. The pond was used to breed fish or grow lotus flowers, which represented Confucian gentlemen, or water shields. Willow or crape myrtle trees were planted around the pond, and pine, bamboo, crape myrtle, and willow trees were planted on the island.

2) Waterfalls

According to *Imwon gyeongjeji*, "a location by noisy, fast-flowing water is not appropriate as a site for a house." However, waterfalls created in the gardens were mostly man-made, scaled-down versions. Some waterfalls were streams that fell directly into a pond below and still others flowed into a pond to create a gentle overflow. Some had underground water seeping in next to the pond, while others were built using a small water mill to channel the water in. Connecting bamboo gutters or stone pipes to stone ponds for lotuses and stone mortars in order to create waterfalls was also a commonly used method.

3) Water Channels

Though natural streams could be enjoyed from inside the house through a lattice wall, they were also diverted into the garden or dammed to form an artificial water channel.

Larger gardens sometimes had natural water channels such as brooks or small streams. These were called *seokgan* if they passed through stone or *songgan* (pine) or *jukgan* (bamboo) depending on the object of the scenery. Some water channels were made by digging below the wall so they could flow into the garden directly. Bamboo gutters called *bigu* were used to channel in the water.

Figure 19. Pond for lotuses called Mugiyeondang, Hahwanjeong and Pungyongnu pavilions (1728) in Haman, Gyeongsangnam-do. The island in the center of the rectangular pond, elegantly surrounded by old pines, represents Mt. Bongnaesan.

Meanwhile, curved, artificial water channels called *goksugeo* were made using stones symbolizing *yin* and *yang*.

3. Use of Stone

1) Artificial Mountain

Artificial mountains called *seokgasan* were made by stacking stones, particularly granite, which represented mountain energy and had high aesthetic value. They were widely used in house gardens after the 13th century, and their construction in the courtyard of the men's quarters or around ponds is referenced in such old documents as Kang Hui-maeng's "Gasanchan" (Eulogy for an Artificial Mountain)," Seo Geo-jeong's "Gasangi" (Record of an Artificial Mountain), Hong Man-seon's *Sallim gyeongje* (Farm Management), Jeong Yak-yong's "Dasan hwasa isipsu" (Twenty Poems on the History of Flowers by Dasan) and Kim Jo-sun's *Punggojip* (Collection of Poetry and Prose).

2) Oddly-shaped Stones

After the mid-Joseon era, artificial mountains gradually fell out of use and were replaced with a trend towards oddly-shaped stones that were easier to fit into narrow gardens. These stones featured unusual, naturally occurring shapes, were less than one meter high, and were exceptional in their individual beauty. They were used extensively, placed standing on end alongside flowering plants, on terraced flowerbeds, along walls, around ponds, and in back gardens.

According to *Yanghwa sorok* (A Brief Record on the Cultivation of Flowering Plants), written by Kang Hui-an, the stone had to be green in color, and the shape had to suggest a mountaintop and cliff with hidden clouds in a valley. It also had to be a natural stone with ornamental value that was found on a mossy mountain. Similar descriptions are also found in other works, including *Sallim gyeongje*, *Dasan 4 gyeongcheop* (Album of Four Scenes by Dasan), and *Danwondo* (Painting of Danwon Kim Hong-do).

3) Stone Pots

Stone pots (*seokbun*) smoothed out to hold oddly-shaped stones were placed alongside the walls of the men's quarters (*sarangchae*) and terraced flowerbeds. They were also called *seokham* (stone case) or *goeseokdae* (platform for oddly-shaped stones).

Stone pots had no regular size or form but were commonly made into square, hexagonal, octagonal, or round shapes. Their surface was decorated with symbolic patterns and characters. For example, the characters for *yeongju* (瀛州) invoked the wish for eternal youth, based on the idea of immortality. Fine sand symbolizing water was used to fill the pot that held oddly-shaped stones, representing the ideal world.

4) Stone Pond and Stone Mortar

Seokji, also called *seogyeonji*, were miniature ponds lined with smoothed stones. They were meant for decoration; lotus flowers, aquatic and floating plants, and fish were added to the water. The image of the sky reflected on the surface of the water was part of their beauty. *Seokji* were square in shape and placed in the courtyard of the men's quarters, the courtyard of the women's quarters, or back garden. They were a clever form of waterscape that made it possible for people to feel close to nature even in small spaces.

Figure 20. An oddly-shaped stone that symbolizes a return to nature and eternal youth

Dolhwak, or stone mortars, were also decorative objects that had similar uses as *seokji*. They were small and round and placed in the courtyard of the women's quarters, back garden, and terraced flowerbeds. They served the practical purposes of fire suppression, water supply, and so on.

5) Stone Table and Stone Stool

Stone tables (*seoksang*) were flat stone tables where one could sit and rest, drink tea, or enjoy a game of *baduk* or *janggi* while enjoying the scenery. Stone stools (*seoktap*) were used in a similar way as stone tables but were smaller and higher than the latter. In the case of stone tables, broad, flat stones were cut into uniform sizes, and four supporting stones were placed at each corner. Stone stools were used with appropriately-sized stones or left in their natural state.

6) Others

There were also stone lanterns, stone markers used for dismounting from horses or palanquins (*hamaseok*), stepping stones placed in courtyards or streams to create pathways, and small stone pillars (*seokju*) that played the role of sundials or on which lines of verse or the name of the location were carved.

4. Pavement

Paving materials for the courtyards of traditional houses included white clay, flat slab (*bakseok*), black brick (*jeondol*), and quicklime. White clay pavement, or long-weathered granite which had turned into fine earth, was the most preferred method. Also common was thin, flat slabs of granite or natural stone used in its rough state. Black bricks and quicklime were also used for paving.

5. Pavilions

Pavilions were used for a multitude of activities, including appreciation of the natural surroundings, scholarly discussions, recital of poems, and education of younger scholars. They were built in the courtyard of the men's quarters, the courtyard of the separate house, and the back garden.

Pavilions were mainly built from wood, but the roofs were either tiled or thatched using perennial herbs. The floor was made from either wood or an *ondol*-heating system. Pavilions were usually square, but some were built in rectangular, hexagonal, octagonal, cross or fan shapes.

Used for the appreciation of nature, pavilions themselves were works of art that were pleasing to the eye. In "Saryunjeonggi," Yi Gyu-bo (1168-1241) records a mobile pavilion on wheels, which could be moved to take advantage of the changing scenery. This shows how pavilions were used to enjoy the beautiful natural scenery that differed according to season, location and time.

6. Introduction of Landscape

Natural scenery was often brought closer to everyday life for people's enjoyment and appreciation. Two different methods were used to accomplish this. First was the *yugyeong* method, which entailed retiring to or visiting scenic places in the surrounding area, while the second was the *chwigyeong* method, where natural scenery was brought directly into house gardens.

The *chwigyeong* method of incorporating natural scenery into a garden included four different styles: *chagyeong,* or "borrowing the landscape," used the scenery that lay outside the house, village or fields; with *sagyeong,* or "copying the landscape," a natural scene was recreated inside the garden; *seongyeong,* or "selecting the landscape," meant choosing one outstanding scenic element; and *uigyeong,* or "imaging the landscape," used abstract or symbolic elements of natural scenery.

Vertical elements such as buildings, trees, hills, doors, windows, walls, and latticed fences were used to make small or narrow gardens appear larger and deeper by visually combining and overlapping hidden and exposed landscapes.

Both moving and still views were considered in the making of gardens, and different vantage points were created based on distant, middle and near views.

Figure 21. Gyeongjeong and Seoseokji in Yeongyang, Gyeongsangbuk-do

Other viewing directions included looking up, looking down, looking front and looking back.

In particular, special aesthetic touches could be found throughout the garden. Outside scenery was brought in where it could be appreciated up close. Overly artificial elements were avoided and scenic elements that harmonized natural and man-made beauty, such as terraced flowerbeds, walls, ponds, decorative objects, pavilions and trees, were placed in the garden.

Specifically in the case of the men's quarters (*sarangchae*), which had an advantageous location for observing the outside scenery, natural scenery was kept at a distance, and trees were planted in the courtyard for its abstract or symbolic beauty. If the door of the main wood-floored hall (*daecheong*) was opened wide, one could see all the way up to the back garden. The use of empty

Figure 22. A lotus pond and a pavilion built in *sarangchae* of the *yangban*'s house

Figure 23. Square-shaped stone pond and round-shaped stone mortar

space and hidden views created a sense of imagination and profound beauty.

When the door on the side of terraced flowerbed is open, decorative objects in the back garden appear inside the frame of the door, the image of which is connected to a hill in the back covered with bamboo and pine forests and wild flowers, suggesting a vision of graceful purity. This picture-frame effect is also seen in the back garden, where oddly-shaped stones, lotus ponds, chimneys, and a neatly organized platform for clay jars are placed, and the garden of the separate house that feels like a still-life, with pine and crepe myrtle trees planted on an island in the center of the pond.

IV. Conclusion

Korean villages were traditionally built with a mountain in back and a river in front. The natural surroundings with open land in front of the village created a sense of tranquility. In addition, the combination of residential sites, surrounding area, and land under cultivation with nature, economy, community, and environment resulted in a living space that ensured safety. In other words, by maintaining a principle of unity among heaven, earth, and humans in harmony with nature and the order of the universe, and by preserving natural scenery within residential spaces, a sound and sustainable living culture was established.

Figure 24. Painting of Okhojeong by Kim Jo-sun

Gender segregation and social status were applied to traditional houses, where spaces were clearly divided. These living spaces also reflected the hierarchy of principal, subordinate, and additional, based on direction, altitude, closeness, and decoration. The entire space of the household was a compound of building and yard units; this combined the inner spaces of the *haengnangchae, sarangchae, byeoldang, anchae,* and *sadang* with the outer spaces of the *haengnang madang, sarang madang, byeoldang madang, an madang, bakkat madang,* and back garden.

The landscape architecture of the house metaphorically expressed people's views of religion nature, and the universe in an objective space. It was also a practical and aesthetic space for cultivation of the heart and mind and, in particular, the expression of the desire for utopia and eternal youth, integrity and seclusion. Landscape design incorporated inner and outer courtyards, inner and outer gardens, and inner and outer surrounding areas as part of the natural scenery. In addition, decorative objects, pavilions, waterscapes, terraces and flowerbeds were used for aesthetic appreciation.

Pavilions and ponds in particular were artistic and literary spaces that brought people into contact with nature. The selection of materials and colors, the use of plants with symbolic or traditional geomantic meanings, and the use of native plants such as deciduous trees and fruit trees also reflected the idea of unity with nature.

The *chagyeong* method for borrowing the natural scenery and introducing it into the garden, and the *yugyeong* method of enjoying the scenery from within it, were often used. The picture-frame effect, the creation of scenery in a selective and metaphorical way due to the dislike of excessive, artificial skill, and symbolic scenery that reflected the dignity or ethics of the maker were emphasized.

As such, Korean landscape architecture sought harmony with nature while using metaphysical design techniques that transcended formative beauty. This resulted in the creation of gardens that were natural and ecologically sound.

References

Chung, Dong-o. 1986. *Hanguk-ui jeongwon* (Korean Gardens). Minumsa.

Heo, Gyun. 2002. *Hanguk-ui jeongwon* (Korean Gardens). Dareun sesang.

Hong, Man-seon. 1643-1715. *Sallim gyeongje* (Farm Management).

IFLA Korean Organizing Committee. 1992. *Hanguk jeontong jogyeong* (Korean traditional Landscape Architecture). Doseo Chulpan Jogyeong.

Jeong, Jae-hun. 1990. *Hanguk-ui yet jogyeong* (Ancient Korean Landscape Architecture). Daewonsa.

Kang, Hui-an. 1974. *Yanghwa sorok* (A Brief Record on the Cultivation of Flowering Plants). Translated by Yi Byeong-hun. Seoul: Eul Yoo.

Korea Institute of Landscape Architecture. 1992. *Dongyang jogyeongsa* (History of East Asian Landscape Architecture). Mun Un Dang.

Min, Kyung-hyun. 1991. *Hanguk jeongwon munhwa* (Korean Garden Culture). Seoul: Yekyong.

Shin, Sang-sup. 1991. "Jeontong jugeo-ui oebu gyeonggwan guseong chegye-e gwanhayeo" (On the Structure of External Landscape of Traditional Residences). Ph.D. diss., Korea University.

Yi, Jung-hwan. 1971. *Taengniji* (Ecological Guide to Korea). Translated by Yi Ik-seong. Seoul: Eul Yoo.

Yoo, Byung-rim, et al. 1989. *Joseonjo jeongwon-ui wonhyeong* (The Archetype of Joseon Era Gardens). Environmental Planning Institute, Seoul National University.

Yun, Kuk-pyong. 1977. *Jogyeongsa* (History of Landscape Architecture). Ilchokak.

Authors

Shin Sang-sup
(Woosuk University)

Shin Sang-sup is a professor in the Department of Landscape and Urban Design at Woosuk University. He received his Ph.D. in Agriculture from Korea University. He was a visiting professor at the Colorado State University (2000-2001). He is currently Vice-President of Korean Institute of Traditional Landscape Architecture and also a member of the Cultural Properties Committee. He is the author of *History of East Asian Landscape Architecture* (1996), *Korean traditional Ecology* (2004), and *Traditional Village and Cultural Landscape of Korea* (2007). E-mail: ssshin@woosuk.ac.kr

Hong Hyeong-Sun
(Joongbu University)

Hong Hyeong-Sun is a professor in the Department of Environmental Landscape Architecture at Joongbu University. He received his Ph.D. in Engineering from Cheongju University. He is currently working as an editor-in-chief at Korean Institute of Traditional Landscape Architecture and technician at the National Land Development.

Chapter 4

THE SPATIAL AND LANDSCAPE CHARACTERISTICS OF WALLED TOWNS

I. Introduction

1. What Is *Eupseong*?

As Korea has so many different kinds of *seong*, or fortress walls, it could be called a "country of fortresses." So far, there are approximately 1,200 known fortresses spread throughout all the provinces of South Korea. They served multiple functions as residential, administrative, and military sites throughout history, and site selection and spatial arrangement were based on the most effective use of these functions. Therefore, fortresses still remain an important element for examining the traditional landscape structure in Korea.

Eupseong were fortress walls built around the regional boundary of a local administrative unit called *eup*, within which government offices and commoners' residences were built. *Eupseong* differed from traditional villages, because they were concentrated at the living center of a centralized society that was responsible for both administrative control of the surrounding areas and military defense.

The formation of *eupseong* appears to be based on the implementation of political and administrative functions that reflected the centralized ruling structure centering on the monarch. According to the local administrative system, the country was divided into eight *do* (provinces), which were again divided into *bu, daedohobu, mok, dohobu, gun,* and *hyeon*. Among these, *bu* (including *yusubu*) served a strategic function in defending the capital city and *mok* were historical administrative centers. *Daedohobu* were centers of defense for the whole nation, and *dohobu* were regional defense strongholds. The basic unit of the local administrative system was *gun* and *hyeon*.

Accordingly, *eupseong* were the product of a linear administrative system that followed a direct line from the capital (king) to the *do* (provincial governor), and then to *bu, mok, gun,* and *hyeon* (local magistrates). It differed from the manorial system of medieval Europe or Japan's feudal system where a certain degree of regional autonomy was possible. In general, *eupseong* were specially designated traditional cities, as more than half of pre-modern cities in Korea were surrounded by fortress walls. The *eupseong* described in this chapter, however, were administrative centers of *gun* and *hyeon*, which were slightly bigger than villages. They also served the lowest administrative function in the local administrative system of the Joseon era and had the features of cities which differed from traditional villages in both size and characteristic.

2. Location and Type of *Eupseong*

As the center of administration of *gun* and *hyeon* during the Joseon era, *eupseong* were located in agricultural areas, and were especially concentrated along riversides, which were strategic points for land and water transportation to facilitate trade. They were also located at important military points, as well as places such as markets, stations, and ferry crossings.

Though it is true that most *eup* were surrounded by walls, they were originally built without them, as they served a solely residential function when communities were first formed. It was from the early Goryeo that the form of *eupseong*, with the outskirts surrounded by walls, began to take root, becoming very popular by the end of Goryeo or during the early Joseon. In early Joseon,

160 out of 330 *eup* were surrounded by fortress walls, and according to *Dongguk yeoji seungnam* (Expanded Survey of the Geography of Korea), written during King Seongjong's reign, the total number of *eupsong* reached 179, which meant that more than half of all local administrative units had fortress walls. However, most of them were destroyed throughout the process of modernization following Japanese occupation, and only a few remain today.

There were three types of *eupseong*: *sanseong*, located on mountainous terrain, *pyeongjiseong* on flatlands, and *pyeongsanseong*, which was a combination of the two. There were two different construction methods for *sanseong*: *temoe* and *pogok*. *Temoe sanseong* were built almost horizontally, two thirds of the way up the mountain. The name of this method was derived from its resemblance to a headband, as the wall appeared to wrap around the mountain. The length of the walls usually ranged between 400 and 600 meters, but they sometimes reached over one kilometer.

Mud was most commonly used to build the fortresses, which were built on hilly areas below 200 meters above sea level. Due to their small size, this type of *sanseong* could be built easily, but their small internal area made them ill-suited for long-term battles. In this regard, *pogok sanseong*, which were suitable for long-term battles with their wide inner area and abundant water supply from the valley, were devised. Gochang Eupseong was a typical example of this style, which prioritized wartime defense over residential purposes, making it difficult to form a village within the walls.

Pyeongjiseong are most commonly found in Nagan Eupseong of Jeollanam-do and Jeongui Eupseong of Jeju-do. *Pyeongjiseong* were usually located in open fields, and settlements could develop inside as they had both defensive and residential functions. It was rare that such *eupseong* were built on entirely

Figure 1. Illustration of the configuration of *eupseong* and the surrounding mountains and rivers. *Map of Seonsan-bu*. Possession of Gyujanggak, Seoul National University.

open land. Rather, they were usually built with a mountain range to the back so that the wall surrounded both the field and the base of the mountain. Haemi Eupseong in Seosan-gun, Chungcheongnam-do is a typical example of this style. In the case of large-scale *eup*, they were built in this style for defensive purposes, and the capital of Hanyang is a good example of the style.

3. Size of *Eupseong* and its Social Characteristics

On the hierarchical scale of community size, that is, village → town → city → capital city, *eupseong* were medium in size, bigger than natural villages and smaller than big cities such as *bu* and *mok*. As they were made up of two to three villages, they were situated in the middle of the hierarchy. They were typical of urban communities, in contrast with rural communities.

In general, the physical size of *eupseong* varied between 6 and 15 hectares, and the diameter was between 300 and 500 meters. According to modern urban planning theory, *eupseong* were the size of a neighborhood unit and covered a distance that could be easily walked (400-800 meters). As they belonged to a certain territory within the city, they formed a collective settlement that created a degree of intimacy, allowing residents to share a sense of "we-feeling."

The inside of the *eupseong* was divided into two or three parts by the main axis and the secondary axis, forming separate villages. In addition, a number of villages (north, west and east villages) were spatially demarcated. These were divided again into numerous sections by curved paths. Three to twelve households formed a cluster, with a hierarchical order ranging from cluster to village to neighborhood.

Regarding population size at the end of Joseon, there are presumed to have been between 800 and 1,500 people of 300 to 500 households living in one *eupseong*. Those who lived inside *eupseong* primarily held so-called "third industry" occupations, including administrative, military, communications, education, and commerce. Other typical inhabitants included tenant farmers who worked for a small number of landowners, as well as merchants, peddlers and innkeepers who fulfilled non-productive and consumption-based

Figure 2. An example of the spatial structure of *eupseong*. *Map of Seonsan Eupseong.* Possession of Gyujanggak, Seoul National University.

occupations, in addition to providing services to the surrounding areas. In *eupseong* there were such facilities as Hyanggyo, a local Confucian school, Seonghwangdan, an altar for the village guardian deity, Sajikdan, an altar for the god of earth and the god of crops, and Yeodan, an altar for wandering spirits who had no one to perform rituals for them, all of which contributed to forming a sense of unity based on regional ties.

In this context, social stratification as a distinct form of class division took place between the ruling class, which was made up of bureaucrats and *yangban* land owners, and the ruled class of farmers. *Eupseong* were thus characterized by a degree of isolation, unlike purely agricultural villages. Community consciousness and consanguinity with regional or blood ties based on land economy, common in other traditional villages, were also rare in *eupseong*. Rather, as a socially-alien settlement that was relatively larger than a village, it revealed distinct characteristics of urban society.

II. *Eupseong* of Korea

1. Nagan Eupseong

Nagan Eupseong, located in Nagan-myeon, Suncheon-si, Jeollanam-do, belonged to the county office during the Joseon era. Part of its central facilities, including residential areas and Gaeksa, the guesthouse for government officials, are still preserved in their original state. Nagan Eupseong was called Buncha-gun during the Baekje era, Bullyeong-gun after Unified Silla, and Nagan-gun (or Yangak) under Naju-mok during the Goryeo era. It became Nagan-gun, Naju-bu in 1895 and was downgraded to Nagan-myeon, Suncheon-gun in the April of 1914. In August 1949, it became Nagan-myeon, Seungju-gun when Suncheon-eup was elevated to Suncheon-si, and when Suncheon-si and Seungju-gun were integrated in 1995, the name of its administrative zone was changed once again to Nagan-myeon, Suncheon-si.

The walls were first constructed when General Im Gyeong-eop was serving as the county magistrate in 1626 (the 4th year of King Injo's reign). However, it is assumed that General Im rebuilt what had already been constructed long before early Joseon, given that *Dongguk yeoji seungnam*, which was written in 1481 (the 12th year of King Seongjong's reign), mentions the location of Naganseong as well as the construction method used to build the wall.

According to *fengshui* theory, the surrounding topography including Nagan Eupseong is in the form of *ongnyeo sanbal*, meaning that the land resembles a woman who has let her hair down before applying make-up. The *eupseong* itself is described as the form of *haengju*, as it resembles a boat crossing the sea. Mt. Geumjeonsan (670 meters high) stands to the north as the guardian mountain, with Mt. Myeoraksan (Obongsan) and Mt. Gaeunsan to the east and Mt. Baegisan (584 meters) and Mt. Geumhwasan to the west. A vast field opens up in the south with a low hill (Mt. Oksan, 59 meters) in the middle. Nagan Eupseong demonstrates the *pyeongjiseong* type, found in the open fields. Mt. Buyongsan (195 meters) and Janggunbong peak (414 meters) are located in Beolgyo, past the front mountain, or Mt. Oksan, and Ongnyeobong peak lies beyond Mt. Geumjeonsan in the north. Dongcheon stream flows in from the southeast of Mt. Geumjeonsan, while Seocheon stream comes in from southwest. Both streams flow outside the east and west sides of the fortress wall, and pass the front of Mt. Oksan before crossing the field and reaching the sea to the south.

The periphery of Nagan Eupseong measures 13,700 meters. The fortress wall itself is four meters high, three to four meters wide, and 135,000 square meters in size. There are three gates to the east, west and south, and the east gate is an *ongseong*, or a semi-circular chemise built to protect the gate. There are also one pond and two springs inside the fortress. The guesthouse for government officials (Gaeksa) and nine thatched houses, which appear to have been built during the Joseon era, have been designated important folklore materials, along with a building that housed the stele of General Im Gyeong-eop. Nagan Hyanggyo and Chungminsa shrine for generals Im Gyeong-eop and Kim Bin-gil are also cultural assets located to the east of the fortress.

Figure 3. Overview of Nagan Eupseong I

Figure 4. Overview of Nagan Eupseong II

The kinds of occupations that would belong to today's tertiary industry—military, communication, education and commerce fields—were popular among the inhabitants of this village. Those in these fields totaled between 62 and 124, forming an important class of inhabitants within the village community.

2. Jeongui Eupseong

Jeongui Eupseong in Jejudo Island was the county government office for approximately 500 years until the *gun-hyeon* system was abolished in 1914 after Jeongui-hyeon, which had been established in Goseong-ri, Seongsan-mycon, Jcju in 1410 (the 10th ycar of King Taojong's roign), was moved to the present location (Asang-dong, Seongeup-ri, Pyoseon-myeon, Namjeju-gun) in 1423 (the 5th year of King Sejong's reign).

Jeongui Eupseong was built in the *pyeongjiseong* type on flatlands, in a 350-meter-long square, and it covered an area of 9 hectares. Ten or so watchtowers were built on the wall, and the gates to the east, west and south were used to control the comings and goings of the people.

According to *fengshui* theory, Mt. Yeongjusan was the guardian mountain, Mt. Hallasan the ancestral mountain, and Namsanbong peak was the front mountain. The village was in the form of *janggun daejwa*, with the two generals, i.e. a blue dragon on the left and white tiger on the right, facing each other with small hills representing soldiers scattered around the area. The village was also said to resemble a boat with the rudder and anchor at Mt. Namsan. The bow of the boat pointed northwest, and Namsanbong peak was the stern. This characterized the natural landscape outside the wall.

Figure 5. Overview of Jeongui Eupseong I

Figure 6. Overview of Jeongui Eupseong II

The main public facilities inside the fortress included the magistrate's office, Hyangcheong (Local Agency), Gaeksa (guesthouse for government officials), a Confucian shrine, and annex buildings. All three gates had two-story tower gates, and four stone grandfathers (*dolharubang*) were located inside each gate. The size, shape and living conditions of Jeongui Eupseong were similar to those of Nagan Eupseong.

Though *eupseong* were typically divided into three parts, small irregular paths that extended from the main axis divided it into nine small villages or clusters. These villages had their own shrines based on their public facilities, which must have provided an independent living sphere for each village.

3. Haemi Eupseong

Haemi Eupseong is located in Haemi-hyeon, Seosan-gun, Chung-cheongnam-do, which was a strategic military location. It was built mainly for defense. The *eupseong* is located on the descending ridgeline of Mt. Gayasan. The ridgeline occupies approximately one fourth of the entire inner area, and the fortress was built in *pyeongsanseong* type.

Though Haemi-heyon is only a small village on the west coast of Chuncheongnam-do province, an army commander-in-chief of Chungcheong-do province resided here for almost 200 years, dating from the 18th year of King Taejong's reign to King Hyojong's era during Joseon. The *eupseong* itself was constructed in the 22nd year of King Seongjong's reign (1491). Currently, some features still remain inside the *eupseong*, such as relatively well-preserved walls, recently-constructed three gates, an office for a magistrate

Figure 7. Overview of Haemi Eupseong I

Figure 8. Overview of Haemi Eupseong II

(Dongheon), square-shaped pavilion, and buildings attached to the Dongheon including a prison. It is assumed that people once lived inside the fortress. Also, according to the article on Haemi-hyeon of *Yeoji doseo*, the circumference of the fortress wall was approximately 2,000 meters, with a height of 4.5 meters and an area of 7.3 hectares. It appears that there were six springs and wells but no ponds. Three sites for the village guardian spirit were located inside the fortress, and one site was located outside; they still exist today. Sajikdan, an altar for the god of earth and the god of crops, and Hyanggyo were located outside the east and west gates, respectively.

4. Gochang Eupseong

Gochang Eupseong, located in Gochang-gun, Jeollabuk-do, is a *pogok sanseong* type. It is also called Moyangseong. It is assumed to have been constructed in the first year of King Danjong's reign (1453). As a fortress affiliated with the garrison of Naju, it was connected to Ibamsanseong mountain fortress. It also served as an important military point, being used as a training ground for soldiers. Like Haemi Eupseong, it was also built for defense purposes. Gochang Eupseong, built in the *sanseong* type in a mountainous valley, was unique in that it was mainly occupied by administrative government buildings while the inhabitants formed a village outside the fortress. In this regard, the eupseong itself did not have any urban characteristics as a collective settlement.

The fortress wall was a total of 1,700 meters in length, 3.6 to 4 meters in height, and 16.5 hectares in area. The three fortress gates are restored with two-story tower gates and semi-circular chemises. However, according to the old maps, only the north gate and the east gate had two-story tower gates, while the functionally insignificant west gate was left open. Six protruding bastions (*chiseong*) were constructed inside the fortress, and a moat was added for defense purposes. According to *fengshui* theory, Jangdaebong peak (106 meters) was a guardian mountain located behind the government office. With Jangdaebong at the back and Mt. Seongsan at the front, Gochang Eupseong faced north, thus, the north gate was the main gate for the fortress. According to the *Dongguk yeoji seungnam* (Expanded Survey of the Geography of Korea), there were two ponds and four wells within the fortress. The map of Gochang-hyeon (1788) made during King Jeongjo's reign also confirms that the Dongheon, Gaeksa, and Hyangcheong, three two-story tower gates, and 22 other government facilities were located inside as well. It is thought that the fortress was not a residential one due to its topography and its function as a strategic military site. In villages outside the fortress, five stone *jangseung* (guardian posts) were placed at the center and at each entrance of the crossroad.

According to *fengshui* theory, the village inside Gochang Eupseong looked like *waho eumsu*, or a tiger crouching down to drink water. Today, Hyanggyo and Gochang High School are located on the site of Mt. Seongsan that was considered the "crouching tiger," and Gochang Girls' High School now stands on the site of the pond that was considered "drinking water." The village outside the fortress looked like *haengju*, or a ship at sea. The sites for the village guardian spirits were placed in all four corners and at the center, serving as visual demarcation. The site for the village guardian spirit on Hageo-ri, which was next to the sea, was highest, reflecting a boundary hierarchy.

III. Spatial Characteristics of *Eupseong*

1. Spatial Form of *Eupseong*

When analyzing the form of *eupseong* based on *Yeoji doseo*, a Joseon Dynasty atlas, it is found that most *eupseong* were either round or square: 49 percent were round, 31 percent square, and the remaining 20 percent were irregular in shape. One can speculate that round and square shapes were based on the concept of *yin-yang*, according to which the sky is round and the earth is square.

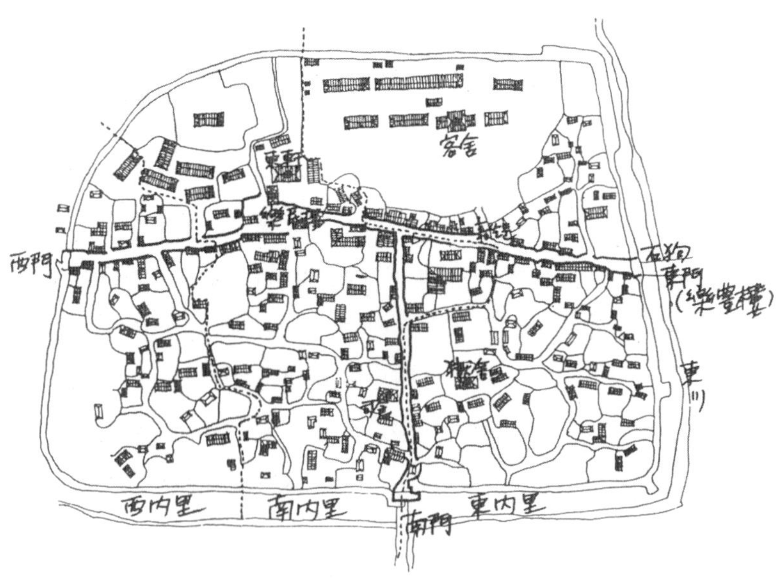

Figure 9. Map of *eupseong* (Nagan Eupseong)

The area inside the fortress was mainly divided by the arterial roads. Most roads were either T-shaped (45 percent) or cross-shaped (36 percent). Because most *eupseong* faced south with a mountain at the back, according to *fengshui* theory and other reasons, the gate could not open to the north. Even when the gate was positioned to the north, it was merely formal and not used.

This basic pattern of round or square-shaped *eupsong* with T-shaped or cross-shaped roads has also been found in pre-industrial cities worldwide. Thus, some believe that this pattern is an archetype belonging to the collective human unconscious.

2. The Spatial Structure of *Eupseong*

The spatial structure and main facilities of *eupseong* included government buildings that serve governmental, military, educational, and religious purposes: Dongheon (magistrate's office) and related facilities, Gaeksa (a guesthouse for government officials), Hyangcheong (Local Agency), a prison, Hullyeoncheong (an office for military training), Hyanggyo (a local Confucian school), Seonghwangdan (an altar for the village guardian deity), Sajikdan (an altar for the god of earth and the god of crops), and Yeodan (an altar for wandering spirits who had no one to perform rituals for them). They were concentrated in certain areas, while the surrounding area consisted of commoners' houses. These all combined to form an entire community.

Among the government buildings, the Dongheon office was also called Jeongdang or Jeongcheong and was where a provincial governor or a county magistrate took care of official affairs. Gaeksa was a guesthouse for government officials. It was used to enshrine the spirit tablet representing the king, and rituals were performed there every first and the fifteenth day of the month. It was situated at the very center of the *eupseong*, and was the most important government facility in terms of size and hierarchy.

Other facilities included Hyangcheong, an advisory committee of local elites, the prison, Hullyeoncheong, an office for military training, the Hyanggyo school, and the Sajikdan altar for observing religious rituals. Though they each had their particular functions, they must have been primary landscape elements that fulfilled symbolic roles for the *eupseong*. In particular, the Gaeksa, Dongheon, and Hyangcheong, which symbolized the king, the magistrate, and the local elites respectively, were central facilities that formed the core of the *eupseong* landscape.

Other facilities were mainly religious or educational, such as Sajikdan, Hyanggyo, and Munmyo (Confucian Shrine). Following the principle of the *Zhouli* (Rites of the Zhou), that is, "Sajikdan to the left and Munmyo to the right," Sajikdan was placed west outside the fortress while Hyanggyo or Munmyo was placed to the east.

There were also other religious facilities, including Seonghwangdan and Yeodan, both of which were located on the guardian mountain behind the *eupseong*. Along with Sajikdan and Munmyo, they made up "three altars and one shrine" (*samdan ilmyo*).

In general, the main village surrounding the government buildings inside the *eupseong* and the village centered around the Hyanggyo outside the *eupseong* formed the main residential area. The residential area inside the fortress had a high population density and markets and houses stood side by side along the roads.

Figure 10. Dongheon (Nagan Eupseong)

Figure 11. Residential area (Nagan Eupseong)

The spatial structure of Nagan Eupseong was divided largely into three parts by main and secondary roads. In other words, the main road that ran east to west divided the space into high and low, the latter of which was again divided into east and west by the secondary road that ran north and south. The two lower spaces consisted of three villages called Dongnae-ri, Namnae-ri and Seonae-ri, and the actual community life of the residents was organized by this division. Therefore, each village had its own ritual space for folk religion. Regarding this division of territory, the residents believed it reflected the concept of Five Elements in the directions of east, west, south, north and center.

The inner spatial structure of these divided villages was created, not by main and secondary roads, but by irregular and naturally formed paths. Within the residential blocks that were divided by such paths, houses with relatively large plots of land were built at the innermost center of the block, repeating the contrasting structure of "center" and "periphery" of the entire *eupseong*.

The *eupseong* roads formed a T-shape where the secondary road to the south gate connects to the main road that runs east and west at a right angle. In the case of Nagan Eupseong, traffic was heaviest from such eastern cities as Boseong and Beolgyo. Therefore, the main east-west road was particularly emphasized (the width was approximately twice that of the north-south road), whereas the secondary north-south road was simply a formality that followed the principle of *Zhouli*. It is evident from old data and the present view that important landscape elements were arranged in a dramatic way along the entrance of the main east-west road, which was the most important in terms of functional and symbolic weight.

IV. Landscape Characteristics of *Eupseong*

Landscape composition of *eupseong* in the Joseon era can be categorized according to the relationships between the physical landscape elements, i.e. visual and structural landscape, cognitive landscape, and behavioral landscape.

This chapter will examine Nagan Eupseong as the main subject of *eupseong* landscape composition based on the following three points: people resided inside the *eupseong*; documents are reliable; and the form of the village has been relatively well preserved. At the same time, the analysis and supplementary explanations of the landscape characteristics of Gochang Eupseong of Jeollabuk-do, Haemi Eupseong of Chungcheongnam-do, and Jeongui Eupseong of Jeju-do will be added.

1. Visual and Structural Landscape Characteristics of *Eupseong*

1) Landscape as Territory

Spatial territoriality that is established by a bordered interior space of landscape is characterized in a limited way by the visuality of that border, which comes to possess the character of an organic substance itself, not simply as a membrane that separates inside and outside. It contrasts with the interior and is expressed as a symbolic element. In other words, while the inside is exemplified as mundane, time-dependent, and secular, the border is seen as possessing elements that are special, independent of time, and sacred.

As an element that restricts territory, the border takes its form in natural elements such as hills, rivers and coastlines. In the case of cities or fortress towns in Korea, natural elements, such as the four cardinal mountains (the guardian mountain, blue dragon on the left, white tiger on the right, and the front mountain) and stream, form the external-most territory as the outer boundary. The fortress wall and gates form a more specific inner territory, while the roads or paths inside the wall demarcate separate areas on the inside. In this regard, when geographical configurations, which were established according to *fengshui* principles, were incomplete as a boundary in themselves, people artificially reformed the landscape. This method is called *bibo* or *yeopseung*.

As mentioned earlier, the macro-scale *fengshui* feature of the surrounding topography including the *eupseong* itself of Nagan Eupseong is called *ongnyeo sanbal*, meaning the land resembles a woman who has let her hair down before applying make-up. The shape of the *eupseong* itself is called *haengju*, which means it looks like a large boat crossing the sea. In general, in the case of *ongnyeo sanbal*, the front mountain (*ansan*) should be shaped like a large comb with thick teeth (月梳型); the mountain on the right should resemble a mirror (面鏡型); and the mountain on the left should be in the shape of a compact and bottle of hair oil (粉匣油壺型). When these geographical conditions are met, this *eupseong* is considered an auspicious site. In the case of Nagan Eupseong, Mt. Oksan, the front mountain, is shaped like a comb with thick teeth, while Pyeongchon pond in front resembles a mirror. Furthermore, it is said that a woman (Mt. Oksan) is putting on make-up before meeting the general (Janggunbong peak) in the south, and the helmet (Tugubong peak) she will give to the general lies over Ogongjae pass nearby. In brief, Nagan Eupseong resembles a woman applying make-up before meeting a general who is about to go to war. This implies Nagan Eupseong's military importance as well as its strategic advantage in defense.

By comprising the four cardinal mountains (Mt. Geumjeonsan, Mt. Myeoraksan, Mt. Baegisan, and Mt. Oksan) and the geographical configurations of these mountains (Ongnyeobong, Janggunbong, and Tugubong peaks), Nagan Eupseong further expands its territory. Also, by overlapping multiple *fengshui* principles while adding the boat shape of the *eupseong*, it emphasizes the territory of *fengshui*. The *bibo* (complementary) and *yeopseung* (repressive) methods are used to emphasize *fengshui* principles as visual territoriality. For example, because the Dongcheon stream, which is located outside the east gate, flows directly south, the *bibo* method was used to divert it to the south gate and thus turn it into a type of moat. Also, Mt. Myeoraksan (Obongsan), which corresponds to the blue dragon on the left, was too steep and treacherous. Therefore, a pair of stone dogs was placed outside the east gate to counter the inhospitable terrain, using the *yeopseung* method.

In Gochang Eupseong, the form of the village outside the *eupseong* is *haengju* (a ship at sea); it is in the shape of a long oval one kilometer by 700 meters. Guardian poles (*sotdae*) were placed at each of the cardinal directions and at the center, defining the visual territoriality of the border as well as emphasizing the border and the center. This is another good example of a landscape style that combines the Five Elements theory, *fengshui* theory, and shamanism.

In Jeongui Eupseong, the village was seen as being shaped like a boat or the *janggun daejwa* type, with two generals sitting across from each other. Therefore, objects symbolizing the rudder and anchor were placed at Mt. Namsan. The bow of the boat faced northwest, and Namsanbong peak was the stern, demarcating the natural, geographical territoriality outside the fortress.

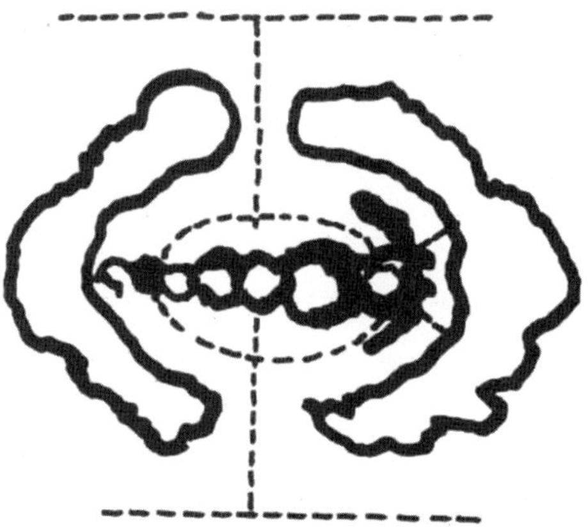

Figure 12. Illustration of *janggun daejwa* type according to *fengshui* theory (Jeongui Eupseong)

In addition to the macro-scale visual territoriality, other objects that marked territory through artificial, micro-level structures included walls, trenches, two-story tower gates, and public facilities (e.g. Hyanggyo, Sajikdan and shrine) located outside the wall. Public facilities reflected a more centrifugal territoriality as a form of negative space, while walls and gate towers expressed a more centripetal territoriality as a form of positive space. At Nagan Eupseong and Gochang Eupseong, Hyanggyo and the Bigak in which a stele was housed were placed at the main entrance outside the fortress, while at Haemi Eupseong, Sajikdan and Hyanggyo were constructed outside west and east gates respectively. This can be interpreted as an effort to supplement the landscape visually and symbolically by creating a "blue dragon on the left and white tiger on the right."

Meanwhile, fortress walls were built in the area surrounding the village for external defense, and another trench was dug outside the wall in order to strengthen defense. This was a strong physical border element that corresponded specifically to the concept of territoriality. The formative symbolism of this boundary was represented most powerfully inside each fortress through the defensive facilities of the fortress wall itself, including *chiseong* (protruding bastions), *jeokdae* (gateguard platforms), and *yeojang* (crenellated parapet).

In the figure published in *Noindangji*, Nakpungnu, the main entrance of Nagan Eupseong, was the east gate. It contained a two-story building with a loft, whereas the south gate, Jinnamnu, and the west gate consisted of only one story. A stone bridge was built outside the east gate, and the Hongsalmun gate, or a red arrow gate, was installed inside.

A pair of stone dogs was placed at the main entrance to emphasize the territoriality of the main entrance in multiple ways. The south gate opened onto

Figure 13. Wall of Jeongui Eupseong

Figure 14. Protruding bastion of Haemi Eupseong

Figure 15. South gate (Jinnamnu) of Nagan Eupseong

farmlands, while the west gate was the least functional and least frequently used apart from its function as a direct passageway to the east gate.

According to old maps, at Gochang Eupseong, only the north gate, main gate, and east gate had two-story buildings with wooden floor, while the west gate had only an entrance. All three gates at Jeongui Eupseong had two-story tower gates, and four stone grandfathers were placed inside each gate. These examples show that gates were physical elements that expressed territoriality in fortresses, and a hierarchy was established according to the importance of each gate.

Apart from the *fengshui* aspects, which defined the boundary between the external and internal parts of the *eupseong*, the roads were anther element that defined the territoriality of each area inside the wall. They appeared in similar forms in each *eupseong*: The structure was a straight T-shape connecting three

Figure 16. Fortress gate and stone grandfathers (Jeongui Eupseong)

gates. Structurally, these main roads divided the village. Though the irregular and secondary pathways that extended from these main roads sometimes formed the territoriality of each village, the living area of the village was largely and exclusively divided into three by the main roads.

2) Landscape as an Axis

An axis is fundamentally a linear element that connects two or more points. It took the form of a passage or city roads and also functioned as the central passage through the landscape. In *eupseong*, the primary landscape axis was the T-shaped central passage that connected the three fortress gates. The road from the south gate to the Gaeksa normally formed the main north-south road with the Gaeksa as the terminus landscape; the main east-west road crossed the north-south axis to form a three-way intersection.

The north-south road and the east-west road did not cross at right angles; they generally formed a bent axis from the starting point of the main gate to the terminus, or Dongheon. The main axis was intentionally bent once or more so that the Dongheon would not be directly visible from the opposite side.

In most cases, Dongheon, the terminus by definition, was placed slightly at the back or to the side, and the assumed terminus Gaeksa building was placed as a visual terminus. The bending of the axis can be interpreted both as an intentional measure to encourage a gradual understanding of the space as the viewer moves through it, and as a defensive strategy.

In general, visual objects were arranged sequentially along or on each side of the axis, either symmetrically or asymmetrically. However, in Korean *eupseong* the asymmetrical arrangement was generally preferred so as to form a more natural dynamic balance.

These axes reflected, depending on their width, the hierarchy between the main and secondary axes. In order to show the central symbolism of the main axis, symbolic structures (Hongsalmun at Nagan Eupseong, Punghwaru at Gochang Eupseong) or symbolic natural elements (a large gingko tree that symbolized the "sail" according to *fengshui* at Nagan Eupseong and the pond at Jeongui Eupseong) were placed at a location which became the node of the axis. Also, the visual weight of the areas to the right and left of the axis (e.g. the building capacity on each side of the axis was almost equal at Gochang Eupseong) or the symbolic weight (e.g. at Nagan Eupseong, the bamboo hill on the main axis was *yang* and the pond on the right was *yin*) was considered.

Consequently, the main and secondary axes of *eupseong* strengthened the unified power of the center by containing the government buildings in one defined area.

3) Sequence of Landscape, Figure and Ground, Positive and Negative Spaces, and Spatial Enclosure

The visual landscape of the *eupseong* can be analyzed using the sequence of landscape, figure and ground in Gestalt psychology, positive and negative spaces, and spatial enclosure.

First, the landscape is formed by the bent axis and landscape structures positioned along the axis. Moving along the axis, viewers experience a sense of anticipation and readiness of mind through the hidden and changing views that emerge, creating a gradual understanding of a landscape that also culminates gradually.

In case of Jeongui Eupseong, facilities and roads inside the *eupseong* were arranged so that the major public facilities were located at the center of the T-shaped road. However, the shape of the road was heavily modified. It bends in a number of places to keep the view dynamic and impenetrable. Consequently, this forms many terminus landscapes at various places inside *eupseong*. Upon entering the south gate, the Gaeksa, the guesthouse for government officials, forms a terminus landscape that reaches the end of the road. Going around it, the Hyangcheong, or Local Agency, stands on the opposite side, and the Dongheon, or magistrate's office, forms the final part of the landscape. When entering from the east gate, the marketplace in front of the Dongheon stands at the end, and one must change direction to reach the Dongheon. Thus, the overall landscape is accomplished through the style of the road.

After crossing the bridge over the Dongcheon stream at the entrance of Nagan Eupseong, one passes a pair of stone dogs in front of the east gate

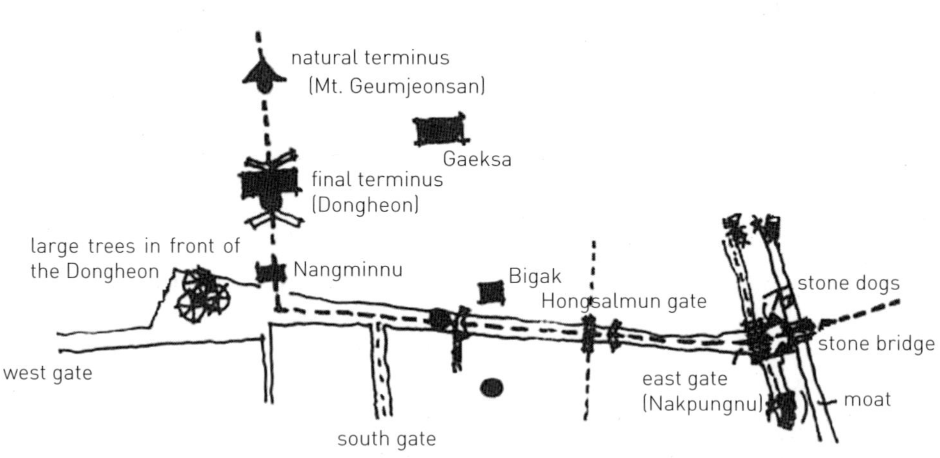

Figure 17. Diagram of sequence of *eupseong* landscape (Nagan Eupseong)

(Nakpungnu), after which the Hongsalmun gate awaits. This double-framed view used at the fortress gate and the Hongsalmun gate respectively emphasizes the feeling of the entrance. Large gingko trees on each side of the road and the Bigak where General Im Gyeong-eop's stele is housed maintain the visual and symbolic weight of the main axis. The Gaeksa, which is the symbolic terminus and the most prominent landscape marker inside the *eupseong*, is isolated on the right side of the road, emphasizing the building's status and authority (the kings' spirit tablets are enshrined here). It is common for the Gaeksa to wield such visual weight in other *eupseong*. It is usually located near the end of the main road that begins at the south gate, and Nagan Eupseong is no exception.

The guardian mountain of the village, Mt. Geumjeonsan, is seen in the background behind the Gaeksa, and it emphasizes the symbolic axis of the village. However, as the village is far away from the guardian mountain, a grove of old, large trees (also used for shamanic rituals) was planted to supplement deficient elements (*bibo*). Lastly, when one arrives at the Dongheon, the final visual point inside the *eupseong* and the terminus of actual administrative activities, one discovers an interesting aspect: A plaza, surrounded by large, old trees and additional administrative buildings, was built to interrupt the view here. From here, one has to turn 90 degrees to pass Nangminnu and approach "the main building" of the Dongheon, the last and actual visual indicator. As a backdrop emphasizing this element, the Dongheon faced the guardian mountain (Mt. Geumjeonsan), the natural terminus, showing a high degree of visual technique.

Figure 18. Gaeksa (Nagan Eupseong)

Figure 19. Spirit tablets enshrined at the Gaeksa (Nagan Eupseong)

Figure 20. Dongheon at Nagan Eupseong

Through this process, "figure" and "ground" interchange continuously according to the intensity of experience and the importance of the objects. In other words, the positive spaces filled with the large, old trees in front of the Dongheon, the two-story gate tower (Nangminnu) in front of the gate of the government office, and the six local offices, are experienced as a "figure." They change into "ground" by turning 90 degrees, and the tower gate and the Dongheon become a new "figure."

Regarding the enclosure that depends on the width of the road in *eupseong*, there is a difference between the main and secondary axes. Enclosure of the main axis is D/H=2, forming a rather tight spatial equilibrium due to its position at the perimeter of the appropriate enclosure. The secondary axis has an enclosure of D/H=1, which forms a strong enclosure that creates expectation and contraction.

Figure 21. Nangminnu in front of the Dongheon (Nagan Eupseong)

Figure 22. Road inside the *eupseong* (Nagan Eupseong)

2. Cognitive Landscape Characteristics of *Eupseong*

1) *Fengshui* Landscape

As capital cities such as Gaegyeong and Hanyang came newly into being, they could be built according to *fengshui*. However, as most villages (*eup*) were established before the Goryeo era, when *fengshui* theory was popular, or even later had already developed into villages of considerable size, it was difficult to rebuild them into ideal cities based on the *fengshui* theory. However, it was customary that at least the administrative site for the village was located on the most geographically auspicious place within the village.

Also, traditionally in Eastern cities, the king's palace or magistrate's office was located to the north so it would receive southern exposure. As most of these northern spaces have their guardian mountain in the north, they are considered central points where life force gathered (*hyeol*) and auspicious sites according to *fengshui*.

In this vein, people tried to stay faithful to the *fengshui* theory as much as possible by constructing the Dongheon and other administrative buildings at the center of *eupseong*, which was considered the best location. The fortress wall was built according to the blue dragon and white tiger concept. Also, the geographical features surrounding the village were used and explained according to *fengshui*, which must have been used in turn to rationalize the good or bad fortune that ensued.

Judging from the style of *eupseong*, their locations were seldom chosen based on the complete *fengshui* principles from the beginning. Instead, *fengshui* was used to create social stability by increasing people's understanding of the landscape; in other words, the relationships between

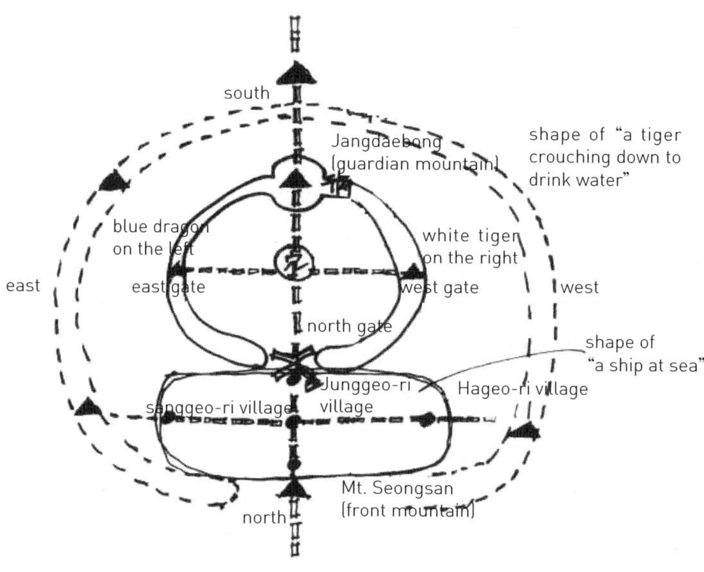

Figure 23. Digram of *fengshui* theory applied to *eupseong* (Gochang Eupeong)

eupseong and *fengshui* were constructed and supplemented by stories of *fengshui*. In visual and structural analysis, the geographical configuration of *fengshui* is largely treated as an element of visual boundaries, whereas in cognitive landscape, the focus is on the meaningful relationships between *fengshui* elements. The four surrounding mountains were called black *hyeonmu* (a cross between a tortoise and a snake), blue dragon (*cheongnyong*), white tiger (*baekho*) and red phoenix (*jujak*). Here, when black *hyeonmu* means master, red phoenix means guest; and when black *hyeonmu* means husband, red phoenix means wife. This also suggests that animism was of fundamental importance from the very start of the application of *fengshui* theory. *Fengshui* can be understood as having created a certain correlative, symbolic landscape, that is, an allegorical landscape.

In the case of Nagan Eupseong, by selecting the two extreme points on the north-south axis that face each other—ancestral mountain Ongnyeobong (a woman) and the far front mountain Janggunbong (a general)—as the main characters of *fengshui*-based folk tales, and by using the surrounding geographical features (Tugubong peak, Mt. Oksan and Pyeongchon pond) as props, a dramatic and allegorical landscape is found, creating relationships of meaning within the surrounding landscape. In addition, by naming places after incompatible animals, such as Bungyebong (rooster) and Ogongchi (centipede), it reflects the dynamic relationships within the landscape.

Gochang Eupseong has a similar form in that the mountain at the back and the mountain at the front represent the opposing concepts of *waho* (crouching tiger) and *eumsu* (drinking water). *Yin-yang* relationships are usually reflected through binary oppositions. The mountain at the back, which is typically the base of the main settlement, is usually regarded as feminine, a concept that originates from the desire for abundant harvests in traditional agricultural society.

According to *fengshui*, the central axis is divided into three parts, i.e. a guardian mountain as the center of the sacred, a sacred tree or a guardian tree as the center of the secular, or shamanism, and the *hyeol* as the center where the sacred and the secular meet. The administrative area of *eupseong* is located on the *hyeol*, which is regarded as the center in *fengshui* theory.

Almost all *eupseong* sites recorded in *Sinjeung dongguk yeoji seungnam* (A Revised Edition of the Expanded Survey of the Geography of Korea) have articles that indicate the number of ponds and springs, and the ponds located on the central axis generally served as an internal water source. The pond under Punghwaru at Gochang Eupseong, the pond near the entrance of the Gaeksa at Jeongui

Eupseong, and the pond to the east near the south gate at Nagan Eupseong are such examples. It was common to have wells or ponds located nearby to connect the internal water source to external water sources. With the guardian mountain and the guardian tree mentioned above, the "sacred three" of popular shamanic beliefs in Korea—the sacred stone (mountain), sacred water and sacred tree — are placed on one axis, creating a system.

2) Landscape as Symbolic Forms or Directions

Among the various elements that influence the *eupseong* landscape from the cognitive perspective, and especially regarding what constitutes its form, there are examples where symbolic forms or directions were considered over practical aspects such as natural environmental elements.

A. Rapport suggested that cultural factors such as religion or ideology can come into play before the logic of geographical conditions, and consequently the landscapes wherein symbolic forms or symbolic directions are applied are often found in traditional spaces. Likewise, according to J. Appleton's habitat theory, people's aesthetic pleasure in an environment is achieved symbolically through an associative application that arises from environments that are immediately felt to be fit for survival, rather than the capacity of the environment that actually provides the necessary conditions for human survival. Based on the habitat theory, Appleton postulated a prospect and refuge theory, according to which the "see without being seen" landscape, which embodies both prospect (observation of the outside, usually a vertical aspect) and refuge (visual concealment from the outside, usually a boundary element), is considered the ideal symbolic landscape that can provide aesthetic satisfaction.

In this regard, when *fengshui* aspects of the *eupseong* and the form of the village within the *eupseong* are applied to the prospect-refuge theory, it can be said that *eupseong* were created as an ideal combination of prospect and refuge elements, with the mountain at the back as the prospect element and the center (局) of *fengshui* as the refuge element.

The landscape was likened to a number of objects including the human body; among these, boats were the most popular. In fact, boat-shaped villages and towns in Korea used masts to supplement the natural landscape, and fortresses such as Jejuseong, Najuseong, and Andongseong had a large number of landscape structures in the shape of a mast. Raising a mast in boat-shaped villages can be understood as establishing a vertical center in order to create a sense of visual unity. This might explain why the mountains surrounding *eupseong* were indispensably secured as strongholds, or why land basins were selected as typical *eupseong* sites. Furthermore, as the residential spaces of the village within the *eupseong* could be viewed from these mountains, they were important for defense and communication; signal fire posts were constructed so that people living further away could be notified in times of emergency through use of signal fire and smoke.

As examples in which the guardian mountain was used as the "prospect" element, there is the case of Haemi Eupseong where the prospect element was reinforced by the Sagakjeong pavilion, and the case of Jangdaebong peak (*jangdae* means a watchtower or sentry tower) in Gochang Eupseong. The examples of the prospect-refuge principle of boat and mast are found in both Nagan Eupseong and Gochang Eupseong. In Nagan Eupseong the guardian mountain is isolated due to its flat topography. Therefore, a village guardian tree serves as the mast for the entire village, which is shaped like a boat. Among the five guardian sites (east, west, north, south and center) found in Gochang Eupseong, the east, west, north and south sites emphasize the "boat" shape and create the characteristic of a refuge, while the center expresses the prospect element of the "mast."

Symbolic direction is A. Rapport's concept, which contrasts with the geographic directions of east, west, north and south. Symbolic directions can be grouped into visual, centripetal, centrifugal, opposing, high and low. The north-facing direction of Gochang Eupseong can be analyzed as symbolically "looking towards the capital."

3. Landscape Behavior of *Eupseong*

A. Rapport categorized the use of the external space of the village into open and outward type, and closed and inward type. He argued that both types tended to co-exist within one region. He also mentioned that while the former appeared in the lower class and folk culture, the latter reflected the upper class and modern culture.

The difference in such spatial behavior can also be seen in the difference between *yangban* villages and commoners' villages. With its relative superiority in terms of economic power and authority, *yangban* villages were allowed many choices regarding the site and landscape formation within the villages and *fengshui* elements were largely applied. As consanguinity and ancestor worship were respected, the sacred position and territorial symbolism of the head family were reflected. Village community festivals such as village rites were not popular among the inhabitants of these villages.

On the other hand, commoners' villages were highly unstable in terms of economic or political power, and they usually consisted of villagers with different surnames. Village rites for the unity of different families were popular, and shamanistic landscape elements were consequently abundant.

Eupseong differed from the above-mentioned villages in terms of social structure in that the landed *yangban* class was weak while the population mostly consisted of bureaucrats, commoners in service positions, and farmers whose lives were based on the surrounding farmland. The high migration rate and the inhabitants with different surnames gave *eupseong* urban characteristics. As they had tribal unities based on region rather than blood, community festivals such as village rites were popular. For this reason, paradoxically, these villages were anti-urban in their environmental formation.

The village in Nagan Eupseong was made up of families with different surnames, and its social and structural features were largely divided into two areas, which were then subdivided into three villages, namely Seonae-ri, Namnae-ri and Dongnae-ri. The village rites of Seonae-ri were held at the village guardian tree (Seonae-ri Hadang) inside the bamboo forest outside the wall. The rites of Namnae-ri were held at the village guardian stone (Namnae-ri Jungdang) north of the village. In the case of Dongnae-ri the rites were held at the site (Dongnae-ri Sangdang) located inside an old nettle tree forest behind the Gaeksa. An old gingko tree (Dongnae-ri Jungdang) served as the center of the entire *eupseong*. The ritual order went from Dongnae-ri Sangdang to Dongnae-ri Jungdang, Namnae-ri Jungdang, and Seonae-ri Hadang.

Tug-of-war was a popular event at community festivals, and it took place at the center of the T-intersection, which was also the center of the entire *eupseong*, pitting east (Dongnae-ri) against west (Seonae-ri and Namnae-ri).

As an agricultural ritual that emphasized the centrality and territoriality of the village by taking the center of *eupseong* as the starting point, and that prayed for an abundant harvest, village rites symbolically expressed binary oppositions by dividing the space of the village into east and west and also by distinguishing the main religious areas. The tug-of-war at Nagan Eupseong clearly defined the dual territoriality between Seonae-ri, Namnae-ri and Dongnae-ri, which took up most of the actual communal living area of the village, and the centrality at the intersection of the road, which was the center of *eupseong*.

V. Conclusion

As collective settlements, Korean *eupseong* fundamentally reflect the natural environment of Korea and collective cultural structure of its people. Though the origin of most *eupseong* can be traced back thousands of years, the traditional, pre-modern social structure revealed a spatial mode particular to East Asia.

Most *eupseong* were built during the Joseon era and are basically centralized, reflecting the characteristics of a *yangban*-bureaucratic nation. Medium and small cities (centered on *gun* or *hyeon*) modeled their form on that of large cities (centered on *do*, *bu*, or *mok*). Large cities in turn were modeled on the capital. In this way, the basic framework was repeated from the capital city to large, medium and small cities.

Such *eupseong* had a large number of public and urban facilities in order to execute their administrative function as well as defensive function, which was one of the important functions of *eupseong*. They were planned and standardized, rather than developing naturally over time. As small-scale cities, Korean *eupseong* were modeled on higher-level cities and further on the capital in terms of urban planning. Traditionally, as Korean capitals were built according to the basic principles of *Zhouli · Kaogongji*, written during the Zhou Dynasty, the *eupsong* did not vary much from this record in their internal shape.

At the same time, *eupseong* in Korea followed *fengshui* principles, which became popular after the Silla era. In other words, Korean *eupseong* depended mostly on *fengshui* theory regarding their location, direction, management of surrounding landscape elements, and the form and the name of various facilities in the city, while remaining faithful to the basic form of *Zhouli · Kaogongji* when it came to the mutual arrangement of public buildings inside the city, and roads and fortress gates. To summarize, Korean *eupseong* combined and applied the two traditional principles of environmental planning by basing their macro-scale location and natural landscape on *fengshui* theory and the specific space of the city and the organization of inner facilities on the basic form of *Zhouli · Kaogongji*.

The landscape structure of *eupseong* can be categorized by form (visual and structural landscape), meaning (cognitive landscape) and behavior (behavioral landscape) with the structural common denominator of *yin* and *yang*.

Firstly, the form (visual and structural landscape) of *eupseong* was divided into inside and outside, and the boundary was based on the four deities by *fengshui* and the fortress wall. The inner structure of the *eupseong* was again divided into upper and lower areas by the road that ran from east to west. The upper area contained administrative buildings and additional public facilities, and the lower area was the residential area where commoners lived. The lower area was divided into two districts by the road that ran north to south, i.e. a service-class village that was heavily subordinate to the local government office and a commoners' village that was independent of it, consequently dividing the spatial structure of the entire *eupseong* into three parts. The sequence of *eupseong* generally began from slaves' quarters near the entrance, followed by the storage area in the service district near the boundary, the Gaeksa which is the symbolic terminus, and led to the Dongheon, or actual terminus, along a bent axis. This sequence reflects the repetition of *yin* and *yang* found in traditional houses, villages and cities in Korea.

Yin-yang structure is also the main element of cognitive landscape. The topography of the *eupseong* itself was conceptualized as *yin* (-) while the visual objects i.e. the front mountain and another mountain in front of it were regarded as *yang* (+). This was based on the concepts of fecundity and abundant harvests in agricultural societies. The *eupseong* was divided into upper and lower parts: the upper part contained the administrative area (+), while the lower part held the commoners' village. Even within each part, high-level facilities were located at the inner space based on the spatial distinction. In the administrative area, the Dongheon was located so that it would function as the *yang*, while the other facilities were *yin*. Also, the landlords' houses were located near the center of the village so they would have the characteristic of *yang* compared to the rest of the village (*yin*). This was the usual method of traditional environmental planning that defined the upper class according to how difficult it was to access the space.

Behavioral landscape also reconfirms the dual structure of *yin* and *yang*. The three villages of Nagan Eupseong were divided into two large communal living areas, both of which were distinct, as reflected dramatically by the tug-of-war festival. In other words, the central space of the entire *eupseong* in form and meaning meets at the junction of the T-intersection, where the two sides of Seonae-ri and Namnae-ri (*yang*) and Dongnae-ri (*yin*) perform a tug-of-war. Thus, the dual structure of *yin* and *yang* is represented symbolically.

References

Appleton, J. 1972. *The Experience of Landscape*. University of Oregon Press.

Ban, Yeong-hwan. 1978. *Hanguk-ui seonggwak* (Fortress Walls of Korea). The Society for the Commemoration of the Great King Sejong.

Eliade, M. 1961. *The Holy and the Profane*. New York: Harper & Row.

Gochang-gun County Office. *Gochang gunji* (Records on Gochang-gun County).

IFLA Korean Organiging Committee. 1992. *Hanguk jeontong jogyeong* (Traditional Landscape Architecture of Korea).

Jeju-do Provincial Office. 1980. *Seongeup minsok ma-eul bojon mit yukseong gibbon gyehoek* (Basic Plans for the Preservation and Development of Seongeup Folk Village).

Jellicoe, G. A. 1970. *Studies in Landscape Design*, volume II. London: Oxford Press.

Oh, Hong-seok. 1980. *Chwirak jirihak* (Village Community Geography). Seoul: Kyo-hak Sa.

Park, Chan-yong. 1984. "Joseon sidae eupseong jeongjuji-ui gyeonggwan guseong yeongu" (A Study of Eupseong Landscapes during the Joseon Era). *Hanguk jogyeong hakhoeji* (Journal of Korea Institute of Landscape Architecture) 12.1.

Park, Chan-yong, and Kim Han-Bai. 1987. "Joseon wangjo sidae-ui do-eup gyeonggwan chegye yeongu" (I) (A Study of the Landscape System of the Capital during the Joseon Dynasty). *Hanguk jogyeong hakhoeji* (Journal of Korea Institute of Landscape Architecture) 15.2.

Ralph, E. 1976. *Place and Placelessness*. London: Pion Ltd.

Rapport, A. 1969. *House Form and Culture*. Prentice Hall.

Schultz, N. 1971. *Existence, Space and Architecture*. Praeger Publisher, Inc.

Seosan-gun County Office. 1981. *Haemi Eupseong nae geonmulji balgul bogoseo* (Report on the Excavation of Building Sites inside Haemi Eupseong).

Seungju-gun County Office. *Nagan eupji* (Records on Nagan-eup).

______________. 1979. *Naganseong minsok bojon maeul josa bogoseo* (Investigative Report on Folk Village Preservation of Nagan Eupseong).

______________. 1983. *Nagan Eupseong gaebal gyehoek bogoseo* (Report on Nagan Eupseong Development Plan).

Author

Park Chan-yong

(Department of Landscape Architecture, Yeungnam University)

Park Chan-yong is a professor in the Department of Landscape Architecture at Yeungnam University. He received his Ph.D. from Korea University. He was the invited artist, National Exhibition of Landscape Architecture in 2005. He was Dean of college of Natural Resources, Yeungnam University from 2005 to 2007. He is currently Vice President of the Korean Institute of Traditional Landscape Architecture.

E-mail: cypark@ynu.ac.kr

Chapter 5

Landscape Architecture of Retreat Gardens

I. Introduction

Byeolseo (別墅) referred to secondary houses built in scenic or pastoral spots away from the main house and used for retreat, seclusion, or communion with nature. *Byeolseo* gardens (hereafter referred to as retreat gardens) were divided into two styles: the villa style and detached house style.

Villa-style gardens were created by influential people from Seoul or Gyeonggi-do province and usually shared the same features as a basic household, including a kitchen, a main house, and storage. Regional villas built for retreat and seclusion were predominately built in this style. Though they were simple gardens that lacked a full household structure, meals could be prepared in the main house nearby, and simple cooking and daily tasks could be carried out. The retreat gardens found in Yeongnam, Honam and Chungcheong regions belong to this category.

Detached house gardens built separate from the main house were intended to express filial piety. Many included a house for dwelling, as in the case of Joseongnu in Nongso village at Seongmun-ri, Doam-myeon, Gangjin-gun.

Retreat gardens were built in scenic or pastoral spots for the purpose of retreat, seclusion, or communion with nature. They were usually located within walking distance (between 0.5 and 2 kilometers) of the main house.

Retreat gardens featured two-story pavilions (*nu*) and pavilions (*jeong*), some of which had rooms. Most were built in an open design without walls or doors so that the surrounding environment could be seen. They were used as a location for appreciating the natural scenery in its pure form.

However, when necessary, ponds, waterfalls, or artificial mountains were created, and decorative objects or trees were added to enhance the scenery. In

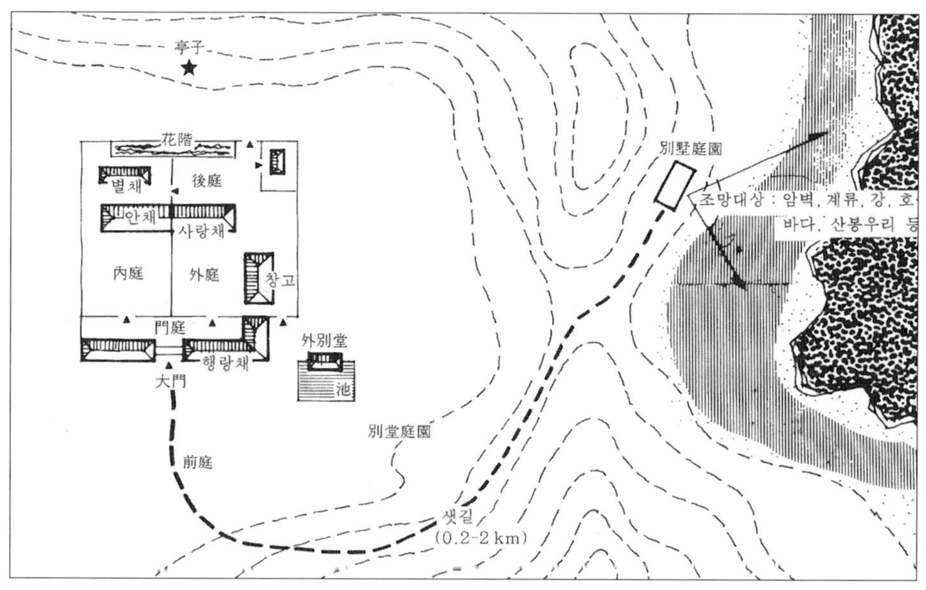

Figure 1. Illustration of the concept of a retreat garden

short, the retreat garden was a detached space set away from the main house, where people could experience both the human and natural environment while communing closely with nature.

II. The Origin of Korean Retreat Gardens

1. Three Kingdoms

The origin of Korean retreat gardens can be traced back to the *imcheon* ("forest and stream") gardens. *Imcheon* gardens were developed under the influence of agriculture, which emphasizes reverence for nature and attachment to the land. After Goryeo, they developed into natural-style landscape gardens, which seem to have been influenced by the turbulent times and landscape paintings of the Joseon era.

After the early agricultural era of field cultivation passed, the Bronze Age (5th century BC) brought about rice cultivation and changes in living conditions. People moved from living in riverside dugouts to building huts on south-facing slopes overlooking rivers. It is estimated that houses with small yards were first built around the first century BC, when the *ondol* heating system was first developed. With the arrival of the Iron Age (AD1st–2nd century), various types of furniture were created and gardens and small farms were introduced. As life became easier, housing styles also developed, and *imcheon* gardens were developed along with these changes.

It is assumed that the first record of retreat gardens was written by Choe Chi-won in *Samguk sagi* (Historical Record of the Three Kingdoms), which says that, upon returning from the Tang Dynasty, Choe felt despair over the social turbulence in Korea and subsequently left his post. He built pavilions in the forests near Gyeongju and Yeongju to enjoy the beauties of nature, and constructed a retreat garden at Masan.

Some members of Silla's upper class enjoyed *sajeol yutaek*, which was another type of detached housing used for seasonal retreats. The name *sajeol yutaek*, which originated during the Silla kingdom, refers to this kind of seasonal housing. They lived in a house in the eastern field in spring, a sunny valley in summer, among the autumn foliage in autumn, and in a snow-covered house in winter. The sunny valley used in summer had a pavilion positioned next to a clear, flowing stream. These aristocratic retreat houses were significant as they became a catalyst for even ordinary members of the upper class to own their own retreat gardens at the end of the Silla period.

2. Goryeo Dynasty

When the Choe family's military regime that emerged at the end of King Uijong's reign in the Goryeo era brought an end to the aristocratic government, a new Confucian literati appeared. They were not only men of scholarly achievement, but also men who were adept at government affairs. In other words, they were *sadaebu*, scholar-officials, who entered politics even more actively after the military regime was overthrown.

A number of *sadaebu* came from the petty functionaries in the local administrations (*hyangni*) who were small or medium-sized landowners or independent farmers with small farms. Their farms were either self-cultivated or managed by tenants or servants. Some continued to enjoy life in their hometowns even after they entered politics. The fact that, among the words for "garden" (*jeongwon*) used in the late Goryeo, terms such as *imcheon* (林泉), *wollim* (園林), and *imwon* (林苑), continued to be used after the mid-Goryeo period is evidence that the highly-educated people of both mid- and late Goryeo enjoyed the use of natural *imcheon* gardens as a retreat.

1) Nongsanjeong

Nongsanjeong is a two *kan* by two *kan* pavilion with a hipped and gabled roof located in the Ongnyudong Valley in Guwon-ri, Gaya-myeon, Hapcheon-gun, Gyeongsangnam-do province. It is said that Choe Chi-won, who studied abroad in the Tang Dynasty and returned to Silla in the 11th year of King Heongang's reign (885) to serve the government after passing the state examination in 874, came to Mt. Gayasan after the fall of Silla and built a pavilion to practice asceticism.

The present pavilion was rebuilt in 1930, and Choe Chi-won's portrait is kept at nearby Haksadang. It is also called Ongnyudong, as Bunok Waterfall and Nakhwadam pond resemble Ongnyucheon stream in Mt. Geumgangsan. Nongsanjeong, which was a retreat garden from the early Goryeo, was also used as a retreat by other scholars who spent their lives communing with nature after Choe Chi-won.

2) The Garden and Flowerbed of Yi Gong-seung

Yi Gong-seung (1099-1183) was sent to the Jin Dynasty as an envoy at the beginning of King Uijong's reign (1147-1170). After taking charges of important official posts, in his final years, Yi built a simple house in the middle of his garden, dug a pond, raised a hill, and planted flowers.

3) Yanggwadongjeong

Located outside Gwangju city, Yanggwadongjeong was built some 800 years ago during the Goryeo era. It is three *kan* by two *kan* with a gabled roof. Traces of bush clover stalks woven with clay are found inside the roof. The pavilion belongs to the Jangheung Ko family, and bears the traits of a village pavilion, as it was used communally by the village. However, its location categorizes it as a mountain pavilion.

Looking around from the wooden floor of Yanggwadongjeong, which is built on a hill facing south, Mt. Mudeungsan is seen in the northeast while a stream flows at the front; an open view of low hills is visible over the field. The pavilion is surrounded by pine, black pine, oak and persimmon trees to the south; black pine, zelkova and Yoshino cherry trees to the northeast; and Chinese arborvitae, black pine and pine trees to the north, which keep the air so cool, even the heat of mid-summer is not felt there.

4) Ki Heung-su's Goksuji

Ki Heung-su (1148-1209) was a famous military officer who lived three generations after King Myeongjong. From a young age, he excelled at calligraphy and spent the later years of his life decorating his garden and raising pets. The garden he created was built on a naturally beautiful spot where a spring gushed out from between a rocky mountain and a forest. Weeping willows and irises were planted around the artificial lake, named Goksuji, and lotus flowers were planted inside the pond. Buildings were built to harmonize with the natural surroundings in locations that were advantageous for observing the natural landscape. In particular, he enjoyed *goksuyeon*, which was the recreational practice of floating wine cups on water while composing poetry, in this garden.

5) Yi Gyu-bo's Saryunjeong

Yi Gyu-bo (1168-1241) was a distinguished writer during King Gojong's reign (1212-1259) in Goryeo. His pen name was Baegun Seonin, but he was also called Samjakho due to his love of poetry, alcohol, and the *geomungo*, a Korean traditional stringed instrument.

Yi had much interest in and knowledge of gardens. In his collection of works, he had recorded some forty types of garden plants, and he arranged the gardens himself and lived there in his final years. His most remarkable record on gardens is "Saryunjeonggi," written in 1201, which describes how he built Saryunjeong. Saryunjeong was a mobile pavilion designed to be moved to different locations in the garden so as to take best advantage of the beautiful landscapes while reading, drinking tea or wine, and playing *baduk*. The pavilion combined sitting and observing the natural landscape with touring around it. It was a unique structure that could be moved anywhere within the garden.

6) Haeamjeong

Haeamjeong is one of the oldest existing garden structures. It was built in the 10th year of King Gongmin's reign (1361) on the shore of the East Sea by Sim Dong-ro while he was living there. It was reconstructed by Sim Eon-gwang in the 25th year of King Jungjong's reign (1530) during the Joseon era, and a name plaque written by Song Si-yeol was hung during King Sukjong's reign. The front is open to the south, but the back and sides are surrounded by pointed stones or large, perforated rocks. As the pavilion stands only one meter above sea level, the waves crashing onto the surrounding rocks during a high wind can create a sense of insecurity. However, the sound of the waves can also bevery refreshing, and its proximity to the sea makes it suitable for fishing.

III. Retreat Gardens of the Joseon Dynasty

1. Background and Sample Sites

If the trend of seclusion as a means of escape from the world, caused by the increasing purges of scholars and party strife, had a direct influence on the formation of retreat gardens in the Joseon era, the development of learning related to Confucianism and Taoism and the idyllic view of nature the scholars held were indirect influences. Also contributing to this trend was the beautiful natural environment of the peninsula. The retreat gardens that were created during the Joseon era are as follows:

Table 1. Retreat Gardens of the Joseon Dynasty

Region	Name of Garden	Location	Year of Construction
1. Seoul/ Gyeonggi Region	Okhojeong	Samcheong-dong 133, Jongno-gu, Seoul	1815
	Seokpajeong	Buam-dong, Jongno-gu, Seoul	Early 19th century
	Seongnagwon	Seongbuk-dong 22, Seongbuk-gu, Seoul	King Sunjo (1800-1834) / King Cheoljong (1849-1863)
	Buamjeong	Buam-dong, Jongno-gu, Seoul	1900s
2. Chungcheong Region	Namganjeongsa	Gayang-dong 65, Daejeon	1683
	Ongnyugak	Birae-dong 1-11, Daejeon	1639
	Amseojae	Hwayang-ri, Cheongcheon-myeon, Goesan-gun, Chungcheongbuk-do	Mid-17th century
	Seoseokji	Yeondang-dong, Ibam-myeon, Yeongyang-gun, Gyeongsangbuk-do	Planned around 1610

3. Yeongnam Region	Choganjeong	Jungnim-ri, Yongmun-myeon, Yecheon-gun, Gyeongsangnam-do	Constructed between 1620 and 1636
	Sohanjeong	Hwaryong-ri, Mulgeum-myeon, Yangsan-gun, Gyeongsangnam-do	1582
	Geoyeonjeong	Gongam-ri, Unmun-myeon, Cheongdo-gun, Gyeongsangbuk-do	Around 1900
4. Honam Region	Buyongdong Garden	Buyong-ri, Nohwa-myeon, Wando-gun, Jeollanam-do	1637
	Dasan Chodang	Mandeok-ri, Doam-myeon, Gangjin-gun, Jeollanam-do	1808-1819
	Imdaejeong Garden	Sapyeong-ri, Nam-myeon, Hwasun-gun, Jeollanam-do	1568
	Myeongokheon Garden	Husan Village, Sandeok-ri, Goseo-myeon, Damyang-gun, Jeollanam-do	Around 1650
	Sosoewon	Jigok-ri, Nam-myeon, Damyang-gun, Jeollanam-do	1520-1557

2. Location and External Space

Retreat gardens are characterized by their location in beautiful scenic spots with striking landscapes, and their short distance from the main houses in which people live. They were neither residential nor everyday living spaces, but instead had the form and traits of temporary or occasional housing. Retreat gardens were separated from villages in three different ways: visually, conceptually, and a mixture of both.

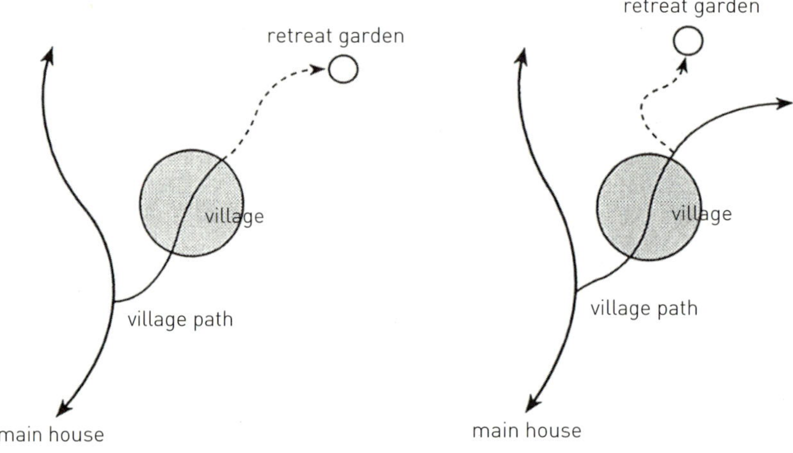

Figure 2. Hierarchy of access to the retreat garden

The structure of the external space of the garden can be divided into three areas: the inner garden within the wall, the outer garden visible outside the wall, and the external area that directly or indirectly influences the garden space. The aesthetic aspects of retreat gardens were not simply limited to the space within the walls but included the landscape outside. This is evident from the fact that poetry, prose and official records often included mention of the landscape that was visible outside the garden, such as the peak of a hill opposite the garden, the stream and field in front, and the sight of the moon setting over a western hill. Therefore, the external structure of retreat gardens should be seen as including the outer garden.

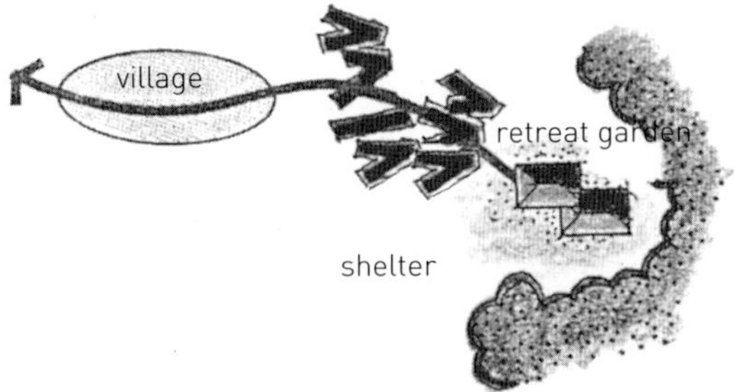

Visual separation (concept map)

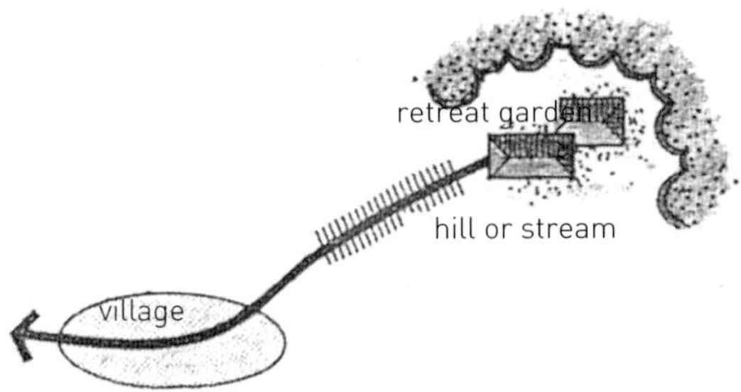

Conceptual separation (concept map)

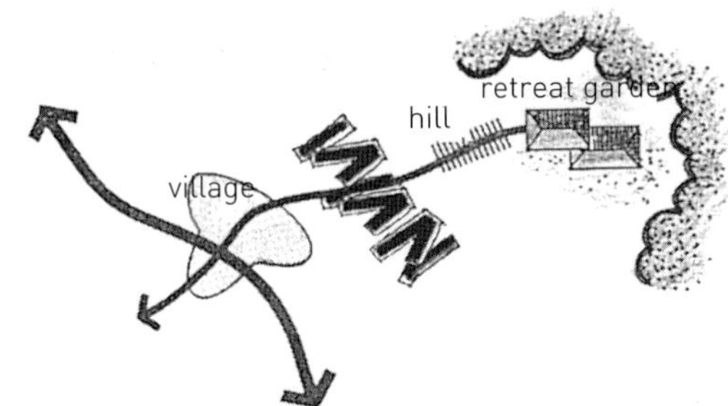

Mixed separation (concept map)

Figure 3. Method I of separation from the village

Figure 4. Method II of separation from the village

Figure 5. Method III of separation from the village

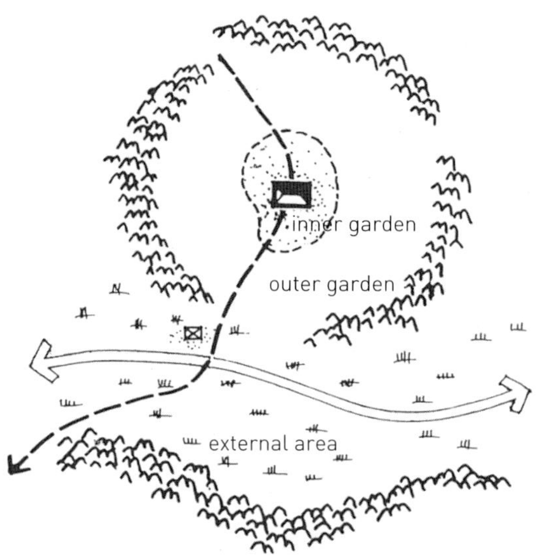

Figure 6. Structure of external space in retreat gardens

3. Landscape Type and Characteristics of Retreat Gardens

Landscape types and characteristics of sample gardens are largely divided into "near water" and "inland," depending on the proximity of water. "Near water" is subdivided into two categories: "adjacent," meaning there was a water source outside the garden, and "inside," meaning the mountain stream was inside the garden. "Inland" can be subdivided into both "mountain" and "flatland," depending on whether the garden is located in a hilly area or on flatlands.

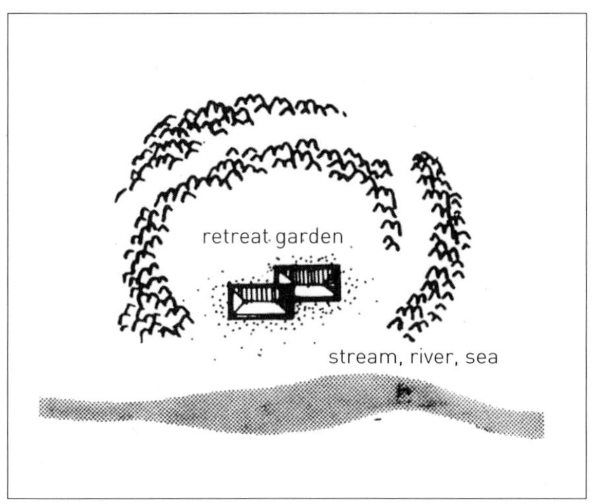

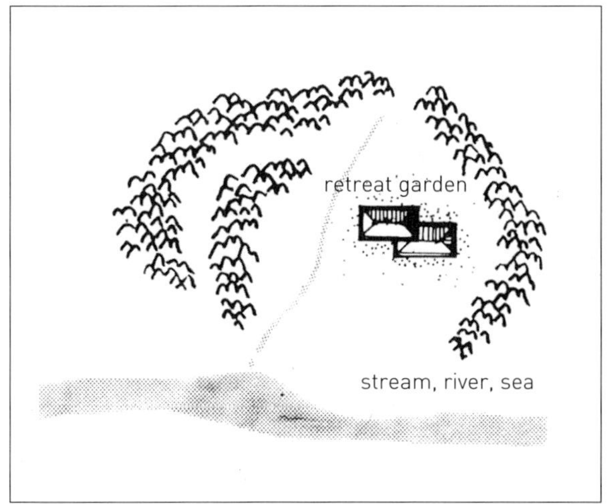

Figure 7. "Near water" and "Adjacent" landscape type (concept map)

Figure 8. "Near water" and "Inside" landscape type (concept map)

4. Structure of Internal Space and Landscape Technique

1) Structure of Internal Space

The garden site forms the basis of the spatial experience and visual character inside the garden. The first element that determines how the site will be shaped is the natural geography, while the second element is the socio-economic background of the owner. Focusing on sample gardens, the site shape consisted of three different types: square, rectangular and A-shaped. This is determined by the ratio of width and depth of the garden's physical borders, which is demarcated by either the garden wall or the natural topography.

As many retreat gardens were located in scenic places that included mountains and streams, their spatial structure was largely determined by the

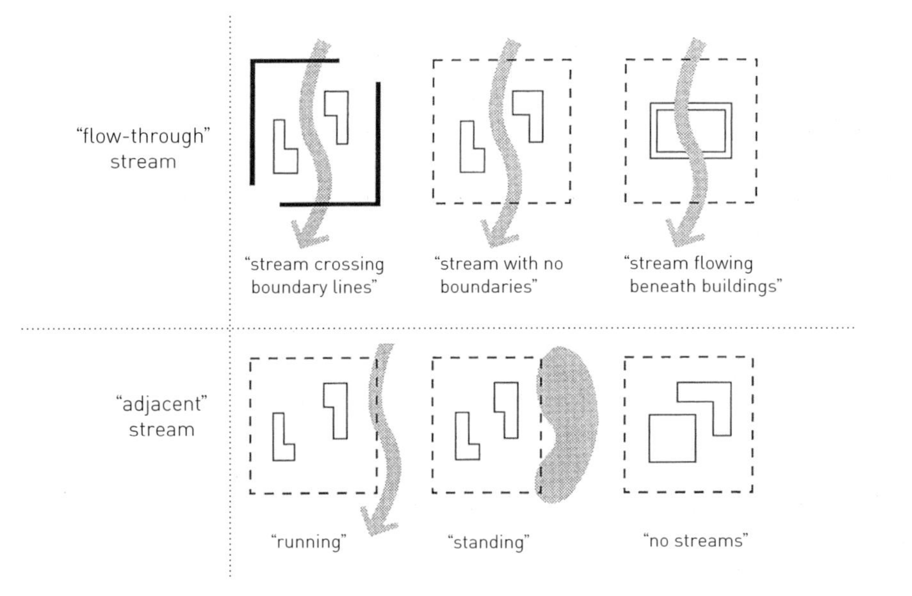

Figure 9. Structure of internal space according to stream type

natural topography and the flow of streams. Sample gardens were divided according to whether or not there was a stream, and in which direction the stream was flowing. Streams were further subdivided into "flow-through" streams that crossed the site itself and "adjacent" streams that passed near the edge of the site. "Flow-through" streams consisted of both those that crossed the garden site and those that passed below the buildings located on the site. "Adjacent" streams included "running" and "standing" water.

Among these many types of retreat gardens, those with multiple buildings and basic household elements, such as Okhojeong, Seokpajeong, Seongnagwon and Buamjeong, marked their boundaries using manmade walls; in contrast, those with a single building, such as a hall or a pavilion, used no artificial boundaries and were instead distinguished by the natural topography, such as hills and valleys.

Namganjeongsa and Ongnyugak are examples of smaller sized gardens with streams that ran below the raised wooden floors of the buildings. At Namganjeongsa, an adjacent stream was purposely diverted into the garden to create a pond; the water was also used to construct an artificial channel that crossed below the building before flowing into the pond. At Ongnyugak, a building was built over the stream in order to maximize the aesthetic sense and romantic atmosphere of the surrounding landscape.

"Adjacent" stream types were those that passed outside the garden; they were divided into two types: running streams that were left untouched and standing streams where the water was diverted to create an artificial pond, within which an island was constructed. Compared to the standing streams, running streams were usually located where there was a wide and plentiful flow of water. Diverse landscape elements in the vicinity included oddly-shaped stones and cliffs; Amseojae, Choganjeong and Geoyeonjeong were examples of this type. Standing streams had relatively small amounts of water and few noteworthy landscape features within visible range. Therefore, water was diverted to create artificial ponds with islands; Imdaejeong and Myeongokheon were built using this method.

2) Structural Elements

Garden buildings included a house that functioned as a residence, a pavilion used for enjoying the scenery or holding educational lectures, and other buildings. In all of the examples listed, more than one pavilion was found except for Buamjeong, where the main building in the men's quarters (*sarangchae*) also functioned as a pavilion. Located outside the capital, Okhojeong, Seokpajeong, Seongnagwon, and Buamjeong were used as temporary residences and therefore contained the basic household elements with buildings required for daily living. However, characteristic of the retreat house was the absence of a family shrine or ritual hall.

Surface Type of the Pavilion

The basic size of the pavilion was three by two *kan*. However, variations included three by three *kan* (Gwangpunggak at Sosoewon), four by two *kan* (Songseokjeong at Seongnagwon, Namganjeongsa, Gyeongjeong at Seoseokji), two by two *kan* (Geoyeonjeong), and one by one *kan* (pavilion with thatched roof).

Except for one-*kan* pavilions, all pavilions contained rooms and were categorized into four different types depending on the location of the room. The first was the "center type," where a one-*kan* room stood in the center. This is found among the pavilions in the Honam region such as Gwangpunggak and

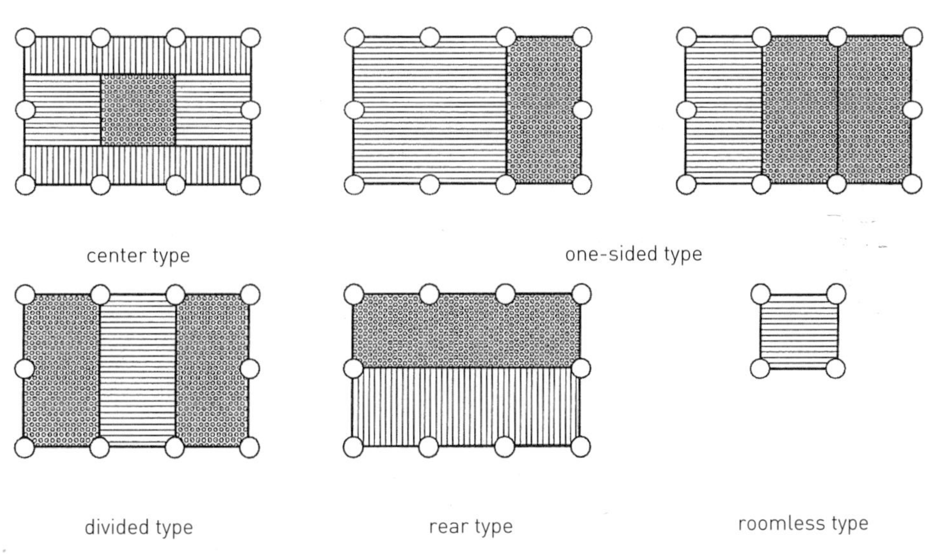

Figure 10. Classification of pavilion types

Imdaejeong at Sosoewon, Myeongokheon, and Seyeonjeong at Buyongdong. The second is the "one-sided type" where the rooms were positioned on either the left or right side of the pavilion. Pavilions found in the Gyeonggi region such as Namganjeongsa, Ongnyugak and Amseojae share this trait; Choganjeong and Jewoldang at Sosoewon also belong to this category. The third is the "divided type" where the rooms are divided into right and left by the wooden floor in the middle; Gyeongjeong at Seoseokji is an example of this type. Finally, rooms positioned along the back wall of the pavilion are called "rear type," which is found at Buamjeong and Geoyeonjeong.

Ponds were used in all of the aforementioned gardens. Seventy percent of the ponds were square, while the remaining thirty percent were natural. Most retreat gardens had square-shaped ponds and islands. This is assumed to be due to the influence of the ideology of immortality and *yin-yang* theory.

The visual experience of the garden was expressed in a unique way by creating a line of movement, called *dongseon*, within the landscape architecture itself. Thus, each type of garden had its own distinctive appearance.

Advanced water landscape techniques were used to divert water into the gardens. In most cases, natural streams were used. When required, water was drawn in from the pond using special engineering techniques. In particular, *higu*, small water channels made from wood, were used for visual effect and to divert water into the pond. This was a unique feature of Korean retreat gardens. Though retreat gardens contained natural streams, ponds were often built, signifying that the natural environment was altered through human power.

Arrangement of Decorative Objects and Rocks

Decorative objects included stone cases, stone pots and oddly-shaped stones. Except for Sosoewon and Sohanjeong, natural stones were not reshaped nor were man-made mountains used. However, a number of engraved rocks have been found. The engravings on these rocks include images of nature, views of life or the Taoist view of the universe; this was used as a way to cultivate the mind.

Engraved rocks are always found wherever large rocks are present. This technique was a way for people to take ownership of nature, that is, by naming it. It was used in some places where the gardens were not large enough and the owner did not have the financial means to create a magnificent garden.

Planting Technique

Selection of trees and planting techniques in retreat gardens were largely determined by symbolic, functional and ecological characteristics. Symbolic meanings were derived from the historical sources related to the plant: the Confucian concept of the gentleman, hermitage and friendship, the *sinseon* concept of eternal youth, Taoism, shamanism, wealth, prosperity, and female beauty. The function of plants was to provide privacy and seclusion. However, this was only possible when it was ecologically appropriate for the local conditions.

Figure 11. Example of tree planting (Okhojeong)

The most preferred plants were pine, zelkova, bamboo, crape myrtle, willow trees and lotus flowers. They were usually planted in groups or individually, or they were divided into dense or sparse groups. Trees were planted in groups at Myeongokheon, Dasan Chodang, Imdaejeong, Sosoewon, and Choganjeong in order to hide the main house and the retreat house. They fulfilled this function regardless of whether they were planted artificially or had grown naturally. Trees planted in groups were often used as a backdrop, and surrounding pine or bamboo forests were also used frequently as a garden element.

According to the *Yanghwa sorok*, a book of gardening written by Kang Hui-an, crape myrtles (Lagerstroemia indica) symbolize the wish for permanent wealth and glory rather than momentary splendor. Weeping willows were planted along streams because they have the power to repel evil spirits. Also, the swaying of their branches in the wind was said to resemble the image of a woman and symbolized hopes or wishes.

IV. Landscape in Poetry and Prose

The external environment was depicted in a more generalized way than the landscape of the garden. Living conditions, the author's view of life, a transcendental view of seclusion, and a perspective on nature were often included rather than the landscape itself.

An in-depth analysis of descriptions of landscapes in poetry and prose generally shows that places and objects were mentioned most frequently, followed by plants and animals. A number of native plants such as pine, bamboo, and paulownia trees and lotus flowers were described, along with

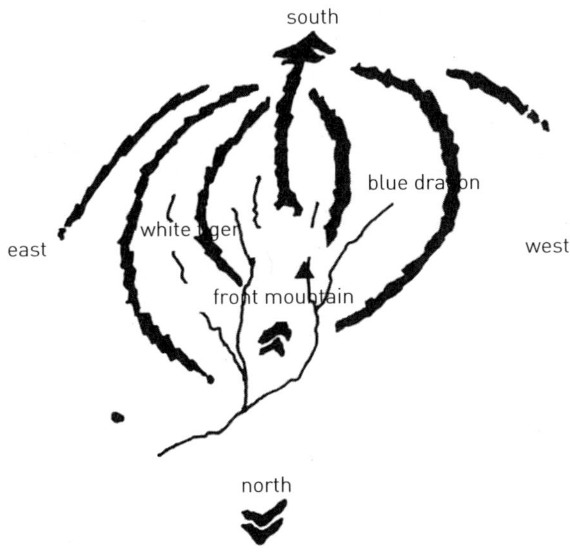

Figure 12. Illustration of *fengshui* at Buyongdong

other species including irises, pomegranates, apricots and peaches. Birds and fish were commonly referred to, and animals that symbolized the world of immortals, such as the phoenix, turtle, dragon, crane and deer, were also popular. The fact that even small creatures like cicadas and ants were depicted shows that the garden comprised all things in the universe.

V. Conclusion

1. The owners of retreat gardens were not only high-ranking officials, but also mostly men of power or scholar-officials who had retired. Their views of nature were based on the idea of adapting to and obeying nature. For the

Joseon era, the gardeners' views of nature can be summarized into the concept of selecting residential sites where the life force of *gi* is generated, Taoist and Confucian concepts of retreat or seclusion, and a transcendental view of nature. The concept of *sinseon* (immortals) is also common in pond construction techniques.

2. The *fengshui* techniques used in retreat gardens emphasized *deuksubeop*, or proximity to water. However, the *fengshui* concept of having a mountain in back to protect the area from strong winds had little influence on gardens.

3. Spatial hierarchy and the flow of movement are revealed in various ways, from the entrance to the place of residence. Here, the flow of the space maintains its own order and dynamic, both of which are characteristic elements of retreat gardens. The boundary and territory of the garden should be extended and interpreted as including the area from the inner to the outer garden as well as the external area that directly or indirectly influences the garden space, encouraging the viewer to appreciate nature and all things in the universe.

4. Another point to bear in mind in terms of spatial analysis is the interpretation of the gardener's concept of garden construction. Until recently, researchers have mainly dealt with the first gardener's status or construction method. However, as gardens were not established within one generation but rather have been succeeded by descendents, the construction activity, space, and change in techniques that took place in later years should also be taken into account.

5. Usage patterns of retreat gardens were diverse, including that of seclusion or retreat, holding lectures and studying, providing a location for new types of activities that originated away from party strife and purges, and hosting a great number of literary and poetry performances.

6. The main purpose for building the gardens was to maintain a secluded and quiet life, avoid the summer heat, live according to one's own will, carry on ancestral customs, and enjoy leisure time. Construction techniques such as the building of pavilions and ponds, naming of stones, and tree planting are significant at the level of modern application.

7. Regional differences were distinct among the various pavilion styles. This seems to have been a cultural difference caused by the divergent formative backgrounds of retreat gardens. Differences in planting style came from discrepancies in climate and geographical conditions, but it is difficult to say whether technical variations in water landscaping, tree planting, and use of decorative objects were based on party or academic differences. In general, retreat gardens in the Yeongnam region during Joseon era were less graceful

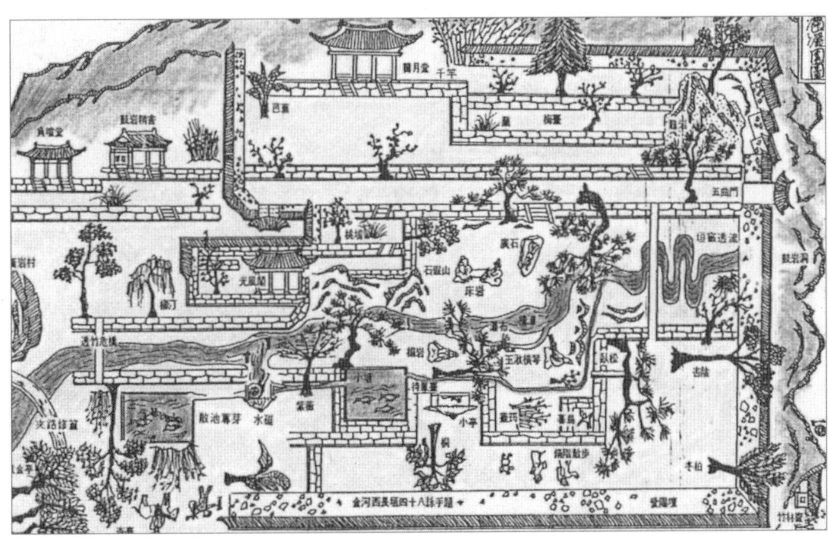

Figure 13. Woodblock print of *Illustration of Sosoewon*

Figure 14. Place for holding lectures and studying

and more masculine than those of the Honam region, which were delicate and feminine in style. Retreat gardens in the capital were built in a villa style with rooms for sleeping, which differed from the separate houses of the Honam region that were built for retreat and seclusion, while the retreat gardens in the Chungcheong region were rather similar to those of the Yeongnam region.

References

Chung, Dong-o. 1986. *Hanguk-ui jeongwon* (Korean Gardens). Minumsa.

Jeong, Jae-hun. 1990. *Hanguk-ui yet jogyeong* (Ancient Korean Landscape Architecture). Daewonsa.

Korea Institute of Landscape Architecture. 1992. *Dongyang jogeyongsa* (History of East Asian Landscape Architecture). Mun Un Dang.

Lee, Jae-keun. 1991. "Joseon sidae byeolseo jeongwon-e gwanhan yeongu" (A Study of Retreat Gardens in Joseon Dynasty). Ph.D. diss., Sungkyunkwan University.

________. 2005. "Hanguk-ui byeolseo jeongwon" (Retreat Gardens in Korea). *Hanguk jeontong jogyeong hakhoeji* (Journal of Korean Institute of Traditional Landscape Architecture) 23.1.

Lee, Jac-keun, and Kim Yong-kee. 1002. "Joseon sidae jeongja wollim-ui jiyeokjeok teukseong-e gwanhan yeongu" (On the Local Characteristics of Arbors in the Joseon Period). *Hanguk jeongwon hakhoeji* (Journal of Korean Institute of Traditional Landscape) 10.1.

Author

Lee Jae-keun

(Department of Landscape Architecture, Sangmyung University)

Lee Jae-keun is a professor in the Department of Environmental Landscape Architecture at Sangmyung University. He received his Ph.D. in Agriculture from Sungkyunkwan University. He is currently President of the Korean Institute of Traditional Landscape Architecture and also a member of the Cultural Properties Committee. E-mail: jklee@smu.ac.kr

The Formation of the Royal Tombs of the Joseon Dynasty and Their Landscape Architectural Characteristics

I. Introduction

The royal tomb where the king and queen were buried after their death maintained its position as the model for all tomb systems. This is not simply due to the formality that people of noble status, i.e. absolute monarchs, were buried there. It was an institution that preceded all other national affairs at a time when the Confucian concept of ancestor worship was the dominant ideology of Joseon society. It is the ultimate expression of the deeply-rooted *hyo* (filial piety) ideology, which says that if ancestors are worshipped with devotion, the blessings will reach future generations. It is also based on the belief that honoring the dead by burying the deceased king and queen in an auspicious place with great formality guarantees the welfare of the present king and royal household. Therefore, when a monarch died, the funeral was held according to the national funeral procedure, and the construction of the royal tomb in particular was a national affair that preceded all other matters.

In this regard, the royal tomb where the monarch was to be buried forever was a space that represented dynastic society, just as the royal palace was the space of living. The location of the royal tomb reflects which site people at the time regarded as a propitious place for the dead. As a silent, solemn, and still space set apart except during rituals, the royal tomb was located in a simple, restricted and unchanging landscape, unlike the magnificent royal palace that reflected regular seasonal changes. This type of landscape was made up not only of the facilities constructed for the royal tomb, but also of the vegetation outside the tomb. In this way, the royal tomb was established as a unique space in the traditional landscape, distinct from other countries in its location, arrangement and landscaping.

II. Historical Changes in the Royal Tomb System

The royal tomb of the Joseon era is composed of three different parts: the upper tomb where the grave is located; the lower tomb which reaches the Jeongjagak (building where ritual offerings are made) from the Hongsalmun (red arrow gate); and the entrance and borders. Various structures stood around the grave in the upper tomb area, whereas the Hongsalmun gate at the entrance of the tomb, the Jeongjagak, and the Bigak where the gravestone is enshrined are placed in the lower tomb area. Meanwhile, the border of the tomb is defined by the *hwaso* (firebreak), *haeja* (moat) and *myeongdangsu* (river or stream that surrounds the tomb).

Figure 1. Overview of Royal Tomb of the Joseon Dynasty

The royal tomb system was consolidated with the advent of the Joseon era. However, the tomb system was already introduced from the Han Dynasty at the end of Goguryeo, and the influence of the Tang Dynasty throughout Unified Silla and Goryeo helped create a unique royal tomb system in Korea. Therefore, in order to analyze the characteristics of the royal tomb system of the Joseon era, it would be appropriate to begin by looking at the changes the royal tomb system underwent before reaching the Joseon era. At the same time, examination of these changes should focus on the burial mound type, the burial method, tomb structures and vegetation.

1. Belief in the Immortality of the Soul and Burial Methods before the Three Kingdoms

Since ancient times, human beings believed that there is another being separate from the physical body. People reflected on life and the world after death, despairing of the temporal and spatial limits on their ephemeral lives. They imagined an afterlife that would follow the present world, and another world separate from the world of the living. However, the human body cannot overcome these temporal and spatial boundaries, giving rise to the belief in an afterlife surpassing the limits of the flesh. In this way, human beings created the idea of a soul in order to explain various human activities and eternal life. The soul was thought to be responsible for the activities of the body and mind, and to continue functioning somehow even after physical activity had stopped. In other words, belief in the immortality of the soul, which means it continues to exist even after the death of the body, came to have a direct influence on funeral methods for processing the body of the deceased.

Burial methods in general entail a number of customs including *tojang* or *maejang* (underground burial), *hwajang* (cremation), *sujang* (water burial), and *pungjang* (open air burial). Various burial methods appeared in Korea according to region and era, but the most common method for the king and the ruling class was *maejang*, i.e. underground burial. This custom, which dates as far back as the Neolithic period, underwent a number of changes over time as religion and the view of the soul were combined.

Dolmens were the dominant burial method used during prehistoric times, especially during the Bronze Age. Dolmens were first created in the northern hemisphere between 3,000 and 2,500 BC and spread throughout the world. They were directly related to Bronze Age people's view of the soul. They believed that there was a multitude of evil spirits in the world that threatened people, and they took particular care to prevent these spirits from playing any tricks when a corpse was buried. As a safety measure, the corpse was bound, and a heavy rock was placed on top to prevent the soul from escaping the body. It is speculated that the belief in the immortality of the soul and fear of evil spirits brought about the practice of burying corpses underground and piling stones on top of the grave; this later developed into dolmens. The large size of the dolmens suggests that they were the graves of the ruling class at the time.

Dolmens in Korea can be categorized into two types: northern and southern, with the Seoul area at the center. Northern-type dolmens were bigger than southern-type ones, and the stones used were slightly trimmed. They follow a relatively regular shape with wide supporting stones on the ground and a much wider, flat capstone on top. In contrast, southern-type dolmens were mostly underground. They are small and were made using natural stones, with small supporting stones on the ground and a capstone on top. Some dolmen lack supporting stones, which makes it difficult to tell whether they are in fact dolmens. In this regard, the southern-type dolmens appear to be less developed than their northern-type counterparts.

Dolmens, which were the main burial method during the Bronze Age, evolved a step further with the next generation into *tomyo*, where the body was buried underground and covered with earth, and *seokgwanmyo*, where the body was placed in a stone coffin. From the end of the Bronze Age to the Iron Age, clay jars were used to bury the bones of the deceased, followed later by wooden coffins and brick coffins.

2. The Royal Tombs of the Three Kingdoms and Unified Silla

1) Goguryeo

Goguryeo tombs are found throughout the Amnokgang (Yalu) river basin, starting from the Jian region in Manchuria, and the Daedonggang river basin around Pyeongyang. They consist of stone mounds and earth mounds. Stone mounds appeared during the early Goguryeo in the Jian area but were succeeded by earth mounds during the late Goguryeo in Pyeongyang. The former succeeded the conventional tomb system of Goguryeo, but in later years, the latter seem to have been influenced by the neighboring Han Dynasty.

Goguryeo's tomb system had two main characteristics: The first was changes in tomb murals, which have been designated a World Heritage site based on both North Korea and China's applications to UNESCO in 2004. In the early to mid-Goguryeo period, the murals were mainly genre paintings that depicted everyday life; they disappeared in the late Goguryeo. Genre paintings were replaced by *Sasindo*, which depicted a dragon, tiger, phoenix and tortoise in the four cardinal directions, as influenced by *fengshui* and *yin-yang* principles.

The second characteristic was the use of *fengshui* (K.: *pungsu*) in selecting the shape and location of the tomb. Tombs were built based on *fengshui* principles of landscape arrangement, according to which the guardian mountain (*jusan*) stood behind houses or gravesites and the front mountain (*ansan*) stood in front. Mountains surrounding a house or a grave on all four sides (*sasinsa*) in order to define the site boundaries were also an important *fengshui* condition for creating a propitious site. The shape of the land, which was determined to be auspicious or not based on whether it resembled an object or animal, was also decided in relation to *fengshui*.

2) Baekje

Royal tombs of Baekje were built in an open style, as influenced by exchange with other countries including Goguryeo and China. Different styles also appeared whenever the capital of Baekje was moved. The early Baekje tombs that spread out from the capital, Seoul, were stone mound tombs as in Goguryeo, but they took such diverse forms as stone chamber tombs, urn-coffin burials, or pit tombs into which the coffin was lowered. Brick chamber tombs appeared after the capital of Baekje was moved to Ungjinseong (present-day Gongju) in 475; a typical example of this style is the tomb of King Muryeong. This demonstrates the close relationship between Baekje and the Liang Dynasty at the time, as Baekje was also influenced by the latter's tomb system. Meanwhile, *fengshui* principles were used to select the location of the tomb. Baekje moved its capital again to Sabiseong (present-day Buyeo) in 538.

Figure 2. Tomb of King Muryeong, a brick chamber tomb, in Gongju

Figure 3. Stone chamber tombs found in Neungsan-ri, Buyeo

Tombs dating back to Baekje's Sabi period (538-660) were found in Neungsan-ri, Buyeo. These tombs are assumed to be royal stone chamber tombs, which differed from the brick chamber tombs of the Ungjin period. Their locations were also chosen using *fengshui*, and a painting of the four deities that guard the four directions (*Sasindo*) is found in the mural of the 6th Tomb.

3) Silla and Unified Silla

Royal tombs and unidentified tombs are spread across various regions starting from Gyeongju. The tombs of the Silla era were characterized by their location either at the center or on the outskirts of the capital, usually on a plain. The outer shape of all tombs took the form of a large earth mound. The inner

Figure 4. Goereung at Gyeongju

structure contained either a wooden coffin tomb with a stone mound or a stone-lined tomb. There were also a few stone chamber tombs.

After Silla overcame and unified Goguryeo and Baekje, becoming Unified Silla, stone chamber tombs were mainly used for the royal family. Their locations were moved to hilly areas outside the city, and a formal tomb system was established, as influenced by Tang culture. In its most developed form during this era, the base of the royal tomb was encircled with flat, square stones, called *byeongpungseok* or *hoseok*, which had relief carvings of the twelve zodiac animals. The twelve zodiac animals were carved onto the *hoseok* to symbolize the space and time of the universe. They were frequently used in the Tang period ornaments that were buried with the body of the deceased, and held symbolic meaning as they guarded the cardinal directions and the tomb.

Figure 5. The stone sculpture of Goereung at Gyeongju

The placement of *hoseok* carved with the zodiac animals was a method established during the Unified Silla.

Also, a *sangseok* (stone table for ritual offerings) was placed in front of the grave, and a *muninseok* (stone statue of a civil official), *muinseok* (stone statue of a military official), stone lion, and gravestone carved with the name and rank of the deceased were placed on each side of the path leading to the grave. Tang-style funeral rituals and tomb types were combined to create the Unified Silla tomb system.

During the reign of King Heungdeok, when the tomb system of Unified Silla was at its height, the selecting of the gravesite also became important, unlike conventional royal tombs. Propitious sites with a mountain in back and a river or stream in front of a grave were selected. The royal tomb was divided

Figure 6. Tomb of King Heungdeok at Gyeongju

into two levels: stone lions were placed on all four sides of the grave just as at the tomb of King Seongdeok, and *hoseok* encircled the lower part of the grave. The twelve zodiac animals were carved in relief on the stones and surrounded by a stone railing, and simple stone sculptures were placed in front of the grave. On the lower level, stone statues of a pair of civil and military officials were placed to the south of the grave, facing each other on either side of the path leading to the grave. The gravestone was placed at the front towards the east. This elaborate arrangement was passed down intact to the later generation along with the *fengshui* methods of choosing gravesites. It was used as the basic form of royal tombs throughout Goryeo and Joseon.

Figure 7. The tomb of King Taejo of Goryeo at Gaeseong

Figure 8. The tomb of King Gongmin of Goryeo at Gaeseong

4) Goryeo

The royal tombs of the Goryeo era faced south with the guardian mountain in back. The left and right slopes of the guardian mountain represent the blue dragon and white tiger, and the *jusu,* or main stream (water flow is an important condition for a good site, according to *fengshui*) and the *gaeksu,* or auxiliary stream, meet in front of the tomb, forming an auspicious site. The royal tomb was located on a slope in front of the guardian mountain, and twelve *hoseok* were placed around the bottom of the grave, following the style of Unified Silla. Standing or seated images of the twelve zodiac animals were carved in relief, or occasionally in intaglio. The carving style was simple and straightforward.

A stone railing, slightly higher than what was typical of Unified Silla, was constructed approximately 0.6 meters away, and a stone table was placed in front of the grave. Octagonal, candleholder-shaped stone posts stood to the right and left of the table. The front of the grave was divided into many levels, unlike the two that were normally used during the Unified Silla era. A stone lantern was placed at the center of the second level, while stone statues of a pair of civil and military officials were placed facing each other on the right and left sides of the third level. The fourth level was wide and flat, and featured the Jeongjagak, where rituals were performed, and Bigak, which was built to house a tombstone. Though the royal tombs of the Goryeo era succeeded the system of Unified Silla, new features such as stone pillars, stone lanterns, the Jeongjagak, and the Bigak were constructed, and stone lions, stone sheep, and stone tigers were arranged around the grave to complete it. Among the royal tombs of the Goryeo era, the tomb of King Gongmin is the most complete and magnificent, and it thus became the model for royal tombs during Joseon. Geonwolleung, the tomb of King Taejo, the founder of Joseon, is a more fully developed model.

III. The Formation and Characteristics of the Royal Tombs of the Joseon Dynasty

1. Historical Background of the Creation of Royal Tombs in the Joseon Dynasty

The royal tombs of the Joseon era are categorized into *neung*, *won*, and *myo* according to the status of the deceased. *Neung* are the graves of the king and queen, *won* are the graves of the close relatives of the king, the Crown Prince and his wife, and their eldest son and his wife, and *myo* are the graves of the prince and princess by the queen, prince and princess by a concubine, and concubines. There are 42 *neung* and two *myo* (Yeonsangun and Gwanghaegun) dating from the Joseon era, beginning with King Taejo's Geonwolleung and including the tombs of posthumously enthroned kings (*chujonwang*) and dethroned kings. Only two of these tombs, Jereung and Hureung, are located in North Korea. The remaining forty *neung* and two *myo* are all found in the south.

Geonwolleung, the tomb of King Taejo, which is a prime example of Joseon's royal tomb system, was modeled after Hyeolleung, the tomb of King Gongmin of Goryeo. However, a *gokjang*, or low, semi-circular stone wall, was added around the tomb as well as stone objects influenced by the Southern Song style in China. Twelve *hoseok* were placed at the base of the high grave mound, and twelve-*kan* railing surrounded the *hoseok*. Two sets each of stone sheep and stone tigers were placed outside the railing to protect the mound, and a *gokjang* wall was built to the east, west, and north of the mound. The stone arrangement around the tomb was largely divided into three levels: One *honyuseok* (wide, flat stone table for the spirit to rest on when it emerges from the grave), five *goseok* (drum-shaped stone) that supported the *honyuseok*, and two *mangjuseok* (stone posts) were arranged on the top level. One stone lantern, a pair of stone statues of civil officials, and a pair of stone horses were placed on the middle level. Finally, the lower level had a pair of stone statues of military officials and a pair of stone horses. However, though the royal tomb system was established according to this rule, it continued to change throughout the Joseon era according to historical circumstances.

2. Location of the Royal Tombs of the Joseon Dynasty

Joseon's *Gyeongguk daejeon* (National Code) regulated the distance of tombs from Hanyang, their geographical features (e.g. location and direction of the mountains on which tombs are located), and other restrictions, which were all related directly and indirectly to the location of the royal tombs of the Joseon era.

First, regarding the distance from the capital city, the royal tomb was to be placed between a radius of ten *li* (4 kilometers) and 100 *li* (40 kilometers) from the capital city, where the royal palace was located. This is supported by the fact that, with a few exceptions, all royal tombs of the Joseon era are found within a 100 *li* radius of the four main gates of the capital city.

Second, grave sites were chosen in relation to *fengshui*, the traditional view of geography. In East Asia, *fengshui* is related to mountains, water and the cardinal directions. According to long-held beliefs, all things in the universe operate according to *gi* (Ch.: qi, life force), though it cannot be seen by human beings. *Gi* is believed to move along mountains and stop when it meets water. It was also believed that mountains are always connected and continuous. Therefore, a good location is one where good *gi* is collected, and this can be detected by examining the shape of the mountains and water. Theoretically, according to *fengshui*, propitious land is surrounded by mountains on all four sides. The mountain at the back (*jusan*) is the master and therefore should appear confident and powerful. In contrast, the mountain at the front (*ansan*) should appear modest, like a guest. This traditional human geography was based on comparing the shapes of mountains to human beings or objects in order to determine whether the mountain had good or bad *gi*.

Figure 9. "opographical Map" in *Changneungji* (Records of Changneung Tomb), which shows the flow of the four cardinal mountains and the mountain at the back

Figure 10. Illustration of a propitious gravesite that shows how the four cardinal mountains flow from the guardian mountain at the back to the royal tomb

Regarding the guardian mountain, which was the most important element in deciding the location of the royal tomb, its shape and root were very important. Just as the master of the royal tomb has the status of an absolute being, the root of the guardian mountain at the back also had to be the highest in the hierarchy of the mountains. Therefore, according to *fengshui* theory, the royal tomb of the king and queen had to have mountains in all four directions and the guardian mountain at the back in particular had to be the best among mountains.

Mt. Geomansan, the guardian mountain of Geonwolleung (the tomb of Taejo Yi Seong-gye, the founder of Joseon), which was the first royal tomb of the Joseon era and the model for all Joseon tombs, originated from Mt. Baekdusan, which was considered the source of all mountains on the peninsula. Most other royal tomb locations have guardian mountains, of which their origin is related to the hierarchy of mountains.

3. Structural Elements and Characteristics of the Royal Tombs of the Joseon Dynasty

The royal tomb was generally divided into upper and lower areas. The upper tomb area included a *gokjang* wall, stone objects, and stone steps around the grave mound. The lower area included the Jeongjagak where rituals were performed, the Bigak where the gravestone was enshrined, the *sansinseok* (an altar on which the ritual for the mountain spirit was performed), the *mangnyowi* where the ritual paper was burned, the Subokbang where lower officials in charge of the tomb resided, a kitchen where the food used for rituals was prepared, the *chamdo* (ritual path), the Hongsalmun gate, and the *panwi*, which marked the position of the officiant during rituals. Connecting the upper and lower areas is the *sindo* or *singyo*, the path or bridge for the deceased spirit to use, which constitutes a transitional space.

Other tomb features include *eojeong* (a well for the king's drinking water), *jejeong* (a well for ritual water), the Jaesil where the government officials in charge of the tomb resided or where the ritual officiant stayed the night before the ritual, a firebreak and moat demarcating the tomb, a river or stream surrounding the tomb, and a stone bridge located before the Hongsalmun gate.

1) Boundary and Entrance of the Royal Tomb

The typical elements that mark the boundary and distinguish the territory of the royal tomb are *hwaso* and *haeja*. *Hwaso* is a firebreak built to prevent damage from wildfires. It was built by digging a moat around the *neung, won,* and *myo,* as well as by burning adjacent trees or clearing the land outside to prevent grass from growing. *Haeja* is a moat that was dug inside the firebreak.

Figure 12. Stream flow and location of stone bridge in the "Topographical Map" in *Changneungji* (Records of Changneung Tomb).

As the royal tomb was located at a propitious site according to *fengshui*, water was always present near the mountain. Symbolically, water is related to purification, as it divides secular and sacred spaces. In *fengshui*, it prevents the good *gi* (life force) of the propitious site from seeping out. Therefore, water was treated as the most basic element. In this context, it was absolutely necessary for the royal tomb to have a stream flowing at the front with a stone bridge (*geumcheongyo*) over the stream. Also, it was preferable to have water flowing in from the left and right sides to form a closed shape. This feature originated from the *fengshui* principle of preventing the good *gi* of the royal tomb from escaping by blocking it in with water.

2) Upper Area of the Royal Tomb in Joseon

Neung of the Joseon Dynasty

The *bongbun*, or mound, is the central feature of the upper area of the royal tomb. Though the form of the mound was fixed during the Joseon era, it still took on different shapes in terms of type.

The first was the single mound type, where either the king or queen was buried alone. The second is the double mound, where their mounds were buried next to each other, along the mountain ridge. One modification on this was the triple mound, where the mounds of the king, queen and the second queen (if the king remarried after the first queen's death) were laid together. In the case of double or triple mounds, two or three mounds were created with one *gokjang* wall. The third type, called *dongwon igang*, was a mound placed at the base of a mountain ridge on either the left or right side of the mountain behind the Jeongjagak; a low wall and stone objects were placed independently. This type was the largest in size and had a separate wall and stone objects but the same Jeongjagak and Bigak. The fourth type was *hapjang*, where the king and queen were buried together in one mound. In this case, *honyuseok* were placed in front for each person buried there; everything else was the same.

Out of 42 royal tombs of the Joseon era, the single mound was the most common type at fifteen, followed by fourteen double mounds. There were six *dongwon igang* graves, beginning with Gwangneung, and seven *hapjang* graves. The single-mound and *dongwon igang* graves that were large in size and required a great deal of money and effort to construct were mostly built when the country was at peace. In contrast, the double-mound and *hapjang* types, which required the least amount of labor and materials, were mostly

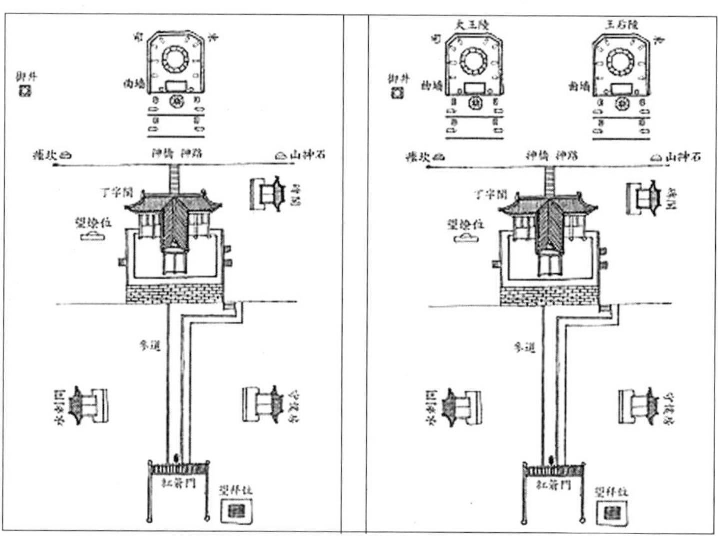

Figure 13. Typical types of tombs of Joseon Dynasty

built during the late Joseon. This shows that the mound type of the royal tomb was directly related to the vicissitudes of the dynasty.

Stone Screens and Stone Railing

Byeongpungseok or *hoseok* were stone slabs encircling the lower part of the mound like folding screens. Twelve zodiac animals were carved on each stone, which faced out in twelve directions, and a Taegeuk (Great Ultimate) symbol was painted at the center. It was also typical to have a railing surrounding the stone slabs. This method began during the Unified Silla and was established with the tomb of King Gongmin of Goryeo. It was also used at King Taejo's Geonwolleung of the Joseon era and was generally used for royal tombs. However, abiding by King Sejo's dying wish to observe frugality, stone screens

Figure 14. Front view of Geonwolleung

Figure 15. Overall view of Geonwolleung, as seen from behind the mound

Figure 16. Geonwolleung complete with stone screens and stone railing

Figure 17. King Sejo's Gwangneung. Following his wishes, stone screens were eliminated, and only the stone railing with the twelve zodiac animals was constructed.

and stone coffins were eliminated. Though they appeared again later when royal authority and discipline had to be strengthened at the royal court amid the confusion over royal succession, this style was consistently used after King Sejo.

Gokjang and Seokgye

Gokjang, also called *gokdam*, is a low wall that surrounds the mound on the back and sides except the front.

Seokgye is a one or two-step stone staircase built around the back, on the east and west sides inside the *gokjang*, depending on the topography of the tomb. *Seokgye* are thought to have first been created as a structural element to prevent the wall from collapsing under the pressure of the earth on top of the tomb. However, flowers and trees were not planted here, unlike the terraced flowerbeds in the royal palace.

Stone Sculpture Arrangement

Stone sculptures included stone sheep, stone tigers, stone tables, stone candleholder-shaped posts, stone lanterns, stone statues of civil officials, and stone statues of military officials. According to the *Gukjo oryeui* (Five Rites of the State), which dictated the proper mode of conduct for major state rituals during the Joseon era, two pairs of stone sheep and tigers were placed on the east and west sides of the mound inside the *gokjang*. Sheep, which are regarded as gentle animals, symbolized sacrificial offerings, whereas tigers represented the guardian spirit of the mountains and the protector of the tomb.

In ordinary graves the stone table on which offerings were placed during rituals was called *sangseok*. However, as all rituals at the royal tomb took place at the Jeongjagak, the stone table was called not *sangseok* but *honyuseok* and

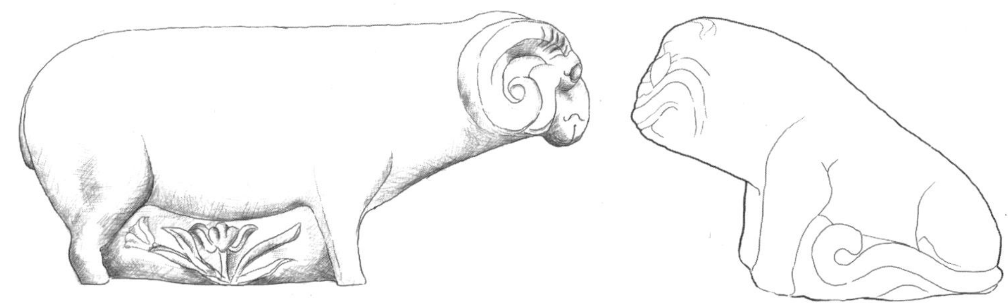

Figure 18. Stone sheep at Myeongneung

Figure 19. Stone tiger at Myeongneung

functioned not as a place for rituals but a place for the spirits of the dead to rest or play.

Mangjuseok are a pair of stone posts placed on either side of the front of the mound. They were arranged symmetrically to the right and left. As they were shaped like candleholders, they are sometimes regarded as lighting the mound, but their exact meaning is not clear. Their foremost function seems to have been decorative.

Jangmyeondeung symbolized prayers for the happiness of the deceased in the other world. Their origin can be traced to the stone lanterns placed in front of the funerary stupas of monks (*budo*), a custom that continued from the end of Silla throughout Goryeo. During the Joseon era, they were placed in front of the stone table. In particular, they succeeded the stone lanterns of temples.

Stone statues of civil officials (*muninseok*) and military officials (*muinseok*) were positioned on each side of the stone lantern. The civil officials were depicted dressed in the official uniform, holding a wooden mace that signified

Figure 20. *Honyuseok* and supporting stones at Gyeongneung

Figure 21. Stone lantern at Myeongneung

Figure 22. Stone post at Myeongneung

the status of a Joseon government official; military officials were shown wearing armor and holding a sword. In the case of *neung*, *won* and *myo*, a hierarchy is apparent as *neung* had one pair of civil and military official statues; *won*, only one pair of civil official statules; and *myo* had none.

To summarize the overall characteristics of the stone sculpture system of the Joseon era, Heolleung, the tomb of King Taejong, following the Hyeolleung and Jeongneung system of Goryeo, has two sets of stone lanterns and four sets of stone sheep, stone tigers and stone horses, which is twice as many as the other royal tombs. At Hongneung and Yureung, which were built after Emperor Taizu's tomb of Ming Dynasty, changes in the placement of stone statues of the civil and military officials, giraffes, elephants, lions, unicorn-

Figure 23. Stone statue of civil official at Myeongneung

Figure 24. Stone statue of military official at Myeongneung

Figure 25. Stone objects at King Sejong's Yeongneung

Figure 26. King Gojong's Hongneung built in the style of an emperor's tomb

lions, camels and horses on each side of a path leading to the mound, are apparent. However, the stone sculpture system tended to abide by the Geonwolleung system, except in the case of the tombs of dethroned kings (Yeonsangun and Gwanghaegun), or the tombs of posthumously enthroned crown princes and princesses (Gyeongneung and Jangneung).

3) Lower Area of the Royal Tombs of the Joseon Dynasty

Jeongjagak and Sindo

Jeongjagak is a ritual building in the shape of the Chinese character ㅜ, located in front of the royal tomb. It has the form of a *jeongjeon* (space where the ritual table is set and offerings are presented), which is three *kan* by two *kan*, and a *baejeon* (space where one bows), which has pillars but no walls or windows and is situated to the south of the central *kan*. This building has a gabled roof.

Figure 27. Spirit path at Sunchangwon

Figure 28. Spirit path at Gyeongneung

Unlike such shrines as Jongmyo (Royal Ancestral Shrine), the tomb is the space where the previous kings or queens are buried. Therefore, unlike at Jongmyo or other scholar-officials' shrines, the *sinmun* (door used by spirits) was always made into a sliding door at the back of the Jeongjagak, through which the spirit of the ancestor buried in the grave would directly enter.

A symbolic path or bridge for spirits was built between the end of the Jeongjagak, where the door for spirits was located, and the start of the ridgeline of the grave.

Bigak, Yegam and Sansinseok

The tombstone at the royal tomb was called *sindobi*, which was protected by the Bigak outside. The head of the *sindobi* was carved in the shape of a dragon, and a turtle-shaped supporting stone was placed at the bottom. The Bigak was constructed to the east of the Jeongjagak, usually facing west.

Figure 29. A stone for burning the ritual paper at Heolleung

Figure 30. Yegam, Jeongjagak and Bigak at Myeongneung

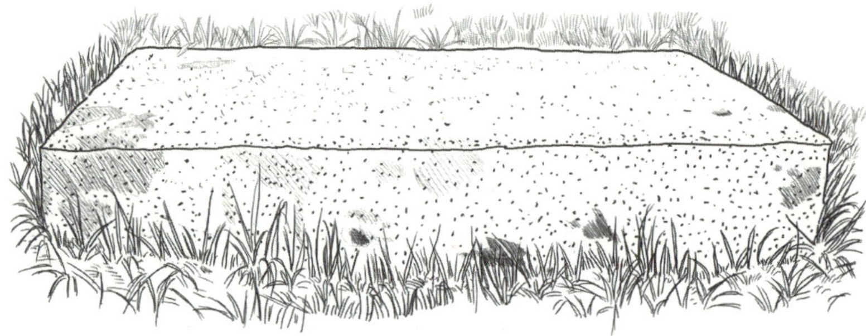

Figure 31. *Sansinseok* at Hongneung

The ancestral ritual begins by washing the hands and presenting an offering of a glass of wine; it then ends by burning the ritual paper over a fire pit called *yegam*. This ritual begins in the east, which represents water, and ends in the west, which represents fire. This was a symbolic ritual performance and the principle of spatial structure was based on *yin-yang* theory. The ritual procedures that began with burning incense and pouring wine on the ground were based on the concept of *yin* and *yang*, and signified calling the heavenly god down to earth using the scent of the incense, and calling the earthly god to the surface using the scent of the wine poured on the ground. In general, *yegam* was situated to the left of and behind the Jeongjagak when facing the grave.

Sansinseok came to take its place as part of the tomb in relation to indigenous beliefs along with various Buddhist shrines such as Sansingak (Shrine of the Mountain Spirit), Chilseonggak (Shrine of the Seven Star Spirit) and Samseonggak (Shrine of the Three Divinities). It was built to pay respects to mountain spirits before constructing the tomb, and it was located to the right of and behind the Jeongjagak. It is rectangular in shape like *honyuseok* but smaller.

Chamdo is a path between the Hongsalmun gate and the Jeongjagak. The path on the left is called *hyangno*, the incense path, and the path on the right is called *eoro*, the king's path. The *hyangno* is slightly higher and wider than the *eoro*. *Eoro* is paved with wide, natural, flat stones just like in the royal palace. It turns in front of the Jeongjagak and connects with the east stairs that lead to the Jeongjagak.

The caretaker of the royal tomb, who managed affairs related to rituals and kept the area clean, stayed in the Subokbang. This building is three *kan* by one *kan* with a gabled roof. It resembles a house with a kitchen, room and wooden floor. It is located opposite the Suragan in the east, facing west.

The Suragan is also called *Eoju*. Originally, it meant a kitchen where the king's food was prepared; in this case, however, it was used for the preparation of ritual food offerings. The Suragan and the Subokbang are located south of the Jeongjagak on the east and west. The Suragan generally sits to the west and faces east; it is a low building in the architectural hierarchy, with two to three *kan* in front and one to 1.5 *kan* on the side.

The Hongsalmun is a red arrow gate that is placed in front of a tomb. The Taegeuk pattern is painted at the center. There are two types of the Hongsalmun gate: one is peaked at the center like a mountain, and the other is straight across.

Panwi, or *baewi* is a paved area that marks the position of the ritual officiant.

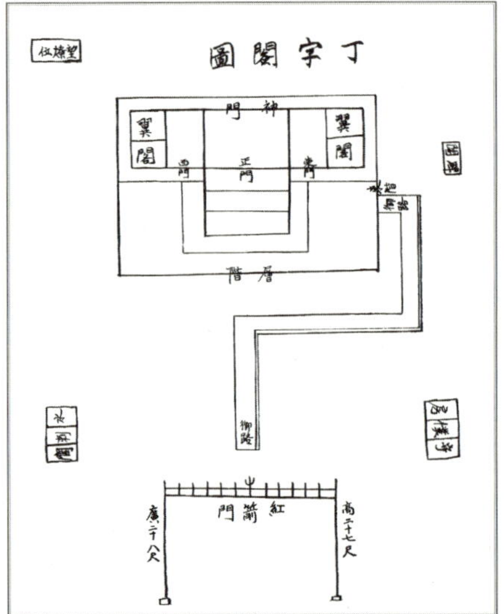
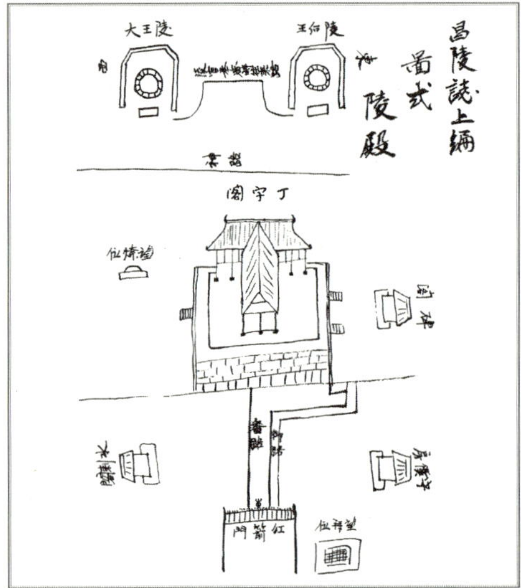

Figure 32. King's path indicated in the "Illustration of the Jeongjagak" in *Ingneungji* (Records of Ingneung Tomb)

Figure 33. Distinction between the incense path and the king's path in *Changneungji* (Records of Changneung Tomb), Vol. 1

Figure 34. *Chamdo* and Jeongjagak at Yungneung

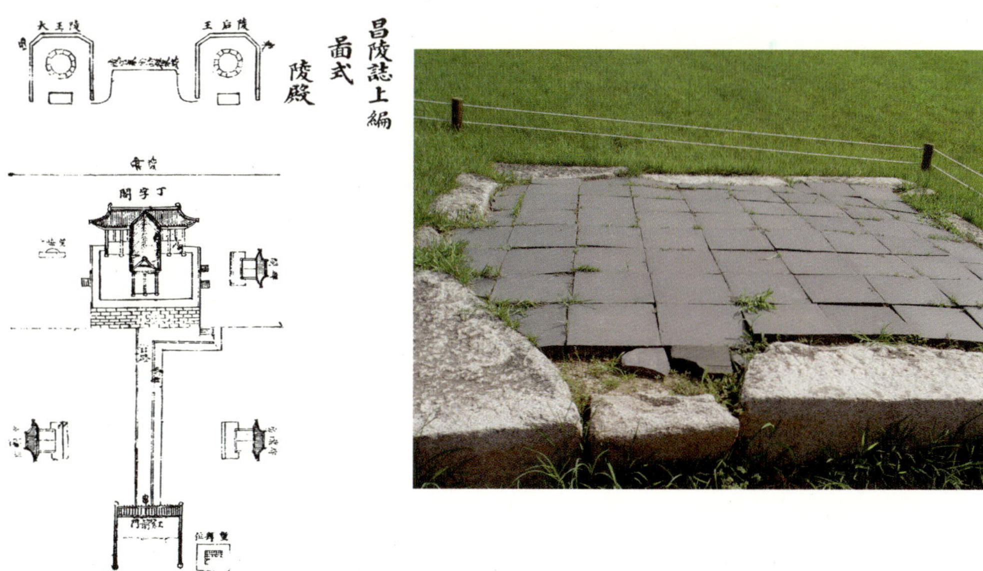

Figure 35. The Hongsalmun at Ingneung

Figure 36. "Illustration of the Royal Tomb" in *Changneungji* (Records of Changneung Tomb)

Figure 37. *Panwi* at Geonwolleung

4) Jaesil and Other Facilities

Jaesil

The Jaesil was normally used as the office of the *chambong*, a government official who guarded and managed the tomb, but ritual officiants also stayed here during the ritual. It was attached to the royal tomb and included an office where officials in charge of the management of the tomb worked, a space for the ritual officiant to stay, and a storehouse where various ritual vessels and other necessary articles were kept. Also, a terraced flowerbed (*hwagye*) was attached to the Jaesil. Rather than elaborate decorations, the flowerbed consisted of two simple, modest levels that were either left empty or planted with azaleas or Chinese juniper trees. Zelkova or Chinese juniper trees were

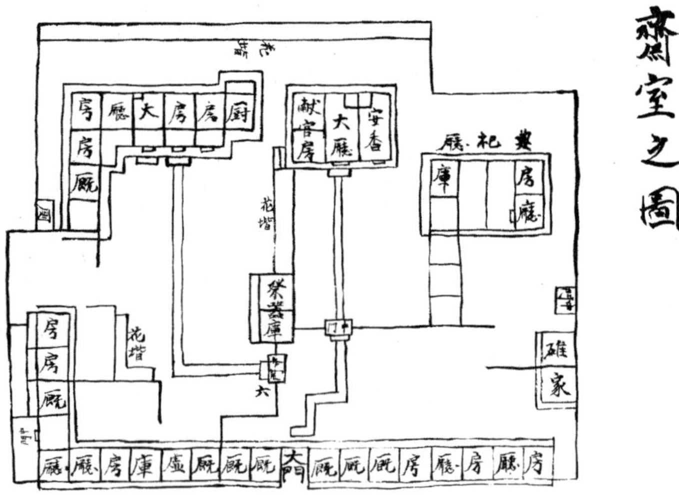

Figure 38. "Illustration of Jaesil" in *Myeongneung deungnok*

Figure 39. Jaesil at Donggureung (Present-day Administration Office)

sometimes planted in the yard, and symbolic trees such as gingko, fir, elm, or zelkova were planted at the entrance of the Jaesil.

Pond and Ritual Water

The traditional function of ponds can be found in *Imwon simnyukji*, an agricultural encyclopedia of the Joseon era, in which it is stated that the advantages of digging a pond are, first, the appreciation that comes from breeding fish, second, providing water to paddies and fields, and third, purifying one's heart. However, ponds built within the space of the royal tomb seem to have had more diverse functions. In *fengshui*, ponds fulfilled the function of *bibo*, or making up for weak areas and minimizing strong areas. They could also be used in the event of a fire and added a scenic element.

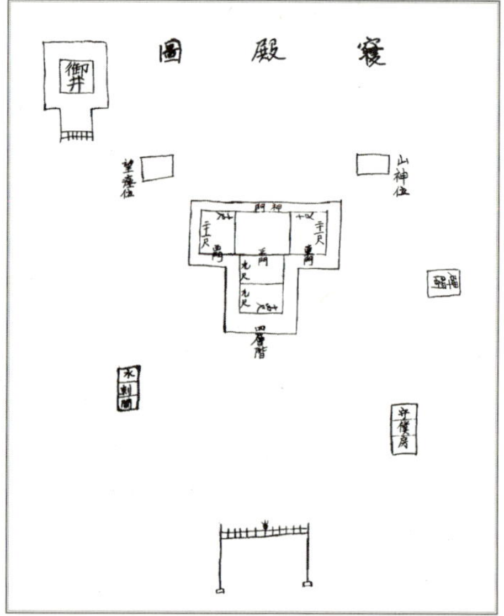

Figure 40. Pond at Gwangneung

Figure 41. Well for the king's drinking water in "Illustration of the Residence for Ritual Officiants" in *Hongneungji* (Records of Hongneung Tomb)

As rituals took place regularly at the royal tomb, a constant supply of ritual water was needed. Therefore, a clean well was dug near the royal tomb, and was called *jejeong*. Also, as the king regularly performed rituals at the royal tomb the *eojeong*, or well for the king's drinking water, was situated in the Jaesil or near the tomb.

IV. Characteristics of the Plants at Royal Tombs of the Joseon Dynasty

1. Records of Plants Used at Ancient Royal Tombs

People have long regarded trees as sacred. Historically, the relationship between people and trees is a multifarious one. Trees were a source of life, and they provided the material for everyday tools and equipment, as well as housing. They also served as a refuge for people seeking shelter from bad weather, predators, and even enemies. Consequently, people began actively cultivating trees and came to deify, worship and protect them. Deification of trees commonly occurred not only in Korea but in other countries where trees were given symbolic significance. Trees have been called "world tree" or "tree of life", and each culture has its own myths regarding trees. In the East in particular, trees usually signified eternal life, and there is much evidence that people planted trees near graves.

Trees appear often in the murals of the Goguryeo people, who are thought to have regarded the afterlife as being connected to the world of the living. Pine,

Figure 42. Pine trees painted on the west side of the northern wall of the burial chamber, Jinpari Tomb No. 1, Goguryeo

Figure 43. Trees painted on the right mural of the front chamber, Jangcheon Tomb No. 1

birch, and cinnamon trees, which were thought to also exist on the moon, were often painted in Goguryeo murals.

Songbaek (pine tree and Chinese arborvitae) deserve mention when discussing the relationship between ancient tombs and trees. A record stating that the people of Goguryeo planted *songbaek*[1] is found in the article on Goguryeo of *Sanguozhi* (The Records of the Three Kingdoms) of China, and the record saying that pine trees were planted around the royal tomb also appears in the writings of Choe Chi-won of Silla. It is also recorded in *Samguk yusa,* written by Iryeon, that pine trees were planted around graves.

As such, many examples are found of planted pines and Chinese arborvitae trees. According to *Sinjeung dongguk yeoji seungnam* (A Revised Edition of the Expanded Survey of the Geography of Korea), which mentions Jinjumyo, the tomb of King Dongmyeong of Goguryeo, pine trees and Chinese arborvitae trees were planted along the central axis in front of the tomb, and Chinese arborvitae trees were planted in a straight line on the right and left sides in front of the Bigak. Also, seven rows of pine trees were planted in front of the tomb of King Gogugyang of Goguryeo.

It is recorded that a number of pines and Chinese arborvitae trees were planted at the royal tomb in China, and deforestation was prohibited. Records show that during the Han Dynasty, pines and Chinese arborvitae trees were planted in rows after the grave was built. Chinese arborvitae trees (big cone pines) were considered an auspicious tree from the Kunlun Mountains in Chinese

---

1 *Songbaek* is usually translated as pines and big cone pines. Though *baek*(柏) initially designated Oriental arborvitae in China, it was mistranslated a long time ago as big cone pines and *songbaek* thus is interpreted as pines and big cone pines. Today, however, both cone pines and Oriental arborvitaes are used to signify *baek.*

myths and legends. It seems that the planting method used in the tombs of the Han Dynasty directly influenced that of Korea's ancient tombs. This is also in line with the fact that the mound style of the late Goguryeo was changed to an earth mound under the influence of the Han's tomb system. It is assumed that the planting method was introduced along with the mound style. That pines and Chinese arborvitae trees were the main species used and that they were often planted in rows can also be related to the influence of the Han Dynasty at the time.

2. Characteristics of Planting at the Royal Tombs of Joseon

Based on *Joseon wangjo sillok* (Annals of the Joseon Dynasty) or various records of the royal tombs, plants at the royal tombs during the Joseon era can be summarized as follows. First, a mound was raised and trees were planted within approximately 300 meters of the mound. The main species were pine and Chinese arborvitae trees. King Taejong ordered that miscellaneous trees be cut down and pine and Chinese arborvitae trees be planted. However, as the pines grew in gradually, faster growing chestnut trees were planted first to create a forest more quickly. This method is similar to today's ecological planting methods.

Fir and alder trees were planted along with pine and Chinese arborvitae trees around the royal tomb. Miscellaneous trees (mostly broadleaf) were also planted as needed, such as to prevent landslides. When it came to planting methods, species such as oaks were planted from seeds. Though cedars, wild walnuts, mulberries and chestnuts were also planted, their numbers were

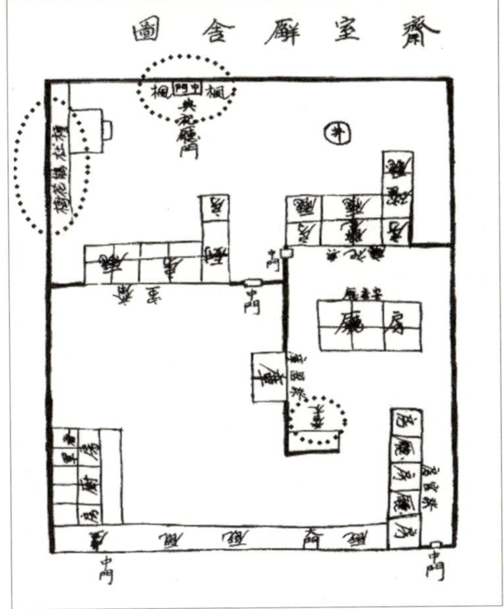

Figure 44. Pine forest at Ingneung

Figure 45. Trees appearing in an illustration of the Jaesil of Hongneung

Figure 46. Alder forest at Ingneung

restricted. Despite the belief that colorful flowering trees should not be planted near graves, azaleas were planted at the entrance of the royal tomb and on the terraced flowerbed of the Jaesil. Chinese junipers were also sometimes planted inside the Jaesil in order to make the incense needed for rituals.

Dense forest was considered important for protecting the royal tomb; thus, the importance of pines, big cone pines, and miscellaneous small trees was emphasized in various historical records. This is in line with today's ecological planting methods used in forest vegetation. Pre-planted trees and growing trees were managed thoroughly. If someone carelessly cut down trees, they were punished severely. This is evidence of the strict and focused tomb management policy.

As it was important to have dense forest around the royal tomb, the cultivation and management of broadleaf trees, which were usually neglected, were ordered when pines and big cone pines were damaged or failed to grow due to blight or harmful insects. Also, alder trees were planted in wetlands, where water flowed on the left or right of the tomb. Alder trees were planted because they are ecologically suited to wet areas, but they also helped to hide the tomb from view because they are fast-growing trees.

The planting methods for the royal tombs of the Joseon era can be briefly summarized as follows. First, a pine forest was planted to mimic a screen. As such, they were positioned behind the grave. Second, trees were planted facing each other and in pairs in front of the Jeongjagak to create rows of trees. Finally, a third method involved planting trees randomly along ridges or hilly areas.

References

Historical Records

Changneungji 昌陵誌 (Records of Changneung Tomb).

Changneung salleung dogam uigwe 昌陵山陵都監儀軌 (Records of the Superintendency of Changneung Tomb).

Daejeon hoetong 大典會通 (Comprehensive Collection of National Codes). Photoprint (1990). Seoul: Bokyung.

Gyeongneung salleung dogam uigwe 敬陵山陵都監儀軌 (Records of the Superintendency of Gyeongneung Tomb).

Hongneungji 弘陵誌 (Records of Hongneung Tomb).

Iwangjik (Yi Royal Household), ed. *Gyeongneungji* 敬陵誌 (Records of Gyeongneung Tomb). Photoprint (1910).

__________. *Ingneungji* 翼陵誌 (Records of Ingneung Tomb). *Myeongneung deungnok* 明陵謄錄, (Records of Myeongneung Tomb).

Myeongneungji 明陵誌 (Records of Myeongneung Tomb).

Sunchang wonji, 順昌園誌 (Records of Gardens in Sunchang).

Books and Articles

Academy of Korean Studies. 1990. *Yeokju gyeongguk daejeon* (National Code, Translated with Notes). Academy of Korean Studies.

Choi, Jong-hyun. 2002a. "Gomunheon-e natanan sungmok sasang yeongu" (A Study of the Tree Worship in Historical Documents). *Gukto gyeheok* (Land Planning) 37.2.

__________. 2002b. "Gomunheon-e natanan jeontong baesik yeongu" (A Study of Traditional Planting Methods in Historical Documents). *Gukto gyeheok* (Land Planning) 37.5.

Chun, Young-woo. 1993. "Joseon sidae-ui sonamu sichaek" (Pine Tree Policy of the Joseon Era). In *Sonamu-wa uri munhwa* (Pine Trees and Our Culture). Sup-gwa Munhwa Yeonguhoe (Society for Forests and Culture).

__________. 1997. *Sallim munhwaron* (On Forest Culture). Kookmin University Press.

Cultural Heritage Administration. 1986. *Joseon wangneung* (Royal Tombs of Joseon). Ujin Munhwasa.

__________. 2002. *Changdeokgung, jongmyo wonyu* (Gardens of Changdeokgung Palace and Jongmyo Shrine).

__________. 2003. *Seooreung sallim saengtae josa yeongu bogoseo* (Research Report on the Forest Vegetation of Seooreung Tomb).

Eun, Gwang-jun. 1985. *Joseon wangneung seongmulji* (Records of the Stone Objects at the Royal Tombs of Joseon). Minsokwon.

Goyang City Government. 1987. *Goyang-gun ji* (Records of Goyang-gun County).

Guri City Government. 1996. *Guri-si ji* (Records of Guri City).

Gyeonggi-do Provincial Government. 1988. *Ginae neungwonji* (The Royal Tomb Sites of Gyeonggi-do).

Han Kook-mun Won. 1995. *Wangneung* (The Royal Tombs). Han Kook Mun Won.

Han, Young-woo. 1996. *Dasi channeun uri yeoksa* (Korean History Revisited). Kyung Sae Won.

Jang, Gi-in. 1997. *Hanguk geonchuksa daegye VII (seokjo)* (Historical Outline of Korean Architecture VII: Stone Sculpture). Boseonggak.

Jang, Yeong-hun. 2002. *Wangneung pungsu-wa joseon-ui yeoksa* (*Fengshui* of the Royal Tombs and the History of Joseon). Daewonsa.

Jeon, Ho-tae. 2003. *Goguryeo gobun byeokhwa yeongu* (A Study of Goguryeo Tomb Murals). Sakyejul.

Jeong, Jae-hun. 1998. *Hanguk jeontong-ui won* (Traditional Tombs of Korea). Hwangeyong-gwa Jogyeong.

Jeonju Yissi Daedong Jongyagwon. 1999. *Joseon-ui taesil*.

Kim, Yeong-bin. 1990. "Pungsu sasang-eseo bon joseon wangneung wonmyo joseong gibeop-e gwanhan yeongu" (A Study of the Construction Methods for the Royal Tombs of the Joseon Era from the *Fengshui* Principle). *Nonmunjip* (Hyosung Women' s University).

Kim, Young-mo and Lee Seon. 2004. "Gojeung-eul todaero han seooreung neungyeok siseol-ui jeongbi bangan yeongu" (A Study of the Management Plan for the Facilities of Seooreung Tomb Based on Historical Research). *Hanguk jeontong jogyeong hakhoeji* (Journal of Korean Institute of Traditional Landscape Architecture) 22.1.

Lee, Seon and Kim Young-mo. 2004. "Joseon sidae neungyeok gonggan-ui sikjae mit gwalli sasil-e gwanhan yeongu" (On the Planting and Management of the Royal Tombs in the Joseon Era). *Hanguk jeontong jogyeong hakhoeji* (Journal of Korean Institute of Traditional Landscape Architecture) 22.1.

Mok, Eul-su. 1988. *Goryeo joseon neungji* (Records of the Tombs of Goryeo and Joseon). Munseongdang.

Na, Hee-la. 2002. "Godae hanguk-ui saengsagwan yeonghon-gwan-eul jungsim-euro (Views on Life and Death in Ancient Korea: Centering on the Soul). *Yeoksa-wa hyeonsil* (History and Reality) 47.

Yi, Chang-hwan. 1998. "Joseon sidae neungyeok-ui ipji-wa gonggan guseong-e gwanhan yeongu" (Research on the Location and Spatial Structure of the Royal Tombs of the Joseon Era). Ph.D. diss., Sungkyunkwan University.

Yi, Ho-il. 2003. *Joseon-ui wangneung* (Royal Tombs of Joseon). Garam.

Yi, Yeong. 1992. "Joseon sidae wangneung neungyeok-ui geonchuk-gwa baechi hyeongsik yeongu" (On the Architecture and Arrangement Methods of the Royal Tombs of the Joseon Era). Ph.D. diss., Department of Architecture, Seoul National University.

Yoon, Jang-sup. 1996. *Hanguk-ui geonchuk* (Korean Architecture). Seoul National University Press.

Authors

Choi Key-soo
(Department of Landscape Architecture, University of Seoul)

Choi Key-soo is a professor in the Department of Landscape Architecture at the University of Seoul. He served as Director of the Institute of Korean Studies, Dean of the College of Urban Sciences, and President of Korean Institute of Traditional Landscape Architecture. He is currently a member of the Cultural Properties Committee. E-mail:kschoi@uos.ac.kr

Kim Young-mo
(Department of Traditional Landscape Architecture, Korean National University of Cultural Heritage)

Kim Young-mo is a professor in the Department of Traditional Landscape Architecture, Korean National University of Cultural Heritage. He received his Ph.D. from the University of Seoul with the dissertation entitled "Structure Principles of the Traditional Spaces." He has written many books and articles on royal palaces, Royal Ancestral Shrine, royal tombs, royal temporary palaces, etc. E-mail: ymkim1683@nuch.ac.kr

Chapter 7

Landscape Architecture of Nu, Jeong and Dae

I. Introduction

Ancient Korean people enjoyed singing and dancing and pursued a lifestyle of taste and aesthetic enjoyment of nature. Koreans were rich in emotions and flexible in how they lived their lives. They preferred to live in the mountains where forests flourished and streams flowed rather than cities bustling with people.

Shall we go live there?
Let's live in the green mountains!
With wild grapes and thyme,

Figure 1. People enjoying the beauty of nature, as depicted in Gyeomje Jeong Seon's painting

Let's live in the green mountains!

Yalli yalli yallaseong yallari yalla

(Cheongsan byeolgok [Song of the Green Mountains], Goryeo era)

Koreans delighted in living close to nature away from the mundane details of everyday life. One example is Yun Seon-do (1587-1671), who created well-known gardens during the Joseon era. Human beings make subjective judgments about nature, which is itself objective. Nature follows the principles of the universe; if people do not live close to nature, they can never become one with it. In other words, it is only when human-centered thinking is abolished that people can live naturally. This is called a state of unity between subject and object. It is in this context that Yun Seon-do wrote the following in *Eobu sasisa* (The Fisherman's Calendar): "*Jigukchong, jigukchong, eosawa!* / Do the carefree gulls following me, or is it I who is following them?" He could not have sung those words without having achieved the unity of subject and object.

Autumn comes to the river village; the fish grow fat.

Weigh anchor, weigh anchor!

Leisurely hours spent on broad waters.

Jigukchong, jigukchong, eosawa!

I look back on the world of men; the farther off the better.

("Autumn," The Fisherman's Calendar)

The phrase, "I look back on the world of men; the farther off the better," clearly reflects the poet's attitude regarding life as a hermit. He considered the life hidden within nature a true life, which was unknown to people living in the

Figure 2. *Sijungdae* (Enjoying the Moonrise by the Lake) by Jeong Seon

human world. From this, we can surmise that our ancestors viewed nature as the ultimate garden.

Nature to humans is like a mother's bosom. Nature gives unsparingly, protects us, and listens to our meaningless complaints. The ancestors of modern Koreans often retreated to *nu*, *jeong* and *dae*, which were located away from the mundane world, to commune with nature. *Nu*, *jeong* and *dae* were spaces where they could take a break surrounded by nature, and where they could enjoy nature directly and become one with it.

People were united with nature while staying at *nu*, *jeong* and *dae*. They lived affluent lives together with nature and built a number of *nu* and *jeong* at scenic locations. They also named distinctively shaped rocks, giving them the suffix "*-dae*." The names represented the location the rock resembled so that its

Figure 3. Jukseoru. Pavilions were built in places with beautiful natural scenery, and gardens for sightseeing or leisure were developed in Korea.

landscape-like features could automatically be detected. For example, the name "Sinseondae" meant a place where *sinseon* (a Taoist immortal) either lived or strolled. This type of place was regarded as being somewhat apart from the human world, therefore the image the name suggests is that of a place high above a cliff with a panoramic view of the surrounding scenery. For example, Sinseondae at Busan has a panoramic view of the wide ocean and small islands (Oryukdo and Jodo) on a clear day, one can see as far as Tsushima Island of Japan. The name "Gahangnu," located in the Yeongdong region, means a pavilion that appears to be riding on the back of a crane. When visiting Gahangnu, one can feel the illusion of flying on a crane.

Nu, jeong and *dae* are not fenced in gardens. They are spaces of philosophy and beauty where the distinction between natural and artificial is not so clear. As palaces such as Changdeokgung or private academies such as Sosu Seowon

Figure 4. Entrance of Yonggongsa temple in the true-view landscape painting by Jeong Seon

also have *nu*, *jeong* and *dae*, it is easy to think of them as gardens hidden behind fences. However, the fact that such scenic spots as the "eight scenic views of Gwandong region" were also named *nu*, *jeong* and *dae* shows that they were not confined gardens.

Given the diverse seasonal changes in Korea, it is tempting to get out and enjoy nature. People often yearn to escape into nature when their lives feel heavy and tiresome. The definition of *pungnyu* is the enjoyment of nature itself. Since Korea has such a rich natural environment, it seems inevitable that gardens in this sense would develop.

II. Differences in *Nu*, *Jeong* and *Dae* of Korea, China and Japan

Korean *nu, jeong* and *dae* differ from those of China and Japan. When comparing their scenic aspects, it can be said that the Korean style is more extroverted and the Japanese style more introverted, while the Chinese style contains elements of both.

As the Korean style was more externally oriented, the natural scenery was considered important. In the case of Dongnakdang, because the wall next to the *sarangchae* (men's quarters) concealed the natural scenery, vertical bars were installed in the wall to allow a view of the natural surroundings from inside the garden. Also, a two-story pavilion gate at the front of private academies (*seowon*) allowed for an open view. Just as pavilions were built facing outward, houses were also built on hills in back gardens or on the outskirts of the village. Windows were made as wide as possible, and the walls were kept small so that it was easier to enjoy the natural scenery. *Dae* also reflected this extroverted style, as they were built on a natural rock bed to allow a good view of the surroundings.

Figure 5. Panoramic view from Gyeongcheondae at Sangju

On the other hand, *nu* and *jeong* in China were built with regard to how they would look from the outside as well as how the outside would look from within the building. As they emphasize both inside and outside, they are introverted and extroverted at the same time. Figure 6 shows a pavilion called Yusheitongzuoxuan at Zhouzhengyuan (Humble Administor's Garden), a Chinese typical garden. As seen from the outside, the building and windows are in the shape of a fan; the outside scenery is framed by this fan when viewed from inside the building. This reflects both an internal and external orientation.

Nu, jeong and *dae* were not as developed in Japan as in Korea. Due to the importance Koreans placed on natural scenery, the middles of walls were often omitted, as in the case of Dosan Seowon, or an extra door was made to allow for a view. In contrast, Japanese gardens were made by first erecting a fence

Figure 6. Yusheitongzuoxuan pavilion at Zhouzhengyuan, China

around the planned area. Objects of appreciation were located within the garden, much as one might reflect on oneself in a darkened chamber such as a tearoom.

Figure 7 shows Aihozi Garden, created in 1313; it was one of the early works of Musoukokusi, a famous Japanese garden designer. The cascade falling from the cliff is not clear in the picture, as the stream was not strong enough when the photograph was taken. The pond at the bottom of the cliff is in the shape of a reclining dragon. There is a pavilion at the top of the cliff but its name is unknown. If this were in Korea, the pavilion would include a hanging tablet, writings from a number of visiting poets, and engraved wooden plates. Also, with Korean pavilions, the spaces between the pillars are left open so that the scenery is visible. These are the differences between Korea and Japan. Though Musoukokusi tried to create a view in his garden, he was not very successful. Aihozi Garden has no more than a one-kilometer view, which is not much compared to the eight-to-ten-kilometer views from Korean *nu* and *jeong*. Again, this can be attributed to the introverted characteristic of Japanese gardens.

Figure 8 is Kogetsudai in the well-known Ginkakuji temple at Kyoto. Its name suggests facing the moon or an image of a person facing the moon. However, as it is made from sand, it is impossible to climb it, where one might get a view of the moon. This would be unheard of in traditional landscape in Korea. Also, if a similar name were used in Korea, *gwangpung jewol* would have been selected instead of *hyangwol*. *Gwangpung jewol* means a bright moon in a clear sky and a cool breeze blowing after the rain has stopped. The sky after the rain is the clearest as the rain has washed away all the dust in the air. The moon, too, is clearer and brighter, and the wind adds to the freshness.

Figure 7. Pavilion at Aihozi, Japan

Figure 8. Kogetsudai in the Ginkakuji temple at Kyoto

Korean traditional gardens excel at such scenery. Regarding the example shown in figure 8, man-made objects that have no practical use do not suit the Korean style. Thus, Sosoewon, a typical Korean garden, features Gwangpunggak and Jewoldang; also, Jewoldae is found at Goesan, Chungcheongbuk-do, and Gwangpungjeong and Jewoldae are paired at Seohu-myeon, Andong. Jewoldae, featured in Figure 9, is located on a cliff behind the village and faces east, offering a good view of the moonrise. The Gwangpungjeong building is found below this one. Figures 8 and 9 clearly reflect differences in the *dae* of Korea and Japan.

Chinese and Japanese gardening styles also use *chagyeong* to adapt the natural scenery to the garden. However, *chagyeong* means "borrowing scenery when there is none or when it is insufficient." As natural scenery was abundant

Figure 9. Jewoldae found at Seohu-myeon, Andong

Figure 10. Autumn foliage at Tongdosa temple

and was the main focus of Korean *nu*, *jeong* and *dae*, "borrowing landscape" was relatively unnecessary. Figure 10 shows the autumn colors at Tongdosa temple. The trees behind the wall are an example of borrowed scenery. However, the term *chagyeong* was not even used in this case, as the natural landscape was such a given in Korean traditional gardens. Therefore, the word is not found in ancient documents. For China and Japan, however, as they were not solely extroverted, *chagyeong* was used to supplement the existing landscape.

III. Historical Context of *Nu*, *Jeong* and *Dae*

1. Historical Records

In order to understand how Korean *nu, jeong* and *dae* developed, it is necessary to first examine the historical records. The *Shijing* (Book of Odes), the oldest compilation of Chinese poetry, recorded the existence of *yeongdae* (靈臺), *yeongyu* (靈囿) and *yeongso* (靈沼) in the Zhou Dynasty between 1000 and 600 BC Here the character 靈 can be seen as a prefix that signifies "divine spirit" or "soul"; therefore, *dae, yu* (a type of pasture) and *so* (pond) probably existed in early ancient Chinese landscape architecture. This also means that *dae* preceded *nu* and *jeong*.

In Korea, the very first record of *dae* also appeared 500 years before that of *nu* and *jeong*. It is written in *Samguk sagi* that "birds called *nansae* gathered at Wangdae" during the reign of King Dongmyeong (28 BC). Though it is difficult to know exactly what type of birds *nansae* are, they seem to have been birds that brought good omens. As King Dongmyeong experienced much difficulty in founding Goguryeo and conquered neighboring countries after this record was made, it has a positive meaning. When looking at the picture of Onyeosanseong mountain fortress (Figure 11), what some call Jangdae (Command Post) must be the Wangdae recorded in *Samguk sagi*. This Wangdae soared 600 meters higher than the surrounding plain in the shape of a hat and was thus a magnificent spot for observing the surrounding area and a strategic point for governing the country.

Figure 11. Wangdae of Goguryeo

Figure 12. Joryongdae of Baekje

The record stating that the platform for shooting arrows was built in the royal court during King Gaero's reign (475) of Baekje shows that *dae* were built while the royal palace was constructed. Other *dae* recorded in *Samguk yusa* during the Three Kingdoms era include Cheomseongdae, the oldest observatory in East Asia; Igyeondae, where King Munmu, who unified the three kingdoms, transformed into a dragon after his burial in an underwater tomb; Joryongdae, which was related to the fall of Baekje; Jaondae, a rock on Sabisu river that became warm when a Baekje king climbed it and bowed toward Buddha on his way to Wangheungsa temple; and the five summits of Mt. Odaesan —Dongdae, Seodae, Namdae, Bukdae and Jungdae—where 50,000 bodhisattvas were said to have appeared. These records show that *dae* of the Three Kingdoms era were not intended for sightseeing or leisure. Such concepts only began to appear with the advent of the Goryeo era (Kim and Ahn 1995, 127-128).

Korean *dae* were developed early for military and Buddhist purposes. Meanwhile, the records on *nu* and *jeong* that appeared between 470 and 480, approximately 500 years after those on *dae,* included the concept of sightseeing and leisure. The oldest record on *jeong* in Korea details King Soji's visit to Cheoncheonjeong during Silla. Cheoncheonjeong is a *jeong* related to Seochulji pond. When the king went to Cheoncheonjeong, he received a letter instructing him to shoot an arrow at a box where a musical instrument was stored. Because of the letter, he discovered a monk, who was committing adultery with the queen, hiding inside the box, and he was able to save his own life. This shows that though it is not clear why the king went to Cheoncheonjeong, it is possible to assume that he spent some time there. There are also records stating that King Jinpyeong (579-632) of Silla enjoyed sightseeing and leisure at Goseokjeong.

Figure 13. Cheomseongdae of Silla

Figure 14. Jaondae of Baekje

The first records of *nu* or *nugak* appear in the above-mentioned record of King Gaero (475), along with a record stating that King Mu (636) of Baekje held a banquet with his subjects at Manghaeru, overlooking the ocean. Thus, this shows that while the *dae* of the Three Kingdoms era had military and Buddhist purposes, *nu* and *jeong* were used for sightseeing and leisure.

2. Definition of *Nu, Jeong* and *Dae*

Yi Gyu-bo (1168-1241), a well-known writer of Goryeo, described *nu, jeong* and *dae* in "Saryunjeonggi." According to Yi, *nu* or *nugak* was a two-story structure with a raised wooden floor beneath which people could pass. In contrast, *jeong* or *jeongja* was classified by its spatial rather than structural characteristics. *Jeongja* were left open, reflecting the spatial characteristic of emptiness and openness. *Shuowen jiezi* (AD 98), the first comprehensive Chinese character dictionary, defined *jeongja* as a resting spot for people. According to a survey on the shape of *jeongja* (An 1990), though *jeongja* were smaller than *nugak*, they were made in a variety of styles and the floor was closer to the ground. They were not very colorful but were usually placed where eight scenic views coud be easily seen.

Yi Gyu-bo, on the other hand, defined *dae* as a high platform built piling flat stones. However, this only describes one of three types of *dae*. As stated in *Shuowen jiezi*, *dae* were located in high places from which the surrounding area could be viewed a particularly high place that cannot be reached by people was also called *dae*.

Figure 15. Geumgangdae, which is an inaccessibly high *dae*, of Mt. Geumgangsan

The difference between *nu* or *jeong* and *dae* was that *nu* and *jeong* were man-made structures, whereas *dae* were not. Though buildings were sometimes constructed on top of a *dae* that was raised on a slab base, an analysis of village maps from 1871 to 1899 shows that nearly 75 percent of *dae* did not have buildings (An 1998, 216).

The difference between Korea and China becomes clear when this definition is compared to that found in *Yuanye*, a book of landscape architecture in China. According to *Yuanye*, there were three types of *dae* (Ji Cheng 1634, 43): The first was built on a stone foundation and was flat on top. For the second type, wooden boards were woven together and a flat board was placed on top. The third type stood in front of *nugak* so people could take advantage of the fresh air.[1] All three were flat on top. However, it is clear that the

---

1 園林之臺 或掇 石而高上平者 或木架高而板無屋者 或襲閣前出一步而敞者俱爲臺

Figure 16. Namipo in Yeongyang, Gyeongsangbuk-do province

second type, where a flat board was placed on top of a wooden structure, was a man-made *dae*. Whereas *dae* in Korea signified the use of natural rocks or cliffs, it referred to artificially constructed structures in China. This is the difference between Korea and China.

3. Distribution of *Nu*, *Jeong* and *Dae*

Table 1 details the characteristics of distribution by totaling by province the number of *nu, jeong* and *dae* in the 1530s recorded in *Sinjeung dongguk yeoji seungnam* (A Revised Editon of the Expanded Survey of the Geography of Korea). In total, there were 317 *nugak,* 237 *jeongja,* and 110 *dae*.

Since there were 330 *gun* or *hyeon*, the local administrative units at the time, there must have been about two *nu, jeong* or *dae* in each *gun* or *hyeon*. As Gyeongsang-do, which had the highest number of *nu, jeong* and *dae*, had 66 *gun* or *hyeon* at the time, it is estimated that each *gun* or *hyeon* must have had three *nu, jeong* or *dae*. This number coincides with Sin Suk-ju's record (1460) that "Yeongnam region has some 60 government offices in small and large villages, and there is no government office without *nu, jeong* or *dae*."

Looking at the regional distribution of *nu, jeong* and *dae* in Table 1, over 10 percent of *nu, jeong* and *dae* were located in the provinces that belong to present-day South Korea, i.e. Gyeongsang-do, Jeolla-do, Chungcheong-do, Gangwon-do and Gyeonggi-do. On the other hand, fewer than 10 percent were located in the North Korean regions, that is, Pyeongan-do, Hwanghae-do and Hamgyeong-do. Also, the provinces with higher numbers of *nu* generally had higher numbers of *jeong*. Therefore, though some *dae* were made for military

Table 1. Distribution of *Nu, Jeong* and *Dae* by province during the Joseon Dynasty (%)

	nugak	*jeongja*	*dae*	total
Gyeonggi-do	21 (6.6)	43 (18.1)	8 (7.3)	72 (10.8)
Chungcheong-do	33 (10.4)	30 (12.7)	15 (13.6)	78 (11.8)
Gyeongsang-do	108 (34.1)	56 (23.6)	20 (18.2)	184 (27.7)
Jeolla-do	71 (22.4)	44 (18.5)	20 (18.2)	135 (20.3)
Hwanghae-do	19 (6.0)	12 (5.0)	5 (4.5)	36 (5.4)
Gangwon-do	30 (9.5)	21 (8.9)	23 (20.9)	74 (11.2)
Hamgyeong-do	16 (5.0)	13 (5.5)	7 (6.4)	36 (5.4)
Pyeongan-do	19 (6.0)	18 (7.6)	12 (10.9)	49 (7.4)
Total	317 (100.0)	237 (100.0)	110 (100.0)	664 (100.0)

purposes, the overall distribution of *nu, jeong* and *dae* did not change much.

The province that did not fit this general trend was Gangwon-do. Though Gangwon-do had fewer than 10 percent of the total *nu* and *jeong*, it had the highest number of *dae* among all eight provinces with 20.9 percent. This is because Gangwon-do had well-developed cliffs along the coast facing the East sea, such as Gyeongpodae and Heoidae of Gangneung, Musongdae of Ganseong, Neungpadae of Samcheok, and Biseondae and Uisangdae of Yangyang, which provided magnificent views of the sunrise. Also, it has splendid mountain scenery such as Geumgangdae and Baegundae at Mt. Geumgangsan. Hence, An Chuk of Goryeo sang of the scenery in Gwandong region in *Gwandong byeolgok* (1330), and later Jeong Cheol of the Joseon era also wrote *Gwandong byeolgok* (1580) after an excursion to Mt. Geumgangsan and the East Sea.

The changes in *nu, jeong* and *dae* in early and late Joseon are shown in Table 2. The data on early Joseon is taken from *Sinjeung dongguk yeoji seungnam* (1530), while that of late Joseon (1871-1899) is taken from village records. Though the number of *nugak* more than doubled from 317 to 715, the overall composition rate dropped from 47.7 percent to 24.6 percent. On the other hand, the number of *jeongja* exploded, increasing by more than five times from 237 to 1,168. Though the overall composition rate of *jeongja* did not change greatly, they were the most numerous. The causes for such change were twofold: First, as Confucianism spread from Hanyang to the provinces, a local Confucian cultural landscape was established, which in turn gave rise to *jeongja*. As *nugak* were mostly built by local administrative offices, or *seowon* (private academies), they were naturally limited in their construction. The number of *dae* increased in late Joseon due to the high proportion of *dae* built for military purposes, such as *bongdae* (beacon posts), *jangdae* (command posts) and *yeondae* (signal fire posts), at 349 of the total. Overall, the total number of *nu*, *jeong* and *dae* of the Joseon era increased more than four times from 664 to 2,906, though *nugak* did not increase as much as *jeongja* and *dae*.

Table 2. Changes in *Nu*, *Jeong* and *Dae* of the Joseon Dynasty (%)

	nu	*jeong*	*dae*	total
1530	317 (47.7)	237 (35.7)	110 (16.6)	664 (100.0)
1871-1899	715 (24.6)	1,168 (40.2)	1,023 (35.2)	2,906 (100.0)

Figure 17. Taegowa, Yeongcheon. The construction of *jeongja* increased dramatically after the eighteenth century due to the spread of Confucianism.

IV. Styles of *Nu, Jeong* and *Dae*

Though *nu, jeong,* and *dae* sometimes stood independently in natural locations, they were also used to distinguish spaces related to the royal palace, temples, private academies, cottages, fortress villages, traditional villages and upper class houses.

The royal palace frequently included *jeong* and *nu* but rarely *dae*. The space of the royal palace can be divided into its walls and gates, the royal audience chamber, the king's private quarters, the king's bedroom, attached buildings, and the back garden. While *nugak* existed in such forms as tower gates of fortresses or Gyeonghoeru pavilion, *jeongja* was usually found in the back garden. The ratio of 17 *jeongja* and one *nugak* (Juhamnu) at Changdeokgung well reflects the use of *nu, jeong* and *dae* at the royal palace. Seochongdae, which was built at Changgyeonggung during the reign of Yeonsangun, is the only *dae* at the royal palace.

Nu and *dae* are found at temples more often than *jeong*. Temples are structured in such a way that visitors experience a series of different spaces before reaching the Main Hall. Located opposite the Main Hall, *nugak* is both a gate and a space for religious events. *Sinjeung dongguk yeoji seungnam*, a book of geography from the early Joseon Dynasty, describes each village over twenty chapters. Though *dae* was not explained separately, it appears in thirteen of the chapters. This shows that *dae* were found in diverse and wide ranging areas. In addition, 29 *dae* are described in the article on *nu* and *jeong*, 25 *dae* in the article on historical remains, 25 *dae* in the article on mountains and rivers, and 19 *dae* in the article on Buddhist halls. According to the article on Buddhist halls, some flat rocks located on a cliff near the temple such as

Jwagodae, Jinju, Gyeongsangnam-do, were also called *dae*. Because the rock could be sat upon, it must have been a good place for meditation.

Byeolseo gardens, or Korean retreat gardens, more often featured *jeong* and *dae* than *nu*, because, as mentioned earlier, the public spatial characteristic of *nugak* did not correspond to *byeolseo*, where people went to retreat from the world. Daebongdae, which means waiting for the phoenix, and Sojeong built at Sosoewon (Figure 19), Okseongdae and Gyeongjeong at Seoseokji; Dongdae, Seodae, Seungnyongdae and Dongcheon Seoksil at Bogildo island; and Dongdae, Bukdae, Namdae and Banghwajeong at Sohanjeong in Yangsan, Gyeongsangnam-do are further examples of *jeong* and *dae*. They reflect the more frequent use of *jeong* and *dae* than *nu* at retreat gardens.

The composition of traditional space in Korea is shown in Figure 20. Though residential spaces also incorporated the natural landscape, *nu, jeong* and *dae* were strategically placed to heighten leisure and the enjoyment of nature. Religious spaces were also incorporated into natural and residential spaces; examples of this include *jangseung* (tutelary posts), *sotdae* (village guardian poles), and Seonghwangdang (a shrine for the village guardian deity). These were communal sacred spaces where people prayed for the peace and abundance of the village.

Figure 21 shows a panoramic view from Buyongdae on an approximately 70-meter-high cliff in Hahoe Village. As seen in the figure, the surrounding landscape of the village, including streams, a white sand beach, pine forest, the village itself, and far-off green mountaintops, comes into view at a glance. Buyongdae is well known not only for its panoramic view but also for the special stringed firecrackers that were used by the upper class. The firecrackers were set off on summer nights, and they were very different from present-day fireworks. Whereas the latter are launched into the sky before exploding,

Figure 18. Okganjeong at Yeongcheon. The side facing the stream was used to build a pavilion.

Figure 19. A pavilion on Daebongdae

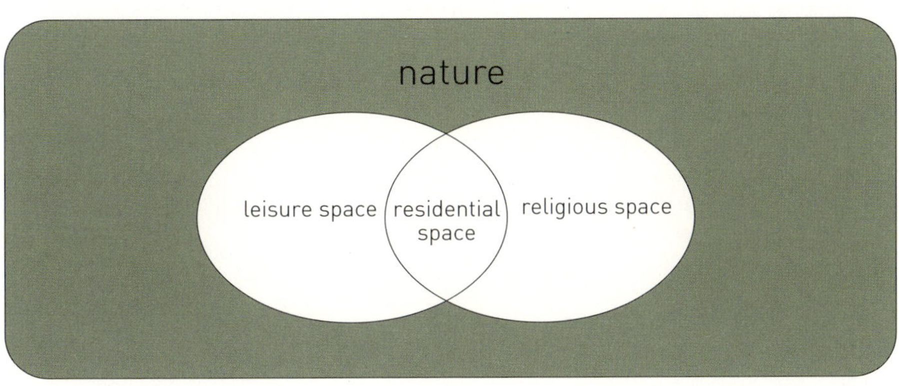

Figure 20. Composition of Traditional Space

Figure 21. Panoramic view from Buyongdae at Hahoe Village

Figure 22. Stringed firecrackers

Figure 23. Setting off stringed firecrackers at Buyongdae, Hahoe Village

Hahoe stringed firecrackers, as seen in the figure, burned slowly along a string that crossed the river; the burning resin is said to give off a pleasant scent. The firecrackers could be ignited while crossing the river in a boat and composing poetry. Also enjoyed were "egg fires," as shown in the figure, where spots of fire floated on the water, as well as "fire flowers," where haystacks were lit and thrown from the top of Buyongdae.

V. *Nu*, *Jeong* and *Dae*, the Center of Nature Excursions and Literature

1. *Nu*, *Jeong* and *Dae* as Natural Cultural Landscape

The Confucian cultural landscape usually meant that *nu*, *jeong* or *seowon* (private academies) were included within Korean traditional villages. However, the problem is that *nu*, *jeong* and *dae* were not limited to villages and the capital. In other words, a problem of classification arises when *nu*, *jeong* and *dae* are found in natural landscapes. It is difficult to classify these cases as examples of either "Confucian cultural landscape" or "natural landscape." What is clear is that they are neither.

The style of Korean traditional gardens, wherein *nu*, *jeong* and *dae* were built in places where people could enjoy and commune with nature, can be understood through the concept of "natural cultural landscape." Clearly, this signifies neither a natural landscape nor a cultural one. Like *nujeong*, which are always included in landscape paintings despite their small size, the landscapes of Korean traditional gardens can be defined as a natural cultural one.

Within this natural cultural landscape is an invisible door that transcends time and space. Gangseondae is one example. Just as there are eight famous scenic places, there are eight *dae* in Busan. One of these is Gangseondae, where it is said that an immortal living in the mountains comes down to rest on the eleventh day of the eleventh lunar month. Gangseondae is also found in other places, including Danyang, Yeongdong and Gareun Gugok at Goesan of Chungcheongbuk-do, Geochang of Gyeongsangnam-do, and Muju of Jeollabuk-do. In the past, Koreans believed that the mountain god came down to rest on cliffs, thus they thought that if they rested there as well, they could become like the mountain god. Reality, idealism and imagination came together at *dae*. Thus, they can be considered an example of a natural cultural landscape.

2. *Nu, Jeong* and *Dae* as the Center of Nature Excursions

Nu, jeong or *dae* are always found at scenic spots in Korea. *Nu* and *jeong* are usually located deep inside hills rather than an exposed or protruding position. In this way, they were designed to harmonize with the surrounding environment. They fit in easily with the surrounding rocks, trees and water. Koreans were not opposed to climbing hills to find *nu* and *jeong*, despite their inherent artificiality. Instead, Koreans looked forward to the natural wonders that would unfold at the top.

This anticipation of the beauty of nature was preparation for communion with nature, that is, the unity of subject and object. Therefore, scholars such as Seo Geo-jeong, Jeong In-ji, and Gwon Geun stated that "all the splendid village scenery is gathered here at this *nugak*," or "it dominates the beautiful scenery of the village," or "all the magnificent, distant scenery is gathered between the beaded hanging screen and the desk." In other words, by possessing such scenery, one cannot help but identify with nature. Again, this implies a unity of humans and nature, subject and object. As *nu, jeong* and *dae* contained all of the beautiful scenery of the village, they were the center of nature excursions. There was no need to visit other places one by one, as they could all be viewed at *nu, jeong* and *dae*. Herein lies the nature of Korean traditional gardens.

In *Dongmunseon*, compiled by Seo Geo-jeong in 1478, Sin Suk-ju spoke of "*nu, sa* and *dae* as places for sightseeing." The term *sa* (榭) is synonymous with *jeongja*, or pavilion. *Sa* was used when *jeongja* were built for academic purposes. Therefore, Sin's records coincide with the purpose of *nu, jeong* and *dae* as places for sightseeing.

Figure 24. Gangseondae, where an immortal came to rest

Figure 25. Baekhwajeong at the summit of Mt. Busosan

Also, in the preface of *Dongguk yeoji seungnam* (1486), No Sa-sin (1427-1498) and others explained, "*Nudae* is a place for entertaining envoys and enjoying the view when there is leisure time." However, a question arises here regarding the use of the term *nudae*. Why did they only use *nudae* in the preface while mostly using *nujeong* throughout the main text? This could not have been a mistake, since it was presented to the king at the royal court and was written with the cooperation of many competent scholars such as Seo Geo-jeong, rather than being penned solely by No Sa-sin. Thus, it can be concluded that *nudae* and *nujeong* were similar concepts that could be used inter-changeably. Therefore, according to the definition set by Sin Suk-ju and No Sa-sin, *nu*, *jeong* and *dae* were used for nature excursions, i.e., to enjoy the view whenever there was leisure time.

The following two thesises prove that *nu, jeong* and *dae* acted as the center for nature excursions. After her research on Toegye's poetry of *nu, jeong* and dae, Yi Jeong-hwa (1998, 132-133) concluded: "Most Korean writers of poetry written in Chinese characters regularly used *nujeong* as a place for enjoying nature, where they wrote and recited lyrical poetry that focused on describing the landscape. However, Toegye's poetry does not stop at simple descriptions of the scenery but was a form of contemplative poetry that explored the coexistence of humans and nature."

In his research on Songgang Jeong Cheol's (1536-1592) literature, Bak Jun-gyu (1995, 228-229) notes that Songgang did most of his writing at Sigyeong-jeong, Hwanbyeokdang and Sosoewon at Damyang, which reflects the importance of the *nu* and *jeong* of Damyang to his work. Approximately 45 *nu* and *jeong* appear in Songgang's writing, including 75 titles and 114 poems, making up a big part of his literature.

VI. Korean-Style Eight Scenic Views and *Nu, Jeong* and *Dae*

"Eight scenic views" (palgyeong) were another element of the natural cultural landscape of Korea. They originated from the "eight scenic views of Xiaoxiang,"[2] and it is presumed that the concept was introduced to Korea during the reign of King Myeongjong (1171-1197), the 19th king of Goryeo. The

---

2 Beautiful scenery that unfolds according to season and climate at eight points where Xiaoshui and Xiangshui meet in the south of Dungting Lake in China.

Figure 26. Gwansuru. Yeonghoru at Andong, Gwansuru along the Nakdonggang river, Yeongnamnu at Miryang, and Chokseongnu above the Namgang river are four well-known *nugak* that date back approximately 1,000 years.

eight scenic views of Songdo[3] were selected in late Goryeo, based on the motif of the eight scenic views of Xiaoxiang. However, though seven of the scenic views of Songdo followed the style of Xiaoxiang (location and landscape), Bagyeon Falls, the last one, was chosen based only on "location" rather than "location and landscape."

The eight scenic views of the new capital, Hanyang[4] of the Joseon era were Korean in style, not Chinese. The Korean-style eight scenic views, based only on location, is also called the "beautiful sites" style (Kang and Kim 1991, 27).

3　紫洞尋僧, 清郊送客, 北山煙雨, 西江風雪, 白嶽晴嵐, 黃郊晚照, 長湍石壁, 朴淵瀑布

4　畿甸山河, 都城宮苑, 列署星拱, 諸坊碁布, 東門敎場, 西江漕泊, 南渡行人, 北郊牧馬

Figure 27. Aneum Songdae at Geochang: painting and actual photograph. Two scholars enjoying nature are depicted.

The eight scenic views of Gwandong[5] and Gwanseo[6] are beautiful landscapes that typify Korea. Out of these sixteen sites, there were seven *jeong*, five *nu*, two *dae* and two others, which meant that *nu*, *jeong* and *dae* made up 87.5 percent of the total. Therefore, it would be no exaggeration to say that the Korean-style eight scenic views were in fact *nu*, *jeong* and *dae*.

---

5 Cheongganjeong at Ganseong, Gyeongpodae at Gangneung, Samilpo at Goseong, Jukseoru at Samcheok, Uisangdae at Yangyang, Mangyangjeong at Uljin, Chongseokjeong at Tongcheon and Wolsongjeong at Pyeonghae.

6 Yeongwangjeong at Pyeongyang, Gangseollu at Seongcheon, Baeksangnu at Anju, Yaksan Dongdae at Yeongbyeon, Dongnim Falls at Seoncheon, Tonggunjeong at Uiju, Inpungnu at Ganggye and Segeomjeong at Manpo.

It is clear that the *nu*, *jeong* and *dae* of the eight scenic views of Gwandong region were the center of nature excursions and literature, with many people traveling to them to enjoy the natural scenery and describe it in literature. Leading examples are *Gwandong byeolgok* written by An Chuk (1287-1348) of Goryeo, *Gwandong byeolgok* by Jeong Cheol (1536-1593) and a true-view landscape painting by Jeong Seon (1676-1759) during Joseon. Figure 28 is part of the true-view landscape painting of Chongseokjeong, the most famous scenery of Gwandong region. People enjoying nature excursions can be seen at the top of the cliff, which is made of volcanic rocks with developed hexagonal joints. Other scenic sites in the Gwandong area are detailed below.

1) Cheongganjeong

The following is recorded in *Suseongji*, which was compiled by Yi Sik (1584-1647): "Changganjeong is a pavilion that was originally attached to the station and is located two *li* (0.5 mile) south of Mangyeongdae. Its name came from its location by the valley water. When Mangyeongnu collapsed, the station pavilion was moved next to Mangyeongdae, which has magnificent scenery. Though the pavilion is only five to six *bo* away from the sea, it has sustained no flood damage as Mangyeongdae stops the sea water. Even large waves caused by strong winds do not go over the steps, thus creating unique scenery… The present pavilion was repaired by the county magistrate Choe Cheon in 1555."[7]

That the station pavilion was moved next to Mangyeongdae to create a scenic view, as shown in Figure 30, shows that the natural cultural landscape was created by blending *nu, jeong* and *dae* with the natural landscape.

Figure 29 shows people enjoying the scenery at the top of Mangyeongdae. A detailed record found in this document states, "There is a tiered stone peak at the front that resembles an embankment. The top is flat like a desk and seems to be so high. Surrounded by the sea on three sides, on a windless day when the water is clear, it is possible to count the fish in the water. The shadows of old pine trees around the Mangyeongdae cross each other. This location used to be called Mangyeongnu, as there was once a small *nu* on the eastern corner by that name. But the name has since been changed to Mangyeongdae." This is a good example of how the name of the same place could change from *nu* to *jeong* or *dae*.

2) Samilpo

Samilpo is a natural lake located on the east coast. It is approximately 4.5 kilometers in circumference and surrounded by thirty-six white granite peaks of all shapes, such as Mt. Geumgangsan.

The name Samilpo comes from the story of the four immortals of Silla, namely Yeongnang, Sullang, Ansang and Namseokhaeng, who were so

---

7 Choe Wan-su (1993), 82.

Figure 29. Part of Cheongganjeong

Figure 30. Cheongganjeong

mesmerized by the scenery during a visit there that they forgot to return for three days. The island in the middle is called Saseondo, and the pavilion on the island is called Saseonjeong; both names are derived from the same story.

Jeong Cheol described Samilpo in *Gwandong byeolgok*:

I travel to Samilpo, leaving Goseong far behind.

The red letters they carved are still vivid, but where are the four immortals?

Where did they go after staying here for three days?

Are they now strolling near Seonyudam or Yeongnangho?

Where did they sit, beside Cheongganjeong and Mangyeongdae?

During the Joseon era, many people visited this place and wrote poems about the four immortals of Silla, who set the example of a nature excursion. Jeong Cheol, who wrote *Gwandong byeolgok*, also wondered where the immortals had gone when seeing the red letters of "永郞徒南石行," still vivid as if just written, and pondered how many places they had visited. The poem reflects Jeong Cheol's desire to visit such places himself, and he wrote *Gwandong byeolgok* after actually traveling to and visiting them in turn. This is a good example of how *nu, jeong* and *dae* were subjects of literature.

I have mentioned earlier that the Korean-style eight scenic sites are closely related to *nu, jeong* and *dae*. In a painting of Samilpo, a pavilion called Saseonjeong is situated on an island in the middle of the lake, which means that Samilpo, one of the eight scenic views of Gwandong, is also related to *jeongja*. Viewed in the true-view landscape painting, painted by Gyeomje Jeong Seon and shown in Figure 32, Saseonjeong appears to have a unique shape. It is a simple structure with four pillars, of which the bottom part was long and made

Figure 31. Samilpo

Figure 32. Saseonjeong pavilion (Part of the painting of Samilpo)

from stone while the top part consisted of short wooden pillars. This type of pavilion is rare in Korea.

3) Uisangdae

The following refers to Uisangdae found in *Gwandong byeolgok.*

Now the pear-blossoms have wilted and the nightingales sing sadly,

I rise in the middle of the night to climb Naksansa temple hill

and sit at the Uisangdae to watch the sunrise.

Auspicious clouds cluster together like the six dragons that pull the Heavenly

Ruler's cart,

making the whole watery kingdom shake as they rise above the sea.

As they soar to the sky, the thin strands of hair in their manes are so bright

I can count them

I fear lest some innocent fleeting cloud gets trampled by their hoofs.

Other records of Uisangdae can be found in the "Two Great Saints of Naksan," *gown* 3 of *Samguk yusa*; "Naksansagi," *gwon* 13 in *Gwanam yusa*, written by Gwanam Hong Gyeong-mo (1774-1851); and in the poem "Eight Scenic Views of Gwandong" by King Sukjong of Joseon era (Choe Wan-su 1993, 84). When these records are combined and compared to the true-view landscape painting, the parts of the painting can be identified. The place with many buildings in Figure 33 is Naksansa temple, and the white flowers in the area surrounded by a pine forest are pear flowers. The place to the right of Naksansa, where people are sitting on top of the cliff enjoying the sunrise, is Ihwadae, and a red sun is rising on the top right-hand side of the painting. On

Figure 33. Uisangdae

the bottom right is Gwaneumgul cave, through which the sea passes, and a pavilion on the cave seems to be Uisangdae, which is related to the story of Monk Uisang of Silla. In his poem, "Visiting Naksansa at Night," Sunam Yi Byeong-seong wrote, "Those who come to Naksansa temple wait for the sunrise each morning." This suggests that Uisangdae was famous for its view of the sunrise, and that many people came to see it during the Joseon era.

Though I have only analyzed the cases of Cheongganjeong, Samilpo and Uisangdae among the eight scenic views of Gwandong region, there are other, similar places. This analysis shows that *nu*, *jeong* and *dae* were the center of nature excursions, and a number of people visited them to enjoy nature including the sunrise and moonrise and to capture the magnificent scenery in literature.

Figure 34. Part of Uisangdae

Figure 35. Viewing the sunrise was a common activity in Korea, where the view is enhanced by its many hills and frequent good weather.

References

Ahn, Gye-bog. 1991. "Hanguk-ui nujeong yangsiksang je teukseong mit gyehoek iron-e gwanhan yeongu" (A Study of the Characteristics and Design of *Nu* and *Jeong* Style in Korea). *Hanguk jogyeong hakhoeji* (Journal of Korea Institute of Landscape Architecture) 19.2: 1-11.

__________. 1993. "Dae yangsik-ui yeoksajeok baldal gwajeong-e gwanhan yeongu" (A Study of the Historical Development Process of *Dae*). *Geonchuk yeoksa yeongu* (Journal of the Korean Association of Architectural History) 2.2: 26-36.

__________. 1998. "Eupjido bunseok-eul tonghan dae-ui wonhyeong-e gwanhan yeongu" (A Study of the Origin of *Dae* Based on Analysis of Village Maps). *Collection of Papers* (Catholic University of Daegu) 57: 207-217.

Choe, Wan-su. 1993. *Gyeomje Jeong Seon jin-gyeong sansuhwa* (True-View Landscape Painting by Gyeomje Jeong Seon). Seoul: Bumwoosa.

Choi, Key-soo. 1989. "Hyeondae gyeonggwan uimi-eseo jomyeonghae bon hanguk-ui jeontong gyeonggwan" (Korean Traditional Landscape Viewed from a Modern Landscape). *Hanguk jogyeong hakhoeji* (Journal of Korea Institute of Landscape Architecture) 17.2: 57-68.

Ji, Cheng. 1634. *Yuanye* (Garden Management). Photoprint. Seoul: Doseochulpan Jogyeong.

Kang, Yong-jo, and Kim Young-ran. 1991. "Hanguk palgyeong-ui hyeongsik-gwa ipji teukseong-e gwanhan yeongu" (A Study of the Type and Spatial Location of Eight Scenic Views in Korea). *Hanguk jeongwon hakhoeji* (Journal of Korean Institute of Traditional Landscape Architecture) 10: 27-36.

Kim, Yeong-suk, and Ahn Gye-bog. 1995. "Dae yangsik-ui yeoksajeok baldal gwajeong mit teukjing-e gwanhan yeongu" (A Study on the Historical Development

Process and Characteristics of *Dae* Style). *Hanguk jogyeong hakhoeji* (Journal of Korea Institute of Landscape Architecture) 23.2: 124-136.

Park, Jun-gyu. 1995. "Songgang Jeong Cheol-ui nujeong jeyeonggo" (Collection of Poems on *Nu* and *Jeong* by Songgang Jeong Cheol). *Gosiga yeongu* (Journal of Classic Poetry) 2/3: 191-230.

So, Gil-su. 1998. *Goguryeo yeoksa yujeok dapsa* (Investigation of Historical Remains of Goguryeo). Seoul: Sakyejul.

Suh, Kyoung-won. 2002. *Landscape Architecture*. Seoul: Damdi.

Yi, Jeong-hwa. 1998. "Toegye si yeongu—nujeong hansi-reul jungsim-euro" (A Study of Poems by Toegye—Centering on the Classic Poetry in Chinese Characters of *Nu* and *Jeong*). *Hanguk sasang-gwa munhwa* (Korean Thought and Culture) 2: 117-132.

Yu, Joon-young. 1981. "Gugokdo-ui balsaeng-gwa gineung-e daehayeo" (On the Origin and Function of the Nine Bends Paintings). *Misul sahak yeongu* (Journal of the Art History Association of Korea) 151: 1-20.

Author

Ahn Gye-bog

(Department of Landscape Architecture, Catholic University of Daegu)

Ahn Gye-bog is a professor in the Department of Landscape Architecture at Catholic University of Daegu. He received his Ph.D. from Seoul National University. He is currently a member of the Gyeongsangbuk-do and Daegu-si Cultural Properties Committee. His main publications include *Traditional Landscape Architecture in Korea* (1992), *History of Landscape Architecture in the East* (1996), and *Landscape Architecture* (2002). E-mail: gbahn@cu.ac.kr

Chapter 8

Landscape Architecture of Buddhist Temples

I. Introduction

As the purpose of landscape architecture is to create landscape, the purpose of the landscape architecture of Buddhist temple is to create Buddhist landscape. More specifically, Buddhist landscape architecture creates unique scenery that majestically represents the Buddhist utopia and Buddhist symbolism in detail at a special location, i.e. the Buddhist temple. Therefore, the landscape of Buddhist temple is a synthesis of Buddhist doctrine and the religious system. Created through a series of architectural processes, it differs from scenery created by ordinary landscape architecture. This is because the background and design principles differ. As the former has a clear purpose, which is to express a view of the universe and the worldview of Buddhism in a visible form, it naturally takes a unique approach.

The landscape architecture of Buddhist temple is determined by the location on which the Buddhist temple is built. As sites to be landscaped in Korea were generally selected through the principles of *fengshui* (K.: *pungsu*), or traditional geomancy, it may seem natural that temples also reflect elements of *fengshui*. However, the Buddhist temple also embodies the concept of sacredness, and the Buddhist landscape architeture is created through a process that refines this concept. This can be interpreted as meaning that a Buddhist temple can only be built where the energy of the earth is sacred and healthy, and consequently the site of the Buddhist temple cannot but possess unique scenery. Once such a site is selected, a building is placed on the particular spot where the sacred energy is focused so that the Buddhist doctrine and religious system can be achieved. At the same time, an external space is created to establish a sacred area in which various symbolic elements are introduced. Afterward, the unique Buddhist landscape architecture is created.

The Korean Buddhist temples that were constructed during the early stages of Buddhism in Korea were formed based on the principles of spatial structure and rules of Chinese Buddhist temples. However, Buddhist temples particular to the Korean climate and culture appeared gradually. Korean Buddhist temples have a three-level structure, which characterizes and distinguishes them from other countries' temples.[1] The path leading to the central space, the external space, the buildings, and the interactions between the buildings and the external space all form different landscapes that appear in the spatial structuring of the Buddhist temple. Furthermore, the scenic style of the Buddhist temple can be observed in geographical landscape elements that were used in creating the space of the Buddhist temple, in water landscape elements produced in the process of water management and usage, in plant landscape elements that render solemnity to the space, in the architectural landscape elements of Buddhist temple buildings, and in various decorative objects.

As such, the landscape of Korean Buddhist temples is created by the overall combination of various scenic styles, and each style is based on a unique principle of landscaping, which in turn shapes the look of the Korean Buddhist temple. However, Korean Buddhist temples differ greatly from Buddhist temples in India and other places where Fundamental Buddhism is found,[2] from Chinese Buddhist temples that introduced Buddhism to Korea, and those

---

1   The three-level structure means the systematic structuring of the space in order to comprise the belief system of upper, middle and lower level within the Buddhist temple space.

2   Fundamental Buddhism designates Buddhism in the regions of Hinayana Buddhism that include Sri Lanka, Thailand, Myanmar and Nepal.

Figure 1. Bulguksa temple

in Japan where Buddhism arrived later than Korea. This is because Korean Buddhist temples are the products of Korean culture.

This article aims to examine the content and form of the landscape architecture of Korean Buddhist temple by dividing it into locationality, spatial structure, and compositional elements of landscape, and analyzing the background and scenic characteristics of each aspect.

II. Locationality

1. Selecting the Location of Korean Temples

People have long believed that by selecting sites that have particular significance, the sacred power of the place would transfer to them. Religion in particular has led to the importance of selecting sites that have special significance in order to ensure the use of sacred, powerful and meaningful spaces. For this reason, it is most often the case that the location of religious spaces is decided after the sanctity of the location is determined. This process is based on the belief that the sacredness of a certain place is transferred to the objects and buildings within the space, thus sanctifying them, and the sacredness is then transferred to the people who come to visit the place. In this regard, a religious space is sacred because the location itself is sacred, and the religious significance of a place cannot be sanctified unless the location is sacred.

In observing the land on which Korean traditional temples are built, it is clear that the locations selected for Buddhist temples had special meanings, unlike ordinary places, and the selection of Buddhist temple locations was based on various influential factors. For example, during the early introduction of Buddhism, Buddhist temple sites were determined by political and social factors rather than solely religious concepts. On the other hand, traditional views of locations at the time seem to have influenced the selection of locations. Later, as Koreans gained a deeper understanding of Buddhism and began interpreting it in their own terms, more locations that better represented the religious symbolism of Buddhism were preferred. In this regard, the location of the temple, the Buddhist seminary, seems to have changed with the development of Buddhism.

In particular, Buddhist temples in Korea began to be predominantly located in the mountains at the end of Silla and beginning of Goryeo, when Seon (Zen) Buddhism was rapidly taking root in Korea. Having an appropriate place of meditation was the most important prerequisite for being able to reach enlightenment, and a quiet place in the mountains must have been regarded as preferable to the crowded cities, spurring the move to the mountains. It is common knowledge that the principles of *fengshui* and *docham* played an important role in the process of selecting temple locations in the mountains. In particular, the *bibo* (complementary) and *yeopseung* (suppressive) methods were also applied to Buddhist temples, which shows that Koreans not only believed temples should be built on good sites, but also focused on improving substandard sites. The construction of the "nine mountain schools," which are the origin of Seon Buddhism in Korea, was completed by Seon masters who had returned after finishing their studies in China. Given the fact that the locationality of the Buddhist temples of the nine mountain schools is similar to that of Seon Buddhist temples in China, the locationality of Seon Buddhist temples in Korea appears to be the result of "Koreanization" of a Chinese concept.

2. Locationality of Temples Built During the Early Period of Buddhism

The locationality of Buddhist temples built during the early period of Buddhism is reflected clearly in Hwangnyongsa temple, which was built at the center of Gyeongju, the capital of Silla. Hwangnyongsa temple was built in the 14th year of King Jinheung's reign (553). Since its construction, Hwangnyongsa temple maintained its Buddhist identity through a number of reconstructions until 1238, the 24th year of King Gogong's reign in Goryeo, when it was destroyed by fire, after which only the site remains without further restoration. It is therefore difficult to know its overall appearance, but its locationality can be clearly grasped.

Hwangnyongsa temple is located near Banwolseong and Anapji. Considering the city structure of the time, the temple was situated at the center of the capital. It is difficult to understand why Hwangnyongsa temple was built there without comprehending the political objective at the time, which was to strengthen the weak royal authority through the power of a foreign religion called Buddhism. The location that best conformed to this objective was the royal capital, the center of politics. Therefore, the royal court of Silla came up with all kinds of reasons to justify and force the construction of Hwangnyongsa temple,[3] and the temple became a spiritual gathering place for the unification of the three kingdoms as a national temple.

---

3 Regarding the foundation of Hwangnyongsa temple, ancient books such as *Samguk yusa* (Memorabilia of the Three Kingdoms), *Samguk sagi* (Historical Record of the Three Kingdoms) and *Haedong goseungjeon* (Lives of Eminent Korean Monks) record that though the construction had begun on the royal palace, it was changed to a temple when a yellow dragon emerged from below the ground.

Figure 2. Site of the nine-story wooden pagoda and Mt. Sogeumgangsan in the north

Figure 3. Mt. Namsan seen over the pedestal of the 16-foot-high Buddha statue and the site of the nine-story wooden pagoda

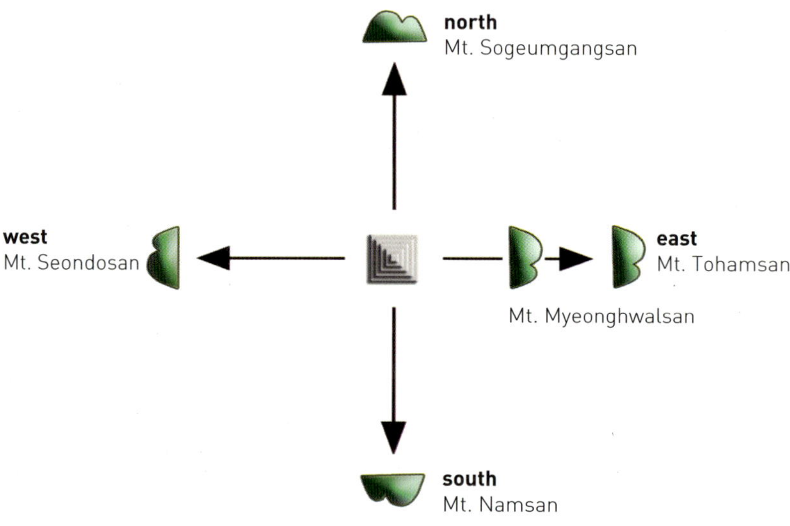

Figure 4. Diagram for the location of Hwangnyongsa temple

Looking at it from another perspective, it is clear that there was a view of locations based on the mutual relationship between humans and nature. The central axis of the nine-story wooden pagoda, which forms the spatial center of the temple, is connected to all four cardinal directions: Mt. Tohamsan in the east over the summit of Mt. Myeonghwalsan, the summit of Mt. Seondosan in the west, the Chilburam rock on Mt. Namsan in the south, and the summit of Mt. Sogeumgangsan in the north. This signifies that the position of mountains was considered during the process of selecting a site for the construction of Hwangnyongsa temple.[4] In particular, as national rituals were held on the five

---

4 It would be far fetched to interpret such mutuality with mountains with the notion of *fengshui* as the theoretical framework to understand the land from the *fengshui* perspective had not yet been

key mountains of Silla, i.e. Tohamsan in the east, Seondosan in the west, Namsan in the south, Sogeumgangsan in the north, and Nangsan at the center, the location of Hwangnyongsa is highly significant in that its sacredness was strengthened when it was aligned with the sacred mountains of the country.

3. Locationality of the Ten Hwaeom Sect Temples

The ten Buddhist temples of the Hwaeom sect were built in the border area of Silla's previous territory, after the three kingdoms were unified. Buseoksa temple, founded by Monk Uisang, is the head temple. Upon examining the locationality of Buseoksa temple, it becomes clear that the temple was built based on an entirely different concept than those built inside the capital city in the early years of Buddhist transmission. Since Monk Uisang built the ten temples in order to promote the Hwaeom sect he brought back from China, it may seem natural that their doctrine, religious system, and thus locationality differ from Buddhist temples built before. However, considering that the theoretical basis of Buddhism at the time was not strong enough to change the locationality of the Buddhist temple according to its doctrine, it may be more appropriate to find the significance of the locationality of those Buddhist temples somewhere else.

---

established when Hwangnyongsa temple was built. Therefore, it would be appropriate to understand the mutual relationship the temple's location had with the surrounding mountains as an expression of the locational perspective that tried to transfer the sanctity of the five mountains that surrounded the royal capital to the temple.

Figure 5. Locational environment of Buseoksa temple

Figure 6. Mountain summit at the front mountain (*ansan*), viewed from Anyangnu

Buseoksa temple is located on a steep slope in the south of Mt. Bonghwangsan, which stands 818 meters above sea level and forms part of the Taebaeksan Mountain Range. A number of mountains of varying height, such as Manseoksan, Eungbangsan and Cheonmasan, overlap and surround the temple to the south, looking as if they are bowing to the temple. In the article on the Buddhist hall in *Sunheung eupji* (Records of Sunheung-eup), it is recorded that "Buseoksa temple is located 35 *li* to the east of the town. Mt. Bonghwangsan curves and stretches south from the Taebaeksan Mountain Range, and stands high with many summits and valleys. The temple is located south of the mountain."

As such, Buseoksa temple is located high up, deep inside the mountain; but it was not simply regarded as a good place to spread Hwaeom thought. This is because Hwaeom thought does not advocate locating temples high inside steep, rugged mountains far away from the human world. Therefore, the significance of the locationality of Buseoksa temple can be derived elsewhere; specifically, the site of the temple was used to manage Jungnyeong pass, which was a checkpoint between old Silla and Goguryeo. In other words, as an important strategic point of the old Silla border, constant maintenance of Buseoksa temple site meant keeping an advantageous position vis-à-vis Baekje and Goguryeo. This argument is persuasive as the same phenomenon is found in the other nine temples of the Hwaeom sect that were constructed by Uisang and his disciples.

At the same time, however, one can see that a unique perspective on location used at the time was applied to the interpretation of the Buseoksa temple site. This can be recognized from the fact that there is a difference of approximately 30 degrees between the axis of the entrance and the axis connecting Anyangnu and Muryangsujeon hall. This was done so the temple would face a special mountain summit, which shows that there already existed a native Korean concept of geomancy that could explain the location of the temple at the time.

4. Locationality of the Nine Mountain Schools of Seon Buddhism

The "nine mountain schools" of Seon Buddhism were monasteries founded by monks who returned from their studies in Tang at the end of Silla. With the introduction of Seon Buddhism to Korea, temples began to move deep into the mountains. The nine mountain school temples are similar in that while they are built deep in the mountains, they are located in particularly flat places. The harmonization of Buddhist temples with the surrounding natural environment is also a special characteristic of these temples. Therefore, it can be said that the central temples of the nine mountain schools were the first to be located on sites that were purely related to nature. This is understandable when considering that the application of *fengshui* began with the establishment of these temples.

That Seon Buddhist temples emphasized the importance of the conditions of location can be seen in an article found in "Relics of Borimsa Temple at Muju Gajisan Mountain in Silla," published in early Joseon. According to the article, "Great Monk Wonpyo founded Gajisan Borimsa during his stay in India. When he was passing through China on his way back to Silla, he came upon a mountain that was similar to one in India. He built a Buddhist temple there and called it Gajisan Borimsa as well. One day, Monk Wonpyo sensed a mysterious

Figure 7. Locational environment of Borimsa temple

Figure 8. Locational environment of Seongjusa temple

energy and followed it over mountains and across the ocean until he found its source; there, he raised the pillar of the temple. As the mountain resembled those in India and China, he built a temple and called it Gajisan Borimsa." He chose the site for Borimsa temple based on the "delicate harmony created by steep mountain passes, long streams and deep valleys."

Another example of the importance of temple locations was Taeansa temple on Mt. Dongnisan. According to the epitaph written by Seon Master Hyecheol, who founded the Dongnisan school, Taeansa temple was located on a site where "a thousand peaks surround it like a screen, a clear valley stream flows, the dragon reveals an auspicious sign and the snake hides its poison, and the pine forest is thick and white clouds are deep, creating an appropriate place for self-cultivation that is cool in summer and warm in winter." These examples show that the energy and shape of sites were important conditions in selecting locations for temples, and such characteristics are commonly found in the temples of the nine mountain schools.

Additionally, the location of the temple on flat land helped create a regular spatial structure. This is because most nine mountain school temples take up the entire space, creating a symmetry and sense of proportion based on a fixed central axis connecting the front and back mountains. The regularity that is found at Seon temples is rare in temples built on slopes. In other words, the regular spatial structure of Seon temples was achieved because the selected locations allowed for it.

5. Locationality of Mountain Temples

As the nine mountain school temples of Seon Buddhism were established and Seon Buddhism became a mainstream in Korea, Buddhist temples were increasingly located in the mountains. Furthermore, through Goryeo and Joseon, Buddhist temples built in the mountains became small in scale and maintained the original purity of Buddhism, unlike ten Hwaeom sect temples or nine mountain school temples in the past. As all such mountain temple sites were chosen based on the suitability of the size of the temple, the focus shifted to the energy of the earth rather than the formality of the temple, as can be observed in previous temples.

Figure 9. Locational environment of Baegyangsa temple

In general, *fengshui* was an important principle in selecting the location of mountain temples. Therefore, the shape and direction of the land on which the temple was to be built was examined and evaluated before building began, and the protection from wind and the access to water were also important.

Thus a good site was chosen and the temple was built. The buildings were constructed according to what the land could accommodate, and the area outside the temple was also organized. However, not all land was considered auspicious or prominent in earth energy. In such cases, a method called *bibo pungsu*, which was based on improving weak, rough or inauspicious land energy, was used at the temples. In *bibo pungsu*, weak earth energy was supplemented by installing Buddhist objects such as pagodas or statues or by raising the land and planting trees; also, evil spirits were prevented from entering. Though the *bibo pungsu* method was largely used at temples, it was later introduced to other areas of Korean traditional landscape architecture and used to strengthen weak energy and prevent evil energy.

III. Spatial Structure

1. Principles of Spatial Structure

The spatial structure of Korean Buddhist temples that were built during the early transmission of Buddhism was modeled after that of Chinese Buddhist temples, which were modified forms of Indian Buddhist temples. However, after constant adaptation and adjustment to Korean environmental conditions

Figure 10. Diagram of Mandala

and cultural characteristics, it was gradually established as a unique Korean form. Korean Buddhist temples can be categorized into three types: the pagoda-centered type (built on flat land with a single pagoda), the pagoda and Main Hall parallel type (built on a low hill with a twin pagoda), and the Main Hall-centered type (built in the mountains). These three types were based on the design principles of mandalas and Mt. Sumeru. Buddhist thought and philosophy are concentrated in these images, which had a decisive influence in determining the surface and three-dimensional structures of the Buddhist temple. From the early introduction of Buddhism to the pagoda and Main Hall parallel type, Korean Buddhist temples were mostly designed to resemble mandalas; in the case of Goryeo and Joseon-era mountain temples, Mt. Sumeru was used as a design principle. Mandalas feature a pattern of overlapping circles and squares

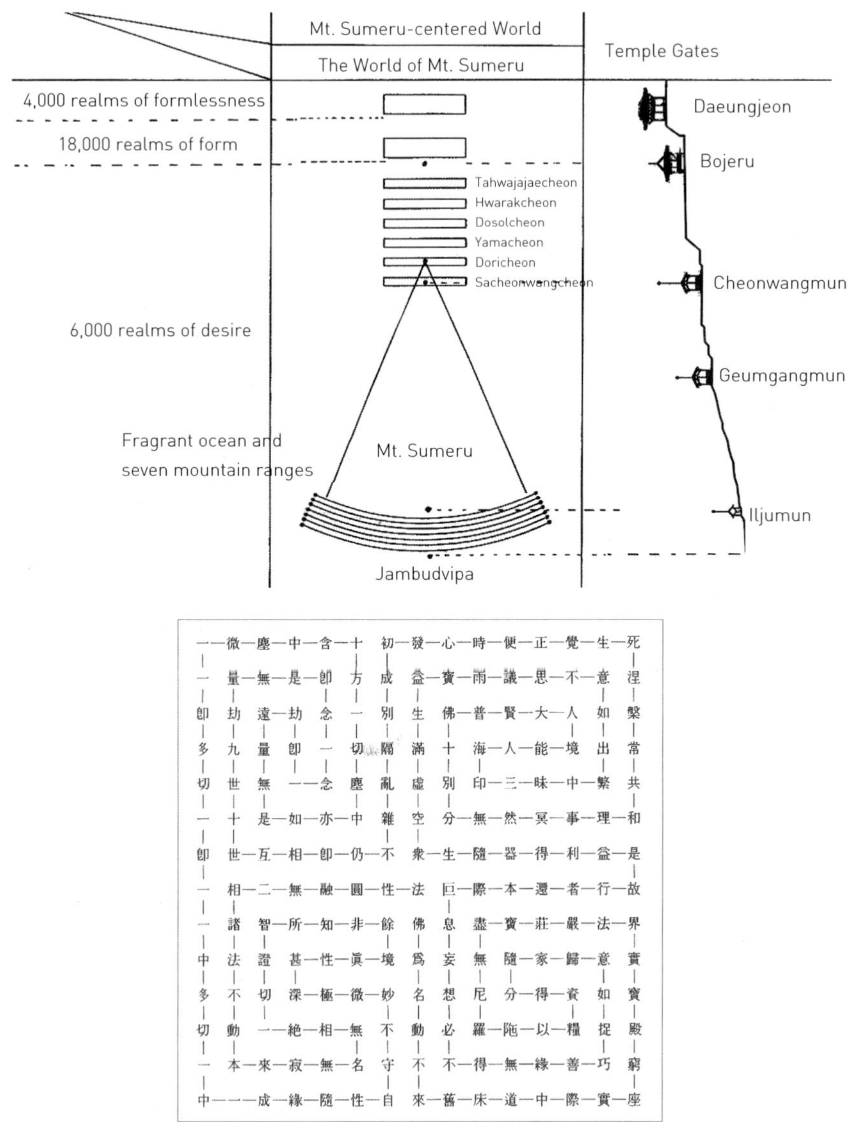

Figure 11. The Structure of Mt. Sumeru

Figure 12. *Hwaeom ilseung beopgyedo* (Diagram of the Realm of Truth as the One Vehicle of the Avatamska Sutra)

which converge inward and expand outward from a fixed point at a regular ratio ($\sqrt{\ }$ times). Their design can be easily applied to the spatial structure of flatland temples. Mt. Sumeru represents the 6 heavens in the realm of desire, the 18 heavens in the realm of form, and the 4 heavens in the realm of formlessness, all of which were applied to the design of mountain temples. Mt. Sumeru is customarily divided into three levels: the top level, of which the object of belief is Buddha and bodhisattva; the middle level, of which the object of belief is the guardian deities of Dharma; and the lower level, which also focuses on such spirits as Seven Star Spirit or Mountain Spirit.

In addition to mandala and Mt. Sumeru, another Buddhist image that was applied to Korean Buddhist temples was the *Hwaeom ilseung beopgyedo* (Diagram of the Realm of Truth as the One Vehicle of the Avatamska Sutra), a diagram that represents the spirit of *haein sammae,* or the state of mental absorption the Buddha entered immediately following his enlightenment. It is based on the *Avatamska Sutra* and contains the truth of the universe in its entirety. *Hwaeom ilseung beopgyedo* is a winding diagram that consists of seven syllables, 30 verses, and 210 characters. It begins with the character 法 (law) at the center of this realm of truth diagram; after winding around, it returns to the character 佛 (Buddha) at the center of the diagram. This corresponds to Monk Uisang's concept that the law and Buddha are not two different things. According to Buddhist doctrine, Buddhist temples were long arranged following the *Hwaeom ilseung beopgyedo*; examples include Songgwangsa and Haeinsa temples. However, few traces of *Hwaeom ilseung beopgyedo* are left in the two temples today, which means that many changes have been made.

Other elements such as harmony with the natural environment, hierarchical order, mutual connection between spaces, and human scale, can be found in

Figure 13. Central axis of Bulguksa temple

Korean Buddhist temples. Harmony with the natural environment was achieved by determining the size and shape of the space and adjusting the axis to suit it, while hierarchical order was realized by adjusting the topographical height and degree of closure, and by changing the size and degree of decoration of the buildings. Connection between spaces was achieved by creating views at the entrances, and by creating a rupture and overlapping effect between small spaces. Finally, a human scale was created by adjusting the distance between each unit of space at the temple or by structuring the angles of elevation and visual width from various points to suit human cognition.

2. Establishing the Axis

Traditional landscape architecture in Korea was systemized according to the axis; the royal palace and Buddhist temples had relatively distinct axis as they consisted of various groups of buildings and as their direction and centrality had to be emphasized.

Though the types of axis that appear in Korean Buddhist temples vary according to the geographical characteristics of the location, size and characteristics, the central north-south axis is commonly emphasized in most temples. In other words, pagoda-centered temples at the beginning of Buddhist introduction, such as the temple site in Cheongam-ri of Goguryeo, the temple site in Gunsu-ri of Buyeo, and Hwangnyongsa temple or Bunhwangsa temple of Silla, share a rigorously straight central axis, along which lie the inner gate, pagoda, Main Hall and lecture hall. Therefore, the entire space of pagoda-centered temples is united structurally through the central north-south axis. This type of straight axis also appeared unchanged in the pagoda-Main Hall parallel type temples, of which the leading examples are Bulguksa, Sacheon-wangsa and Mangdeoksa temples, and the temple site in Cheongun-ri, which were managed by the capital city of Silla. The straight, central axis that appeared in temples built during Silla changed to a bent or single-line axis after the end of Silla and the beginning of Goryeo, when temples began to be built in the mountains. These axes were created when temples were structured according to the topography in which they were built. In this case, diversifying the view by separating the axis of the line of flow and the building axis and maximizing the quality of visual experience achieved at the entrance are advanced landscape architecture methods found in Korean Buddhist temples.

3. Entrance and Path Landscape

When Buddhism was first introduced, Korean Buddhist temples had relatively simple entrances. In the case of pagoda-centered type or pagoda-Main Hall parallel type temples, the entrance was short and simple; visitors passed through the inner gate and progressed toward the Main Hall with the pagoda either at the center or on the east or west side. However, with the introduction of Seon temples and as temples began to be built in the mountains, three gates (Iljumun, Cheonwangmun and Burimun)[5] were built that led to a two-story pavilion gate, followed by the central space where the main Buddhist hall such as Daeungjeon was located. This was completely different from the form seen in previous Buddhist temple types. The system of three gates reflected the image of Sumeru and showed how mountain temples represented the idea of Sumeru in the real world.

The three gates also reflected visual opportunity and direction: that is, while passing through the three gates of Iljumun, Cheonwangmun and Burimun, the view is framed through each gate frame. This style of entrance is only found in mountain Buddhist temples, and it not only creates a continuity of space but also symbolically enables visitors to the Buddhist temple to experience a process akin to a rite of passage. At the same time, the visual effect creates a sense of curiosity, and as such, the entrances to Korean Buddhist temples truly have symbolic and functional aspects.

5　The names of the gates vary according to temples, i.e. Iljumun-Bonghwangmun-Haetalmun (Haeinsa temple), Iljumun-Geumgangmun-Cheonwangmun (Hwaeomsa temple) and Iljumun-Cheonwangmun-Burimun (Beomeosa and Tongdosa temples). However, the fundamental significance of building three gates is the same.

Figure 14. Transitional process of Buseoksa temple

The landscape in the entrance of a mountain temple can also be understood by the distance between knot points. In the case of mountain Buddhist temples, the average distance between the main knot points (such as gate and two-story pavilion) was surveyed and confirmed to be between 25 and 70 meters. Each unit of distance was 25 meters. If, however, the horizontal distance between the main knot points exceeded 25 meters, a platform or decorative object was placed every 25 meters in order to visually vary the space as well as distinguish it. Ashihara Yoshinobu cited this same unit of measurement, when he stated that a distance of 70 to 80 feet was appropriate as one module in arranging the external space, and that this distance made for a human scale.[6]

Table 1. Passage through Pavilion Gates at Main Mountain Temples

Temple	Pavilion Gate	Transitional Pattern
Silleuksa	Guryongnu	Entrance on both sides
Seonamsa	Jonggoru	Entrance on both sides
Hwaeomsa	Bojeru	Entrance on both sides
Ssanggyesa	Paryeongnu	Entrance on left side
Haeinsa	Gugwangnu[8]	Entrance on both sides
Bongeunsa	Beobwangnu	Pavilion gate entrance type C
Bongseonsa	Cheongpungnu	Pavilion gate entrance type E
Yongjusa	Cheonboru	Pavilion gate entrance type C
Songgwangsa	Jonggoru	Pavilion gate entrance type C
Daeheungsa	Chimgyeru	Pavilion gate entrance type A
Buseoksa	Anyangnu	Pavilion gate entrance type F
Bongjeongsa	Manseru	Pavilion gate entrance type E
Yongmunsa	Haeullu	Pavilion gate entrance
Eunhaesa	Bohwaru	Pavilion gate entrance type A

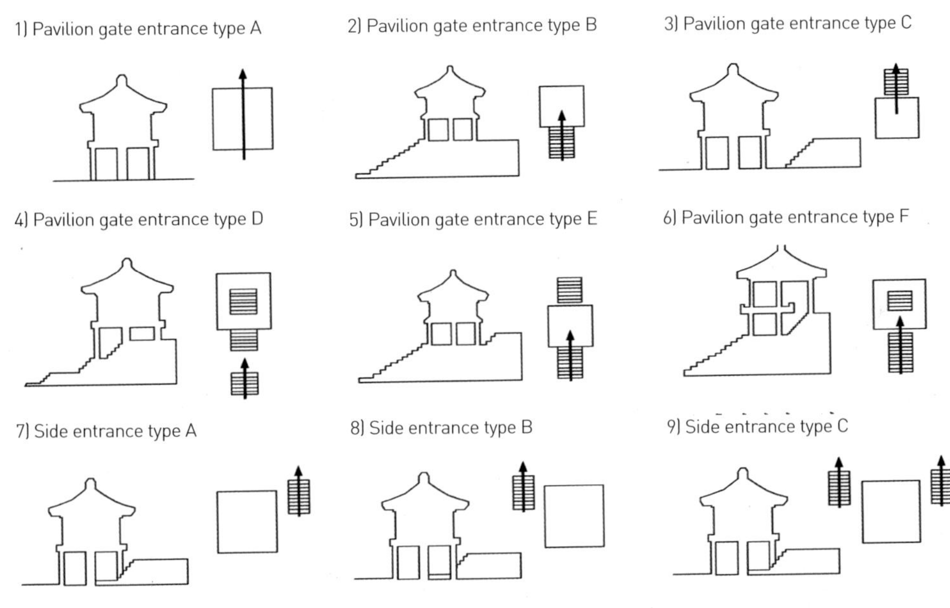

Figure 15. Ways of passing through pavilion gates at mountain temples

Meanwhile, symbolic objects such as stone mounds or guardian posts, which were believed to expel evil spirits, are found at the entrances of mountain temples; mountain gates were sometimes built separately.[7] Furthermore, bridges were built across streams, and all such installations were scenic landscape elements based on the temple entrance.

---

6 Ashihara calls this 70 foot module.

7 Mountain gates mark the boundary of the mountain and are the same concept as *dongcheon* (洞天) appearing in the scenery with Taoist meaning.

8 Gugwangnu used to be entrance through pavilion gate but has changed to side entrance after remodeling.

4. Transition to the Central Space

In order to reach the center of a mountain Buddhist temple, one must pass through a space of entry that leads from the Iljumun gate to a pavilion gate. The entrance passes through several gates and is connected to the center by the pavilion gate. The space of entry of mountain Buddhist temples is thus divided into smaller units by gates. Visitors reach the center by passing through these gates and experiencing the smaller spaces between them.

The entrance gates in mountain Buddhist temples are mostly raised on low stairs consisting of three or four steps, creating a gradual rise. This allows visitors to feel a more acute sense of expectation and curiosity than when climbing a simple ascending path, while also creating a sense of distinct spaces.

Additionally, higher steps are placed before the center of the temple, and a pavilion gate stands at the top of the steps, which causes Daeungjeon to suddenly come into view. Visitors thus feel the height of dramatic transition. Therefore, unlike entrance gates, the pavilion gate is large enough to hide the center completely, and the effect of the gradual increase is complete.

The transition from the entrance to the center includes two methods, namely, the entrance through the pavilion gate, which means climbing the steps below the pavilion gate, and the side entrance, passing the pavilion gate on the right or left or both sides.

Figure 16. Pavilion gate entrance type A: Gugwangnu at Haeinsa temple

Figure 17. Pavilion gate entrance type C: Cheonboru at Yongjusa temple

5. Scale of Central Space

Generally, the center of mountain Buddhist temples is encircled by buildings such as the main Buddhist hall, a monks' residence hall, a meditation hall, and a pavilion gate. These buildings are diverse in style, based on the geography of the temple site or the purpose of the Buddhist temple.

In the case of Buddhist temples located on steep slopes, the entire space of the temple is divided into numerous levels, including the central space. As buildings are constructed on each level, the degree of encirclement is relatively low; Buddhist temples located on flatland, however, have a higher degree of encirclement due to the concentration of buildings.

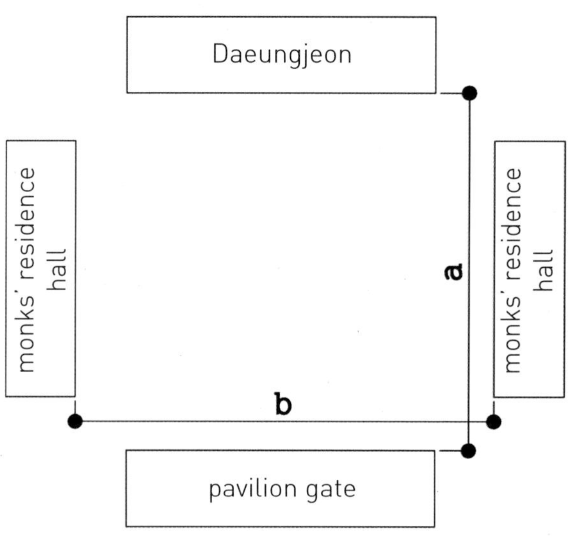

Figure 18. Arrangement of the central space of mountain Buddhist temples

Temple	Width of the Yard (a)	Length of the Yard (b)	a/b	b/a
Bongjeongsa	14.0	13.0	1.08	0.93
Hwaeomsa	45.0	28.0	1.61	0.62
Haeinsa	24.0	23.5	1.02	0.98
Beomeosa	48.0	23.0	2.09	0.48
Ssanggyesa	22.8	40.3	0.56	1.77
Yongmunsa	17.4	17.7	1.00	1.00
Eunhaesa	21.4	22.7	0.94	1.06
Gwallyongsa	16.0	14.0	1.14	0.88
Gounsa	11.8	11.0	1.07	0.93

Figure 19. Central space of Heungguksa Buddhist temple

A survey was carried out on the surface scale of the courtyard (*jungjeong*), and it was found that they measure approximately 25 meters, which again shows that human scale was taken into consideration regarding the size of the central space. The length and width of the center is close to a 1:1 ratio in general, and the shape is similar to a square.

IV. Compositional Elements of Landscape

1. Topographical Landscape Elements

For Korean Buddhist temples, especially those built in the mountains, managing the original topography was an important task for the landscape architecture of Buddhist temple. Topography management was done through such methods as stone platforms, flowerbeds, and stairs. Such elements of topography management are important factors for examining the scenic identity of Korean Buddhist temples.

1) Stone Platforms

Stone platforms were built to stabilize terraced slopes and to improve the aesthetics of the area. As Korean Buddhist temples were usually located on mountain slopes, stone platforms were a common landscape element and were considered a distinct structural element. In particular, stone platforms came in diverse forms depending on the materials or construction method used. Because they functioned as a vertical scenic element, they were easily

Figure 20. Stone platform at Bulguksa temple

Figure 21. Stone platform at Bulguksa temple in detail

Figure 22. Stone platform at Buseoksa temple

Figure 23. Stone platform at Yongjusa temple

recognizable visually. Stone platforms at Korean Buddhist temples were usually made by stacking natural stones, but there were some exceptions, such as Bulguksa, Buseoksa, Bongseonsa and Yongjusa temples.

The stone platforms found at Bulguksa and Buseoksa temples were unique in that they were made using completely different materials and construction methods. At Bulguksa temple, long stones were elaborately trimmed and set using the *mokgagu* style, or wooden furnishing style; stones of varying size were used to fill the spaces in between the long stones. The stone platforms at Buseoksa temple, on the other hand, were made using large, natural stones that were evened out and stacked in layers. In particular, stone bracket arms are used as a decorative element at Bulguksa, turning the stone platforms into a beautiful scenic element. For this reason, the stone platforms at Bulguksa temple are said to have a feminine beauty, while those at Buseoksa temple are said to have a masculine beauty. In addition, royal palace construction methods were used at Bongseonsa and Yongjusa temples, where the stone platforms were built using long pedestal stones, because both temples belonged to the royal family. As the use of carved stones outside the royal palace was prohibited by law during the Joseon era, the fact that they were used means that these temples belonged to the royal family.

2) Terraced Flowerbeds

Terraced flowerbeds (*hwagye*) were a unique structure created during the process of site selection; they have the combined function of retaining wall and flowerbed. Buddhist temple flowerbeds were transitional spaces that connected buildings with yards, yards with yards, yards with the natural environment, and buildings with the natural environment. This was very different from the flowerbeds at the royal palace or the houses of the elites, where they were mostly found at the backs of buildings. This means that temple flowerbeds were used to address the point of contact that connects one space to another; this was necessary as mountain temples were set on a gradual incline.

Among the flowerbeds of Korean Buddhist temples, the one located behind the Main Hall at Bongseonsa temple is the best preserved, and its style and structural aspects are also noteworthy. It was built using long pedestal stones, just as at the royal palace, and it resembled those at the royal palace in terms of height and length. This was only possible because Bongseonsa temple was owned by the royal family. Such flowerbeds are also found at Bongeunsa and Yongjusa temples, which had the same style of flowerbed as they were also owned by the royal family.

Figure 24. Terraced flowerbed with long pedestal stones behind the Main Hall of Bongseonsa temple

For most temples, however, natural stones, rather than carved ones, were stacked in layers to emphasize the decorative aspect of the flowerbed, and fruit trees were planted for their functional aspect.

3) Stairs

Stairs connected upper and lower spaces, and as most were built using stones, they are specifically referred to as *seokgye*, or stone stairs. Each stair varies in height and width so no stair is alike, and as the form and style vary greatly, stairs have high scenic value. Stairs at Korean temples are particularly known for their beautiful stones attached to the both sides of stairs called *somaetdol* on which diverse patterns such as lotus flowers, vines, and the Taegeuk are carved. Images of animals carved on the ends of the *somaetdol* helped determine the aesthetic

Figure 25. *Somaetdol* at Tongdosa temple

Figure 26. *Somaetdol* at the Iljumun gate, Songgwangsa temple

value of the stairs. Among the steps at Korean Buddhist temples, Cheongungyo and Baegungyo bridges at Bulguksa temple are known for their particular beauty.

2. Waterscape Elements

As Buddhist temples in Korea are located in places with beautiful natural scenery, they are well-suited for creating waterscapes. Waterscape elements included valley streams and bridges, lotus ponds and reflecting ponds, valley ponds, waterfalls, stone water containers, and springs.

1) Valley Stream and Bridge

Mountain Buddhist temples were mostly built along valley streams. The Iljumun, temple entrance gate, stands over a stream that flows across the path. This is because mountain Buddhist temples were intended to symbolically represent the world of Mt. Sumeru. From this point of view, the stream in front of Iljumun corresponds to the "fragrant sea" of Mt. Sumeru, thus symbolically distinguishing the sacred from the mundane. Therefore, the temple, i.e. the sacred space, may be intentionally bounded by the valley stream, and the sacred and mundane worlds would be connected by bridges, such as "Bridge to Nirvana" or "Bridge of Deliverance." Seungseongyo bridge at Seonamsa temple in Seungju is known as the most beautiful temple bridge in Korea.

Figure 27. Seungseongyo bridge at Seonamsa temple

2) Lotus Pond

Lotus ponds, which are artificially constructed at Buddhist temples, represent the pond in the Pure Land that is taught in the *Gwanmuryang sugyeong* (Sutra of the Contemplation on Buddha Amitayus or simply, Contemplation Sutra). This sutra contains sixteen contemplations regarding attempts to visualize the Pure Land; the fifth contemplation addresses ponds. In examining the shape of lotus ponds that appear in a few *Gwangyeong byeonsangdo*, paintings from the Goryeo era illustrating the *Contemplation Sutra*, the lotus ponds of the Pure Land are mostly square or round and are full of blossoming lotus flowers. Korean traditional temples always have a number of lotus ponds that represent the ponds of the Pure Land.

Figure 28. Lotus pond at Iljiam hermitage

Figure 29. Guryongji pond at Tongdosa temple

Figure 30. Water entrance of Samindang pond at Seonamsa temple

3) Reflecting Pond

Reflecting ponds were built to reflect the shadows of Buddha statues, pagodas and mountains, the holiest objects in Buddhism. Though the location of reflecting ponds may vary, they are usually built near the Iljumun gate or pagodas, or where mountain tops can be well reflected. A number of Korean temples have reflecting ponds, among which Buryeongji (Buddha pond) at Buryeongsa temple, Gupumyeonji (pagoda pond) at Bulguksa temple, Yeongji (pagoda pond) at Mireuksa temple, Yeongji (mountain pond) at Munsuwon of Cheongpyeongsa temple, and Yeongji (mountain pond) at Haeinsa temples are the most well known.

Figure 31. Reflecting pond at Haeinsa temple

Figure 32. Reflecting pond at the Mireuksa temple site

Figure 33. Reflecting pond at Munsuwon, Cheongpyeongsa temple

4) Valley Pond

Valley ponds are made by damming valley streams. Most mountain temples have valley streams flowing on both the right and left sides of the temple site, and magnificent ponds are created by damming these natural streams. A few temples have such ponds, but the one found at the entrance of Songgwangsa temple is considered the most beautiful. The valley pond at Songgwangsa temple also functions as a reflecting pond; the shadow of the arched bridge on which Uhwagak is built forms a circle where it falls on the pond. In addition, the shadow of Imgyeongdang, where the tablet that reads *yukgamjeong* (六感亭) is hung, also falls on this pond. Yukgamjeong is a pavilion where the six roots (eye, ear, nose, tongue, body, and heart) are calmed in order to wisely self-reflect, while Imgyeongdang is a type of house by the mirror-like water. This signifies

Figure 35. Reservoir used to make the valley pond

that the valley pond at Songgwangsa temple is a reflecting pond that not only reflects the visible surroundings but also a person's heart.

5) Stone Water Container

Stone water containers were made by hollowing out stones. They were usually placed in the courtyard near the convent well or the washing area, and was filled with drinking water. They were usually oblong in shape but were sometimes also round. There were three installation methods: a single container, a combination of two or more containers, and several containers connected by bamboo or wooden pipes.

The stone water container in the backyard of Dalmajeon at Seonamsa temple is famous among Korean Buddhist temples. It is called *samtang* as it

Figure 36. Stone water container at Seonamsa temple

Figure 37. Natural stone water container at Ssanggyesa temple

Figure 38. Couple springs at Ssanggyesa temple

Figure 39. Structure for spring at Yongjusa temple

consists of three upper, middle and lower containers. The arrangement of the stones according to their size and shape creates a highly artistic effect. A similarly-shaped stone water container is found at Iljiam of Daeheungsa temple, where the three containers are also connected by bamboo pipes. The containers in the courtyard of the meditation hall at Ssanggyesa and Bulguksa temples are also well known.

6) Spring

It was common for mountain Buddhist temples to be built in locations that were good for "protection from wind and access to water." Therefore, most mountain temples had different types of springs called *janggunsu*, which means the water helps to build a strong backbone, like that of a brave general, or *myeongansu*, which means the water is good for eyes. Such springs could be left open, but roofs were sometimes built over them to preserve the quality of the water. Couple springs in the courtyard next to the Main Hall at Ssanggyesa temple were left exposed, while a roof was built over the spring at Yongjusa temple. At Okcheonsa temple, a small building called Okcheongak was built over the spring to protect it.

3. Plant Landscaping Elements

Generally speaking, plants were not an important aspect of Korean Buddhist temples due to the fact that buildings formed the center of the temple. As the central space centering on the Main Hall in particular was more architecturally oriented than others, it was even more difficult to introduce plants. However, this does not mean that Korean temples were not landscaped, as plants were always used in terraced flowerbeds. Furthermore, plants were mentioned in the three main Pure Land sutras and the paintings that illustrate the story of the *Sutra of Amitabha*, which makes it clear that plant material and landscaping was used at Korean Buddhist temples.

That Korean Buddhist temples were landscaped was also evident in the following documents. According to the article on Gwallansa temple, which was built by Kim Bu-sik, in *Goryeosa* (History of Goryeo), as the mountain north of the temple was barren, people were mobilized to plant trees such as pines (松), Oriental arborvitaes (柏), cedars (杉), and Japanese cypress (檜), as well as exotic flowers and plants. In *Dongguk yeoji seungnam* (Expanded Survey of the Geography of Korea), it is recorded that at Hwaamsa temple, "irises are abundant around the pond while yellow tree peonies are in full bloom in front of the stone steps, coloring the yard and wall yellow. Peonies have also bloomed red, bewitching the beautiful Xi Shi of Chu State in China." These documents clearly show that plants were used to beautify Korean Buddhist temples.

On the other hand, though there was not much in the way of plants inside the Buddhist temple, it is hard to deny that numerous plants flourished in the natural forests that surrounded the mountain Buddhist temple sites. Therefore, it is understood that the Buddhist temples borrowed the surrounding natural landscape and thus refined the architecture-oriented landscape of the Buddhist temple.

Figure 40. Pine trees planted along the entrance path of Sanasa temple at Yangpyeong

1) Landscaping with Plants along the Entrance Path

Various evergreens and coniferous trees such as firs, Korean pines, pines, cedars, Oriental arborvitaes, and nutmeg trees still stand today along the entrance path of the Buddhist temple. Planting evergreens and coniferous trees along the entrance is an ancient custom that appears to have been intended to emphasize directionality by creating a view around the entrance path.

Maple trees were planted along the entrance paths of Buddhist temples in southern regions, such as Baegyangsa, Naejangsa and Geumsansa temples, in order to take advantage of the new buds in spring, generous shade in summer, and golden foliage of autumn. In particular, harmony with the surrounding environment was taken into consideration when deciding the species of plants used along the entrance path of the temple, creating a sense of co-existence with nature.

2) Plants Used in Terraced Flowerbeds

Terraced flowerbeds were used to recover a sense of nature in the architecture-oriented temple landscape. Short bushes, flowering plants, and herbs were usually planted in flowerbeds, including fruit trees such as plum trees, Japanese cornel dogwoods, citron and gardenias, and medicinal herbs such as tree peonies and peonies. This shows that the plants used in Buddhist temple flowerbeds were not only planted for aesthetic purposes but functional ones as well, as they provided medicinal ingredients.

In addition, linden trees were often planted in the corner adjacent to the wall outside the central space. Linden trees were used to make Buddhist rosaries. As the leaves of the tree were similar to those of *bo* trees that are grown where Fundamental Buddhism is practiced, they were considered a symbol of

Buddhism. The linden trees at Cheoneunsa temple of Mt. Jirisan, Girimsa temple, and Sanasa temple at Yangpyeong are widely known.

4. Architectural Elements

Elements of landscape architecture also include architectural elements such as gates, walls and chimneys.

1) Gates

Buddhist temples in Korea generally have up to three gates. Iljumun

Figure 41. Stone gate at Ssanggyesa temple

Figure 42. Iljumun gate at Ssanggyesa temple

signified the entrance, Cheonwangmun (Geumgangmun) and Burimun (Haetalmun) were located on the knot points of each unit along the central axis, and a two-story pavilion gate stood at the contact point between transitional and central spaces. A symbolic gate that was raised at the entrance of the mountain, which also served as the boundary of the Buddhist temple, was called Sanmun, and this gate symbolized the boundary between the sacred and the mundane. There are also cases such as Ssanggyesa temple where a natural stone is used to mark the boundary of the mountain.

2) Walls

Buddhist temple walls mark the boundary between inner and outer areas

Figure 43. Baegyangsa temple wall

Figure 44. Beopjusa temple wall

Figure 45. Naksansa temple wall

and limited and encircled certain spaces. Walls also stop the gaze and redirect it. They divide spaces according to their function, and the material of the wall itself, the shape and pattern have aesthetic value.

The most well-known, beautiful Buddhist temple wall surrounds Wontongjeon at Naksansa temple in Yangyang. Here, a clay wall stands on a foundation of long, carved stones. Granite blocks were carved into cylindrical shapes and planted throughout the wall to resemble the sun, moon and stars. Other famous temple walls include those at Haeinsa, Baegyangsa, Seonamsa, Beopjusa and Ssanggyesa temples.

Figure 46. Chimney at Magoksa temple

3) Chimneys

Chimneys were used for cooking and heating, and they were traditionally considered a very important visual element in Korea. They can be categorized into three types, i.e. the simple type where an exhaust hole was made either under the eaves or under the wooden-floor veranda, the free-standing type where the chimney was built at some distance from the body of the building and connected to flues underneath the heated floor, and finally the combined type where the wall and chimney were connected in order to combine the two functions. Free-standing chimneys were most popular at Buddhist temples. The best examples are found at Magoksa and Unmunsa temples.

5. Stone Sculptures

Stone sculptures at Buddhist temples were Buddhist symbols and important objects that reflected the landscape of the temples. Various types of stone sculptures included pagodas, *budo* (funerary stupa of Buddhist monk), stone lanterns, and *danggan jiju,* or two pillars supporting a pole from which a Buddhist flag was hung, were most common.

1) Pagodas

Pagodas are sacred objects where the relics of Buddha are enshrined. Originally, pagodas were built at temples to enshrine Buddha's relics or objects that symbolized Buddha (such as the *bo* tree, a wheel-shaped object that symbolizes Buddhist Law, and Buddha's footprints), instead of worshipping the statue of Buddha. Statues of Buddha were first introduced to temples after the first century, when the doctrines of Mahayana Buddhism became popular.

With the introduction of Buddhism, wooden pagodas were built at the center of Korean Buddhist temples (wooden pagoda at the temple site in Cheongam-ri and nine-story wooden pagoda of Hwangnyongsa temple) and were changed to brick pagodas before developing into stone pagodas. There was also a period when, influenced by the Tang Dynasty, twin pagodas were built at Korean Buddhist temples. They became an important object of worship along with statues of Buddha. However, as temples began to move into the mountains and as Seon Buddhism became widespread, the significance of pagoda construction weakened gradually and there were cases where pagodas were not built at all.

Figure 47. Brick pagoda at Bunhwangsa temple

Figure 48. Geumgang Gyedan at Tongdosa temple

Among the pagodas built at Korean Buddhist temples, the nine-story pagoda at Hwangnyongsa temple, Seokgatap and Dabotap at Bulguksa temple, Dongtap and Seotap at Gameunsa temple, a stone pagoda at Mireuksa temple and Palsangjeon at Beopjusa temple are well known for their artistic value.

Meanwhile, among the pagodas used to enshrine Buddhist relics, there is also an altar type called *gyedan*. Geumgang Gyedan at Tongdosa temple and an altar at Geumsansa temple are the most well known.

2) *Budo*

Budo is a funerary stupa where the relics of the head monks of the Buddhist temple are enshrined. *Budo* were built using materials that were easily found in the surrounding area, including granite. Korean *budo* are largely divided into

Figure 49. Budo at Naesosa temple

Figure 50. Jeonghyewonyung Stupa for National Preceptor Bogak at Cheongnyongsa temple

Figure 51. Atypical stupa at Bulguksa temple

two types: one has a simple, unsophisticated, rustic appeal, while the other has an ornate, sophisticated, detailed beauty.

Until the Goryeo era, *budo* were built on the slope on both sides of the main Buddhist hall, which signified worship. But with the advent of the Joseon era, they were built both inside and outside the Buddhist temple. Some were built in groups outside but not far from the Iljumun gate.

Among the *budo* constructed at Korean temples, only eight including the stupa for Monk Yeomgeo were made from stone in the same style as those built during the Unified Silla and have a clear construction date. A number of *budo*, including the stupa for Monk Jingong at Heungbeopsa temple, date back to the Goryeo era, and stone *budo*, such as the Jeonghyewonyung stupa of National Preceptor Bogak at Cheongnyongsa temple, and many others from the Joseon era still stand today, making it possible to study them formally.

3) Stone Lanterns

Stone lanterns were stone sculptures that functioned as outdoor lighting. They symbolized the mission to "enlighten the people and let them choose the right path by lighting the way with Buddha's truth."[9] In general, stone lanterns were located in front of the Daeungjeon, or the Main Hall, around stone pagodas, and at appropriate places guiding the way to the main buildings. They provided light as well as a sense of spatiality, and they lent visual diversity to the space.

The stone lantern, which consists of the pedestal, the part in which lamp or candle was placed (*hwasaseok*), and roof stone, was typically octagonal. The

---

9 This passage is quoted from *Dengzhi yinyuanjing* (燈指因緣經).

Figure 52. Twin-lion stone lantern at Beopjusa temple

stone lantern in front of Daeungjeon at Bulguksa temple was also octagonal. In addition to this style, there were also modified styles, wherein changes were made to the supporting stones on the pedestal with the upside-down drum, twin lions, and human figure.

Among the stone lanterns found at Korean Buddhist temples, those in front of the Gaeseonsa temple site, the *budo* at Bojejonja of Silleuksa temple, Daeungjeon at Bulguksa temple, Muryangsujeon at Buseoksa temple, Gakhwangjeon at Hwaeomsa temple, and the twin-lion stone lantern at Beopjusa temple have clear construction dates and are of particular value in terms of art history.

4) *Danggan Jiju*

Danggan jiju were supporting pillars raised on both sides of the *danggan*. A *dang* was a type of flag hung at the gate of the temple, while *danggan* was a pole, usually made of stone or iron, to which the flag was attached. *Dang* and *danggan* were used since the end of Unified Silla, but only *danggan* and the pillars remain today.

An object similar to *danggan jiju* used at temples is *goebuldae*, a pole on which a large painting of Buddha is hung. *Goebuldae* are usually placed facing each other in the front yard of the Daeungjeon on the right and left sides.

V. Conclusion

1600 years have passed since the introduction of Buddhism and the advent of temple landscape architecture in Korea. Throughout this long history, foreign styles inherited from China were indigenized, and the unique Buddhist temple landscape was developed in Korea, even serving as a model for other architectural spaces. The reason Buddhist landscape architecture came to be indigenized may be because it was adapted and adjusted to Korean culture. Therefore, Korean lifestyles were incorporated into the landscape of Korean Buddhist temples along with the natural surroundings. In this regard, the scenery of Korean Buddhist temples can be said to be distinctly Korean.

Korean Buddhist temple architecture consists of the site where the temple is located, the separate spaces within the temple, and various structural elements that were introduced to the space. As the Buddhist temple was a four-dimensional space defined by Buddhist doctrine and the Buddhist religious system, Buddhist symbolism is embedded throughout the Buddhist temple, lending it a completely different look from other landscapes.

Over the years, Korean traditional Buddhist temples have disappeared, either naturally or by human intervention, and some have been since rebuilt. Considering that Korean temples are not valued solely for their cultural heritage but also function as a religious living space, research on temples should continue.

References

Asihara, Yoshinobu. 1981. *Exterior Design in Architecture*. New York: Van Nostrand Reinhold Co.

Choe, Wan-su. 1994. *Myeongchal sullye 3* (Pilgrimage to Famous Temples 3). Daewonsa.

Cultural Properties Administration. 1980. *Yeongju Buseoksa bosu jeongbi jeonghwa jun-gong bogoseo* (Report on the Completion of the Repair and Maintenance of Buseoksa Temple in Yeongju).

Hong, Kwang-pyo. 1986. "Uuri nara sachal gyeonggwan-ui sigak gujo bunseok-e gwanhan yeongu"(A Study of the Analysis of Visual Structure of Temple Landscape in Korea). *Collection of Papers of Dongguk University* (Gyeongju Campus), vol. 7.

__________. 1991. "Silla sachal-ui gonggan hyeongsik byeonhwa-e gwanhan yeongu" (A Study of the Transformation of the Spatial patterns of Silla's Buddhist Temples). Ph.D. diss., Sungkyunkwan University.

__________. 1992. "Hanguk-ui sachal jogyeong" (Buddhist Temple Landscape Architecture in Korea). *Hanguk jeontong jogyeong* (Korean traditional Landscape Architecture), edited by 1992 IFLA Korean Organizing Committee. Doseo Chulpan Jogyeong.

__________. 1996. "Sachal jogyeong" (Buddhist Temple Landscape Architecture). In *Dongyang jogyeongsa* (History of Landscape Architecture in East Asia), edited by Korea Institute of Landscape Architecture. Munundang.

Hong, Kwang-pyo and Lee Sang-yun. 2001. *Hanguk-ui jeontong jogyeong* (Traditional Landscape Architecture in Korea). Dongguk University Press.

Jeong, Myeong-ho. 1994. *Seokdeung* (Stone Lanterns). Daewonsa.

__________. 2001. *Budo* (Stupa for Monks' Relics). Daewonsa.

Lee, Ki-young. 2001. "Hwaeom ilseung beopgyedo-ui geunbon jeongsin" (Principal Concepts of the *Diagram of the Realm of Truth as the One Vehicle of the Avatamska Sutra*). In

Uisang-ui sasang-gwa sinang yeongu (Research on Monk Uisang's Thought and Religion). Bulgyo Sidaesa.

Seckel, Dietrich. 1990. *Bulgyo misul* (The Art of Buddhism). Translated by Baek Seung-gil. Youlhwadang Misul Seonseo 49. Seoul: Youlhwadang. Originally published as *Kunst des Buddhismus.*

Sunchon National University Museum. 1995. *Gajisan borimsa jeongmil jipyo josa* (Detailed Investigation of the Land Surface of Borimsa Temple at Mt. Gajisan).

Yoon, Jang-sup. 2000. *Ilbon-ui geonchuk* (Japanese Architecture). Seoul National University Press.

Author

Hong Kwang-pyo

(Department of Landscape Architecture, Dongguk University)

Hong Kwang-pyo is a professor in the Department of Landscape Architecture at Dongguk University. He received his Ph.D. from Sungkyunkwan University in 1992. He is currently a member of the Gyeonggi-do Cultural Properties Committee. He has written many books, including *A Study on the Transformation of the Spatial Patterns of the Silla's Buddhist Temples* (1992), *Korean Traditional Landscape Architecture* (2001), *The Centrality of Korean Traditional Buddhist Temples* (2004), *The Spatial Aesthetics of Korean 9 Zen Temple* (2005), *A Study on the Locational Facfors of Gaselgapsa temple, Chungdo* (2006), *and The Planning of Korean Traditional Landscape Architecture* (2007). E-mail: hkp@dongguk.ac.kr

Chapter 9

EXTERNAL SPACE OF JOSEON'S SEOWON AND NEO-CONFUCIAN WORLDVIEW

I. Tradtional Education in Korea and Overview of *Seowon*

People transmit the knowledge and experience they inherited from their ancestors to their descendents by means of education, so that their descendents can continue to live a more dignified life. Education has long taken place at home or in groups but people have created schools and established them as part of the social system for the sake of more systematic and organized education.

Recorded documents show that educational institutions in Korea were already in existence as early as the Three Kingdoms era. Taehak was founded in the capital of Goguryeo (37 BC-668) in 372 (the 2nd year of King Sosurim's reign), and Gukhak was established in Silla (57 BC-992) in 682 (the 2nd year of King Sinmun's reign). Though not much is known about the provincial educational institutions established during the Three Kingdoms era, local schools were started during the Goryeo era (918-1392) as part of a national policy of governance.

After adopting Neo-Confucianism as the fundamental ruling ideology, the Joseon Dynasty (1392-1910) founded the higher educational institution of Seonggyungwan and the secondary educational institution of the Four Schools (*sahak*) in the capital; *hyanggyo* were established in the province as secondary educational institutions. As the *seowon*, or private academies, took root after mid-Joseon, educational institutions expanded.

Hyanggyo, managed by the state, functioned to educate Confucian scholars and cultivate government officials by preparing them for the national civil service examination as well as to perform rituals for sages, including Confucius. It also served as the center of social enlightenment, public discourse and local culture.

Boys who had commoner status (*yangin*) or higher could enter *hyanggyo*, and students over sixteen years of age were called *gyosaeng*. The number of *gyosaeng* varied according to the size of the village where *hyanggyo* was located. According to *Gyeongguk daejeon* (National Code), the quota for *bu*, *daedohobu* and *mok* was 90 students, 70 for *dohobu*, 50 for *gun*, and 30 for *hyeon*. The financial base of *hyanggyo* was land (*hyanggyojeon*) and servants provided by the government. *Hyanggyojeon* was distributed according to the size of *hyanggyo* as well as the number of students. There are 233 remaining *hyanggyo* in South Korea today.

Seowon was a new private educational institution created by *sarim*, the local elite, which was based in rural communities during the Joseon era. The foundation of *seowon* education lies in respect for deceased sages. Therefore, *seowon* were where deceased sages were revered at shrines and their learning was passed on to young scholars. In other words, these functions were the two pillars of the *seowon*.

In order to fulfill these two functions, it was essential that *seowon* had a ritual space where the spirit tablets of former sages, such as respected Confucian scholars or loyal subjects who were revered for their academic or spiritual virtue, were enshrined and rituals performed, and a space for learning and teaching of Neo-Confucianism. In cases where there is only a shrine, or only a building for instruction, the term *seowon* cannot be used.

Though *seowon* were not very different from *hyanggyo*, in terms of the dual function of ritual and learning, there were also many differences. While the rituals at *hyanggyo* centered on Confucius and his disciples, the rituals at *seowon* were held for deceased sages. Also, *seowon* were a private institution,

Figure 1. Learning space at Namgye Seowon

Figure 2. Ritual space at Donam Seowon

and *hyanggyo* were public. Contrary to *hyanggyo*, *seowon* were not exclusively used to prepare for the civil service examinations but were places for individual learning and cultivation. They were located in natural surroundings with beautiful scenery rather than in or near counties, which were under the direct control of the central government, like *hyanggyo*.

Seowon of the Joseon era trace their origin to Baegundong Seowon. It was established in 1543 (the 38th year of King Jungjong's reign) by Ju Se-bung (1495-1554), then serving as magistrate of Punggi County, as a private academy equipped with a shrine and lecture hall in honor of An Hyang (1243-1306), a Neo-Confucian scholar of late Goryeo, in his hometown of Sunheung, Punggi-gun, Gyeongsang-do. Thanks to the efforts of Toegye Yi Hwang (1501-1570), a well-known Confucian scholar, who was appointed magistrate of Punggi County in 1548, Baegundong Seowon received a royal warrant renaming it Sosu Seowon in 1550 (the 5th year of King Myeongjong's reign), thereby making it the first private chartered academy (*saaek seowon*) of the Joseon period.

Saaek seowon are private academies that received a name plaque with the name for the *seowon* that was created and written by the king. When the king presented the name plaque, he also gave servants, land and classical books to the *seowon* to contribute to its management and maintenance of dignity. Receiving a name plaque from the king meant that the private educational institution was recognized by the state, and its social status differed from those unchartered *seowon* in many ways.

In brief, *seowon* were created in the mid-Joseon by scholar-officials, the ruling elite that advocated Neo-Confucianism as a governing ideology and gradually established it as their own. From the macro-historical point of view, the formation of *seowon* can be seen as a historical product resulting from the

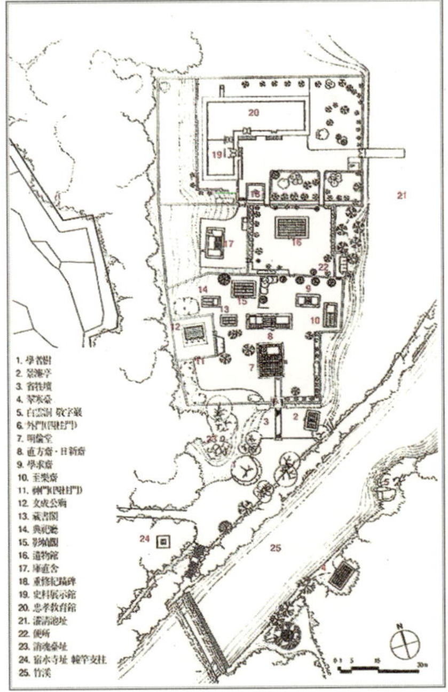

Figure 3. Overview of Sosu Seowon

Figure 4. Site plan of Sosu Seowon

"era of *sarim*," which emerged during the transition from the Buddhist society of Goryeo to the Confucian society of Joseon.

It was Toegye's efforts that enabled *seowon* to take root in Joseon society. Believing that people's minds needed to be corrected in order to reform the disorderly society of the time and turn Joseon into a country of truth, and thinking that *seowon* were needed to teach true learning, i.e. Neo-Confucianism, Toegye led the movement to found *seowon*. He claimed that in order for *seowon* to fully exercise all its functions, it had to have recognition from the government. He also asserted that the government should give the name plaque, books, land and servants to *saaek seowon*, which had to be a national institution rather than belonging to a certain village.

In order for *seowon* to be established and their individual teachings disseminated, Toegye set down the principles of the private academy, stipulating the rules on learning and accommodation, the main principle of pedagogy, and reading methods, all of which displayed the autonomy and specificity unique to *seowon*. The principles developed by Toegye greatly influenced the management of seowon that were established later.

When Sosu Seowon became the first *saaek seowon* (chartered private academy) of Joseon, and Toegye played a leading role in the movement to found *seowon*, they were actively constructed while being recognized as the Neo-Confucian academy of the Joseon era.

As the *seowon* system took its place in Joseon society, the style of *seowon* architecture also came to be established. Baegundong Seowon (which was renamed as Sosu Seowon), the very first *seowon* of Joseon, was not built in the typical *seowon* layout. Its ritual and learning spaces were built in separate areas, so the relationship between the two spaces is not very clear. The main educational building, i.e. the lecture hall and dormitory for students, also had no fixed relationship, and there was the one-*kan* main gate, unlike the three-*kan* main gate of later *seowon*. As such, the connection between the shrine, lecture hall and dormitory is not clear in the architecture of Baegundong Seowon.

However, Namgye Seowon at Hamyang, which was built about ten years after Baegundong Seowon in 1552, played an important role in establishing the layout of *seowon* architecture in the Joseon era. Built in honor of Jeong Yeo-chang (1450-1504), Namgye Seowon has the dormitories facing each other across a central yard. The lecture hall stands north of the yard, while the shrine area is located in separate compounds surrounded by walls on a hill behind the lecture hall. This arrangement was commonly used in the *seowon* architecture that followed.

The *seowon* of the Joseon era spread throughout the country from King Myeongjong's reign in the mid-sixteenth century and King Seonjo's reign at the end of the sixteenth century, continuing on to the reigns of Gwanghaegun, King Injo and King Hyojong. Meanwhile, *seowon* grew into independent institutions free from the interference of local officials and came to play a role in leading Joseon society with the support of the central political power and economic strength as a foothold.

However, *seowon* began to overlap each other and were expanded upon entering late Joseon. Around this time, there were 31 *seowon* that served as shrines for Yi Hwang, 26 for Song Si-yeol (1607-1689), and 21 for Yi I (1536-1584). At the same time, *seowon* were gradually steered away from their original spirit and came to emphasize ancestor rituals more than learning; they became the basis of coteries and factions or of family unity to keep political power in check. They also enjoyed the privilege of tax and public labor exemptions, thus weakening state finance and military force and producing a great number of corrupt political and social practices. Consequently, the kings that followed after the 17th century tried hard to abolish the corruption of *seowon* but without much success; finally, Daewongun (Yi Ha-eung, 1820-1898), who acted as regent to King Gojong (r. 1863-1907) between 1863 and 1873, ordered the dismantling of *seowon*.

Against strong resistance from local Confucian scholars, Daewongun began destroying *seowon* throughout the country. In 1868 (the 5th year of King Gojong's reign), he demolished approximately 1,000 *seowon* that had not received a royal charter, and in 1871, in accordance with the principle of "one person, one *seowon*," which specified that only one chartered *seowon* should be dedicated to one person, he demolished all *seowon*, leaving only 47 behind. Of the remaining 47, 36 *seowon* are in South Korea, and 11 in North Korea. From 1874 on, however, *seowon* slowly began to be rebuilt due to the political and social circumstances at the time, and they remain in existence today. Most have lost their original function of education and continue today only as a place of ritual.

II. Surrounding Geographical Conditions and Location of *Seowon*

Concerning the sites where *seowon* were to be constructed, Toegye said, "*seowon* should be built in places that are related to a respected sage while also being suitable for the *sarim*, the local elite, to live in retirement, cultivate their minds, and read." Toegye's thoughts as such on the location of *seowon* are well represented in his appeal for the royal charter for Baegundong Seowon:

Scholars who want to retreat to search for truth and students who want to discuss and learn about the Learning of the Way do not like the hustle and bustle of ordinary life. Therefore, they carry their books and escape to secluded fields or quiet riversides to sing in praise of the Way of former kings and to study extensively the righteousness and principles underlying the world in order to accumulate virtue and understand benevolence. By doing so, they achieve happiness. This is why they enjoy going to *seowon*. National educational institutions are located inside central or local city walls, and there are age limits for students. But considering that they become distracted and are led astray by the bustling environment, how can the benefits compare to *seowon*?

As such, a number of *seowon* were built in scenic and secluded places that were ideal for self-cultivation and reading, and in places that were related to the sage to whom the *seowon* was dedicated. Such places could include the sage's birthplace or hometown, where he grew up, where he retired to educate his disciples, where he served as a government official, where he was once exiled, where he displayed his loyalty to the sovereign, or where he was buried.

Locations that had a connection to the sage fulfilled the "human factor" that was necessary for construction of *seowon*, while places with beautiful scenery met the "geographical factor." Baegundong Seowon, the first *seowon* of Joseon, and many others that followed were built in places that satisfied these conditions.

The reason *seowon* were located in places with beautiful scenery was mainly due to the fact that Neo-Confucian scholars looked for places where they could live in seclusion, cultivate their minds and bodies, and thus achieve the ideal of "Unity of Heaven and Man" (*cheonin habil*). To Neo-Confucian scholars, as the most important Confucian concept, the ideal of Unity of Heaven and Man was the ideal of human life, in which humans and nature could become one, and all the things of the universe could be harmonized and communicated. Therefore, it was important to pursue the Unity of Heaven and Man through personal awakening. For these reasons, the Neo-Confucian literati constructed *seowon* in the countryside, where water ran through valleys, and in the mountains, where they could put their scholarship into practice and cultivate disciples.

For example, Sosu Seowon sits in a cozy valley surrounded by deep mountains, streams, and clouds. The Jukgyesu stream that originates in the foot

Figure 5. Jukgyesu stream flowing east at Sosu Seowon

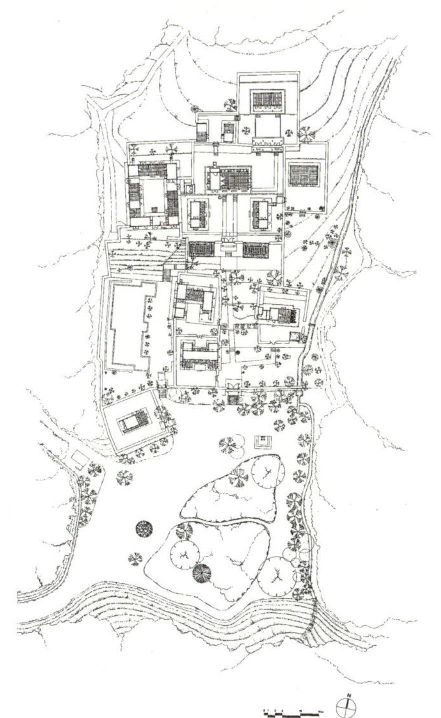

Figure 6. Distant view of Dosan Seodang

Figure 7. Site plan of Dosan Seowon

of Mt. Sobaeksan flows in front of the *seowon*, and the old pines that stand at the entrance look out at the valley. Ju Se-bung chose this site and named it Baegundong because it was "full of clouds, mountains, hills, and rivers, and white clouds always enveloped the valley next to the *seowon*, just as at Mt. Lushan" where Bailudong academy, restored by Zhu Xi (1130-1200), was located.

Dosan Seowon, where Toegye is enshrined, also meets the necessary conditions for a *seowon* site. Originally, Toegye, built Dosan Seodang on a spot somewhat lower than and to the south of the present Dosan Seowon. He began building Dosan Seodang in 1557, when he turned 57, after selecting a spot south of Mt. Dosan; construction was completed in 1561. After finishing Dosan Seodang, Toegye wrote *Dosan jabyeong* (Various Hymns of Dosan), which offers a glimpse into Toegye's thoughts and the scenery around the Seodang:

Looking at the features of Mt. Dosan and its surroundings, the mountain is actually an extension eastward to Mt. Yeongjisan. This mountain is neither too high nor too big, but its valleys are wide and magnificent, with nothing to block the view. The surrounding peaks and valleys seem to hold hands and bow toward Mt. Dosan while embracing the mountain from all sides. Left of the mountain is Dongchwibyeong (East Emerald Screen) and to its right is Seochwibyeong (West Emerald Screen). From Mt. Cheongnyangsan in the east to the mountain's eastern side, and from Mt. Yeongjisan in the west to its western flank, soaring peaks rise up one after the other. These two "Screens" face each other and spiral down towards the south for eight to nine *li*, where the eastern side runs west and the western side runs east finally meet at a wide field in the far south. The stream to the north of the mountain is called Toegye, and the steam to the south is called Nakcheon. The Toegye stream flows around the north of the mountain and joins Nakcheon before flowing to the east of the mountain. The Nakcheon stream, coming from the mountain's eastern side, becomes wide and deep when it reaches the foot of the mountain in the west. A small valley is found here from which a river and the field can be seen. It is deep and cozy yet offers a wide-open view. The foot of the mountain and rocks are distinct and fresh, and the water from a stone well is sweet and cold, making it a perfect place to retire from the world.

Toegye selected an appropriate place for Dosan Seodang only after examining the geographical features of the mountain, water and fields.

In addition, the private academies such as Dodong Seowon at Daegu, Oksan Seowon at Gyeongju, Donam Seowon at Nonsan and Byeongsan Seowon at Andong are prime examples of sublimating appropriate natural conditions into architecture to construct buildings. Among these, Byeongsan Seowon where Yu Seong-ryong (1542-1607) is enshrined is the best example of natural surroundings sublimated into architecture.

Byeongsan Seowon is an architectural example of how much the Confucian scholars of the Joseon Dynasty felt for the natural environment of Korea and attests to the spirit and methods of embedding architecture within nature. The name of the mountain, Byeongsan, is derived from the surrounding landscape where the mountain unfolds like a screen (*byeongpung*) along the riverside where a branch of the Nakdonggang river widens out in the shape of a jar with a strong current. On the opposite side of Mt. Byeongsan, across the river where the mountain's shadow lies deep, a stretch of sandy beach sways with old pines, and the mountain ridge that leads to Hahoe Village begins here.

Figure 8. Nakdonggang river flowing in front of Byeongsan Seowon and natural surroundings

Figure 9. Front view seen from Ipgyodang

Figure 10. Mandaeru at Byeongsan Seowon

Figure 11. Night scene at Mandaeru

Byeongsan Seowon is situated at the foot of the mountain that faces the river and Mt. Byeongsan.

At the base of the mountain and the river, i.e. Mt. Byeongsan and Nakdonggang river, Byeongsan Seowon is built in a way that leaves the space open, thus creating a magnificent external space. In particular, the foreground stretching from a two-story pavilion called Mandaeru to Mt. Byeongsan and the river beyond, which appears between the pillars of the lecture hall of Byeongsan Seowon, Ipgyodang, resembles a folding screen with seven scenes, as it is divided by the open frame of the seven-*kan* building. This creates a dramatic effect in which it is unclear whether one is inside or outside. It also shows how the natural scenery outside the building could be reconstructed as spatial aesthetics.

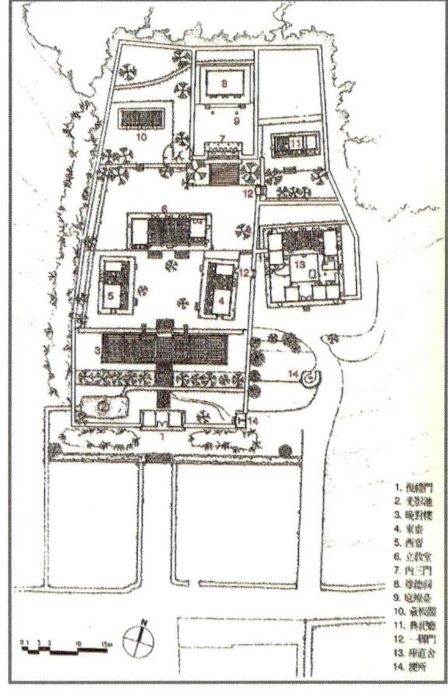

Figure 12. Site plan of Byeongsan Seowon

Figure 13. Stream in front of Oksan Seowon and front view of the academy

Figure 14. Front view of Oksan Seowon

Figure 15. General view of Dodong Seowon

Figure 16. Front view of Dodong Seowon

A low hill stands behind the *seowon* and either a river flows or an open field is in front; the front mountain (*ansan*) is normally located across the field, facing *seowon*. As *seowon* were located in such places, the buildings were arranged to harmonize with the natural setting; if the natural conditions did not allow for this sort of harmonization, the buildings could face any direction, not only favoring southern exposure.

In the case of Oksan Seowon at Angang-eup, Gyeongju, as the main buildings were arranged to face west, they face Mt. Muhaksan over the stream in front of the *seowon* and thus harmonizes with the natural scenery. Dodong Seowon, on the other hand, faces northeast with Nakdonggang river in front of the *seowon* and hence harmonizes most appropriately with the natural topography. Donam Seowon at Nonsan merges with its natural surroundings because it faces east and thus looks out on the open field in front of the *seowon*.

III. Neo-Confucian Worldview and *Seowon* Architecture

Confucianism, the mainstream of Chinese thought, thrived as the practice of propriety-based morality and as the study of ethics during the pre-Qin era (Qin Dynasty: 221-206 BC); but it developed into a metaphysical and cosmological philosophy called Neo-Confucianism, by the Song era (960-1279). The Confucian scholars of the Song era took a step beyond the previous view that understood the content of the Confucian Classics in terms of ethics and morality and interpreted it at a metaphysical level. By restructuring the Confucian theoretical framework to include both the cosmological view and a theory of human nature, they opened the new era of Confucianism.

Seowon, which acted as centers for Neo-Confucian scholarship and the training of students, are also closely related to the cosmological understanding and a theory of human nature pursued by Neo-Confucianism. In order to understand this, it is necessary to understand the ideal of the "Unity of Heaven and Man," which was the ultimate goal of Neo-Confucian scholars.

The Unity of Heaven and Man can be summarized as the ideal of adapting to nature and the Mandate of Heaven. Heaven as conceived by Neo-Confucianism encompasses many meanings, ranging from the physical sky as a visible entity, or a symbolic idea embracing all natural phenomena, to a conceptual and abstract meaning of natural principles, destiny, the origin of morality, or the lord of the universe.

The epistemology of Neo-Confucianism was based on the premise that the principle governing Heaven and the principle governing all things were ultimately no different from one another, and regarded following that principle as the ideal of human life. Although Neo-Confucian philosophers saw nature as being imbued with the principle of Heaven (*cheolli*), their cosmology is not concerned with theories of the creation of the universe, but rather with the relationship between the universe and reality, and especially the problem of values contained here.

For Neo-Confucians, the Unity of Heaven and Man was not simply knowledge but the attainment of an intuitive communion through enlightenment. It was only upon reaching this stage that one attained the highest state of spiritual freedom. What made the Unity of Heaven and Man possible is when nature and humans become one. This is a key point in interpreting the Unity of Heaven and Man pursued by Neo-Confucianism as an "organic thought system"; it is also a basic philosophy that reveals why the architecture designed by humans cannot be thought of as separate from nature, and why humans cannot exist independently from society.

Therefore, Neo-Confucians selected places with beautiful natural settings as sites for learning in order to appreciate nature and build character. Built in such places, *seowon* were a space for reposing leisurely and reciting poetry as well as a place to realize the academic and life ideals held by Neo-Confucians.

Using nature as a medium, Neo-Confucians produced a style of architecture that would materialize the harmony and order of heaven, earth, and nature, i.e. the bases of Unity of Heaven and Man that would connect them with the universe. As a means for understanding Heaven and Man as one, they created architecture in which the natural object and the self communicate through one principle, at a place where architecture and nature could become one. *Seowon* architecture harmonizes well with nature because Neo-Confucians so heavily pursued the Unity of Heaven and Man.

The architectural solutions to achieve this in *seowon* architecture were manifested through site selection, location, and building arrangement.

The *sarim*, local elites who were the main power behind the establishment of *seowon*, built pavilions or private academies in valleys near flowing water and mountains, where they could retreat for study and self-cultivation. This was because, as mentioned by Toegye, such places guaranteed successful learning as they could improve their studies in beautiful, quiet, natural surroundings and, far away from the temptations of the busy, mundane world.

The pavilion, open on all sides and planted directly into nature, was especially conceived as an architectural space onto which the self could be projected and from which the world could be contemplated. Such architecture does not in itself become an object of appreciation seen from the outside, but rather emphasizes looking outside from within the building to appreciate nature and become one with it. Furthermore, Neo-Confucians named the objects that made up the natural setting, such as trees, rocks, water and mountains, in order to incorporate them into Neo-Confucian thought and grant them existential value, so that people could commune with nature in various ways. By personifying nature, Neo-Confucians confirmed the value of an individual in the world and established a space where Heaven and humans came together this quality was an important characteristic of *seowon* architecture.

The way Neo-Confucians retired into nature and built cloisters as well as co-existed in a harmony of architecture and nature was one method of creating a human environment. Such an environment shows that the aesthetic appreciation of beautiful scenery is the highest plane of understanding that leads to the state of Unity of Heaven and Man. The architecture created by Neo-Confucians was one that aimed to personify nature and make people part of nature. To summarize, the ideal of the Unity of Heaven and Man can be interpreted as a philosophy that does not separate culture from nature. A cultural phenomenon is also a natural phenomenon; and natural phenomena express cultural significance. This concept is manifested intact in *seowon* and pavilion architecture.

A good example of the Neo-Confucian worldview and view of nature is observed in Dosan Seodang, a private school founded by Toegye in 1560.

Toegye dug a small square pond east of the *seodang*, planted lotus flowers, and named it Jeongudang, to the east of which he also created a spring called Mongcheon. In 1561, above the spring at the foot of the mountain, he constructed a flat terrace facing the main wood-floored hall of the Dosan

Seodang. He planted plum, bamboo, pine and chrysanthemum on the terrace and named it Jeorusa. The reason Toegye built Jeongudang and planted lotus flowers was because, influenced by the "Ailianshuo" (On Loving Lotuses) of Zhou Dunyi (1017-1073), he wanted to live a humble life like lotus flowers. At the entrance of the Seodang, Toegye built a wicker gate called Yujeongmun, which is seen directly when opening the door on the south side. The Yeoljeong well is found at the entrance of Dosan Seowon, and a path that led to Dosan Seodang was originally located to the south of Yeoljeong. The beautiful scenery at the entrance is described in Toegye's *Dosan jabyeong*:

The trail outside the door follows the stream to the entrance of the village, and the bases of the mountains on each side face each other. If the rocks near the eastern base of the mountain were cleared, there would be enough space to build a small pavilion. However, as I do not have the strength, I left the space as it is. The place resembles a mountain gate, so I named it Gokguam. The foot of the mountain ends a few steps toward the east at Tagyeongdam swamp of Nakdonggang river, above which layers of large rocks overlap each other so high. A platform was built on top, thick pines provide shade, and birds fly in the sky and fish jump in the water. The shadows of the mountain to the left and right sway on the water, bringing the magnificent rivers and mountains together in one view; this place is called Cheonyeondae terrace. The western foot of the mountain is modeled after this and is called Cheon-gwangunyeong terrace, and the scenery is as splendid as Cheonyeondae. Bantaseok rock is at the center of Tagyeongdam swamp. Because it is flat like a saddle, drinks can be exchanged on it while the boat is tied. The platform submerges under water during flooding and reappears when the floodwater is cleared.

Figure 17. *Dosando*, Kim Chang-seok (1652-1720), Yeonsei University Library collection

Figure 18. Front view from Dosan Seodang

Cheon-gwangunyeongdae, also called Cheonundae, is still located outside and to the west of the Dosan Seowon. When standing here overlooking the river, the view opens up and the surrounding scenery can be seen at a glance. Cheonyeondae protrudes toward the river from the east, forming a sense of symmetry with Cheonundae and the Dosan Seodang in the middle. The area below used to have beautiful scenery where the Nakdonggang river twisted and flowed, but it no longer exists today.

Dosan Seodang, created by Toegye, was harmonized with the natural surroundings of Amseoheon, Jeorusa, Yujeongmun, and Cheonyeondae. After finishing Dosan Seodang, Toegye said about this place: "[in spring] mountain birds sing happily, [in summer] plants and trees grow dense and tall, [in autumn] wind and frost make it cold, and [in winter] moonlight shines on a frozen snowscape; the joy is endless as the seasonal scenery is ever-changing." In this place, he could rid himself of worldly afflictions, enjoy everything between the universe and nature, and thus endeavor to find the origin of all things and investigate their *raison d'être*.

IV. Buildings, Facilities and Trees that Constitute *Seowon*

A *seowon* is divided into the ritual space where the deceased sages are enshrined and rituals are performed, the educational space where students pursue learning and cultivate themselves, the pavilion gate where people seek rest and leisure, the auxiliary space for supporting and managing the ritual and educational facilities, and the surrounding space of the *seowon*.

In general, a pavilion gate is located at the very front of the *seowon*, behind which the space for cultivating knowledge and ritual space are located. Each space is enclosed by a wall, and the landscape around the academy constitutes the surrounding area.

The lecture hall is at the center of the learning space, and the eastern and western dormitories where students study and sleep are located in front of or behind the lecture hall. Lecture halls and pavilion gates were built so people could come and go freely, creating a vibrant and open atmosphere. Access to the ritual space was restricted and its construction emphasized a mood of solemnity and dignity.

For the *seowon* built during the nearly 100 years following the end of King Myeongjong's era and King Seonjo's (1568-1608) and King Hyeonjong's (1660-1674) reigns, more emphasis was placed on the lecture halls.

When observing the characteristics of *seowon* site location and building arrangement in this period, the *seowon* were usually built on a slope so the front was lower than the back. The ritual space, or the shrine, was located at the back, the lecture hall was in the middle, and the eastern dormitory and the western dormitory faced each other across the yard in front of the lecture hall. The ritual and learning spaces stood independently, surrounded by walls, and thus the hierarchy of each space was evident. The representative *seowon* built during this period include Namgye Seowon (1552) at Hamyang, Seoak Seowon (1561) at Gyeongju, Yerim Seowon (1567) at Miryang, Dodong Seowon (1568) at Dalseong, Geumo Seowon (1570) at Seonsan, Oksan Seowon (1573) at Gyeongju, Dosan Seowon (1574) at Andong, Deokcheon Seowon (1576) at Sancheong, Seogye Seowon (1606) at Sancheong, Byeongsan Seowon (1614) at Andong, and Nogang Seowon (1675) at Nonsan.

By contrast, the *seowon* built during the seventeen-year period from King Sukjong's reign (1675-1720) to 1741, the 17th year of King Yeongjo's reign, when many *seowon* were destroyed, centered on the shrine. The number of *seowon* increased dramatically around this time, which in turn weakened their learning function and strengthened the ritual function, which took a relatively superior place. Consequently, the clear division between main and subordinate spaces disappeared.

Around this time, the rituals for deceased sages became a main function of the *seowon*, rather than education. As a result, the style, wherein the eastern and western dormitories were placed behind the lecture hall was introduced, displacing the previous model that put the lecture hall in the middle. Also,

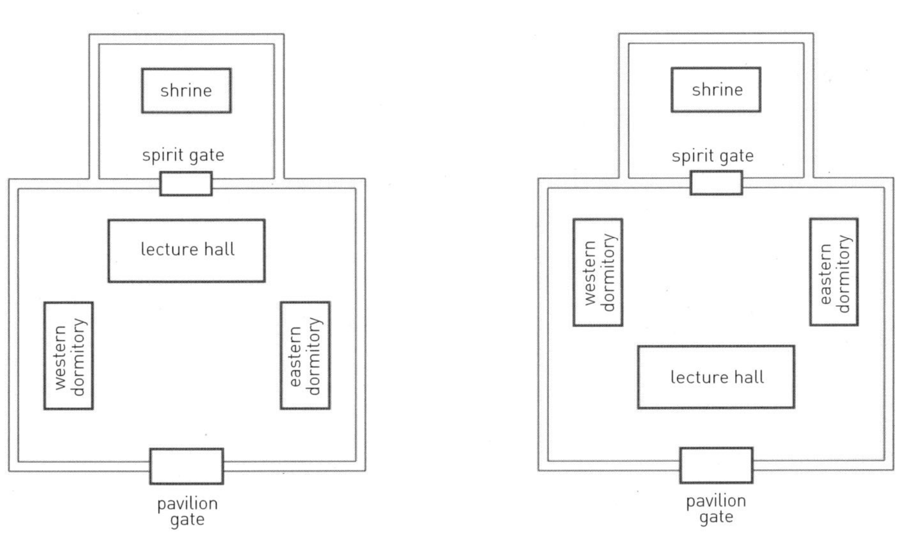

Figure 19. Building arrangements of *seowon* where the dormitories are located in front of the lecture hall (left) and behind the lecture hall (right)

whereas the number of buildings related to the educational function started to decrease, the space for rituals tended to increase. The most well-known *seowon* at this time were Piram Seowon (which moved to its present location in 1672) at Jangseong, Simgok Seowon (1650) at Yongin, Deokbong Seowon (1695) at Anseong, Bongam Seowon (1697) at Jangseong, and Heungam Seowon (1702) at Sangju.

The buildings, facilities and trees at *seowon* reflect a few common characteristics related to the location, arrangement and external space of *seowon*.

To summarize, *seowon* were usually located in beautiful, natural settings away from the secular world, and a hierarchical order was implied in the building layout and spatial organization. This hierarchy was further reflected in the repetition of yards, which were external empty spaces, demarcated by buildings and walls. As a result, *seowon* architecture employs an arrangment that achieves harmony with the natural surroundings, and express clearly the mutual relations between buildings that produce diverse external spaces.

Though the *seowon* buildings are symmetrically arranged, they do not form a rigorous geometrical symmetry but rather defy it, thus appearing both artificial and natural. As such, both an active, lively space within the learning space and a refined, dignified space within the ritual space are created, forming a spatial system that repeats dynamism, tension and relaxation throughout the entire *seowon*.

In this spatial system, moderate and simple architectural styles and order based on principles and the Neo-Confucian worldview, which aims to unify the natural and the artificial, are reflected vividly. This is based on the aesthetics of moderation and clarity the elites of the Joseon era pursued in order to practice propriety in an honest way.

1. Entrance

1) Hongsalmun Gate

The *seowon* begins at the Hongsalmun gate. Hongsalmun is a gate that symbolically marks the *seowon* as a solemn and sacred space. It appears first on the way to the *seowon* entrance. The Hongsalmun gate does not have any actual doors or roof. It consists of two poles on either side of the road, connected with each other at the top by two horizontal bars, on which are planted a row of wooden arrows. The entire structure is painted "red" (*hong*) and studded with "arrows" (*sal*), giving it the name Hongsalmun. These gates were usually raised at the entrances of royal tombs and *hyanggyo*, or county schools.

2) Dismounting Stone

The *hamaseok* is a stone marker to indicate that those passing in front of shrines, where the spirit tablet of a deceased sage is enshrined, regardless of their status, should dismount from their horse or descend from the palanquin in order to show their respect. *Hamaseok*, also called *hamabi*, are usually erected near the Hongsalmun at the entrance of the *seowon*.

In general, one or two gingko trees are planted in front of the *seowon* or near the Hongsalmun or *hamaseok* to signify that this is a place of education. With their strong energy that stretches toward the sky, gingko trees symbolize the fostering of many upright and high-mined scholars; also, because the tree bears much fruit each year, it also symbolizes the wish to produce many scholars every year.

Figure 20. The Hongsalmun gate at Piram Seowon

3) The Outer Gate, Pavilion Gate and Two-Story Pavilion

The outer gate (*oemun*) is the main gate of the *seowon*. It usually consists of three *kan*, or the space between pillars, and is thus sometimes referred to as *oesammun*. Because *seowon* were meant to be built in places close to nature with beautiful natural settings, the most appropriate form of architecture in this regard was *nu*, a two-story pavilion open on all sides with a loft. There, scholars could engage in debates, have poetry meetings, or relax and absorb the scenery. Pavilions were used for rest and leisure, where scholars could take a break from learning while appreciating nature and strengthening their minds and bodies. They were located at the entrance of the *seowon*, close to nature.

Some *seowon* do not have an outer gate but instead use the pavilion gate as

Figure 21. Pungyeongnu, the pavilion gate of Namgye Seowon, seen from the lecture hall

an entrance gate. Some have a separate pavilion inside the outer gate, and others have no pavilion. Pungyeongnu at Namgye Seowon, Suwollu at Dodong Seowon, Hwagyeollu at Piram Seowon, and Hyeongaru at Museong Seowon are all pavilion gates that serve as the main gate, while Mubyeollu at Oksan Seowon and Mandaeru at Byeongsan Seowon are examples of pavilions behind the outer gate.

4) Lotus Pond

Some *seowon* featured a lotus pond at the entrance to symbolize and appreciate the principle of nature and the universe. The most famous of these lotus ponds are the two below Aeryeonheon (meaning "to love lotuses") and

Yeongmaeheon (meaning "to chant about plums"), the elevated, wood-floored verandas in the eastern and western dormitories at Namgye Seowon, which was built in honor of the scholarship and virtuous conduct of Jeong Yeo-chang (1450-1504). Influenced by the Song Dynasty's Confucian scholar Zhou Dunyi's (1017-1073) "Ailianshuo" (On Loving Lotuses), Jeong Yeo-chang is said to have loved plum blossoms and lotus flowers. This is reflected by the names of the verandas of the dormitories, Aeryeonheon and Yeongmaeheon, the plum blossoms planted around the pond, and the lotus flowers inside the pond. At some *seowon*, crape myrtles were planted around the lotus pond. The white bark of these trees represented the dignity and holy nature of Confucian literati. Lotus ponds are also found at the entrance of Simgok Seowon at Yongin, Byeongsan Seowon at Andong, and Jungnim Seowon at Damyang.

2. Study Compound

After passing the outer gate or pavilion gate, the study compound appears. As the area where students read and cultivate their minds, it consists of a lecture hall and dormitories. As for the arrangement of these buildings, in most *seowon*, the lecture hall is in the middle with the dormitories in front. However, in some *seowon* built in the late Joseon, the dormitories were positioned behind the lecture hall.

1) Lecture Hall

The lecture hall is the main building where students learn the Confucian Classics and where the president and vice-president reside. Most lecture halls

Figure 22. Lotus pond seen from Aeryeonheon in the eastern dormitory at Namgye Seowon

Figure 23. Study compound, seen from the lotus pond at Namgye Seowon

Figure 24. Example of dormitories in front of the lecture hall, Oksan Seowon

Figure 25. Learning space at Oksan Seowon

1. Hwagyeollu (pavilion gate)
2. Cheongjeoldang (lecture hall)
3. Jindeokjae (eastern dormitory)
4. Sunguijae (western dormitory)
5. Naesammun (spirit gate)
6. Udongsa (shrine)

Figure 26. Example of dormitories behind the locture hall, Piram Seowon

Figure 27. Learning space at Piram Seowon

have a five-*kan* front, but some are larger or smaller depending on the *seowon*. For a five-*kan* lecture hall, the three middle *kan* make up the main wood-floored hall (*daecheong maru*), and the one *kan* on each side are *ondol*-heated rooms. Looking towards the lecture hall from the yard in front, the room on the right is used by the president, and the one on the left by the vice-president. The main wood-floored hall is used for lectures and discussion between teachers and students and to perform rituals.

2) Dormitory

The dormitory (*jaesa*), as a place where students slept and studied, was usually equipped with a wooden floor and *ondol*-heated rooms. There are usually two dormitory buildings called eastern dormitory (*dongjae*) and western

Figure 29. Lecture hall and Geouijae, the western dormitory, at Dodong Seowon

dormitory (*seojae*), and they face each other across a yard in front of or at the back of the lecture hall. They varied in size but were usually two to five *kan* in front and one to three *kan* on the side. The dormitories were usually built so the ground floor was a step lower and smaller than the lecture hall, and they had gabled roofs, while the lecture hall had a hipped and gabled roof, reflecting the Confucian hierarchy.

3) Jangpangak and Jangseogak

Since the *seowon* was where Confucian students studied, the collection, storage, maintenance, and printing of books was an important task. The Jangpangak was used to store printing woodblocks, and the Jangseogak, which was part of the learning space, was a library for printed books and documents.

Figure 30. The Jangpangak at Dosan Seowon

Large *seowon* had separate Jangpangak and Jangseogak to store printing blocks and books.

3. Ritual Compound

Behind the study compound, the ritual compound appears including the shrine, separated by a wall. The ritual compound consists of a spirit gate, a shrine, and Jeonsacheong, the building for the preparation of ritual offerings.

1) Spirit Gate

As the main gate leading to the shrine, the spirit gate (*sinmun*) functions as a boundary marker between the study and ritual compounds. As the spirit gate is the innermost gate of the *seowon*, it is called inner gate (*naemun*) as opposed to outer gate (*oemun*), the main gate of the *seowon*. Also, because it usually has three *kan*, it is also referred to as *naesammun*.

2) Shrine

The shrine (*sadang*) is the center of the ritual compound where spirit tablets or portraits of the deceased sages, who were the spiritual guides of the *sarim*, are housed and where rituals are held in spring and autumn. It is located in the innermost area of the *seowon*. Unlike the Seonggyungwan or *hyanggyo* established by the state, where Confucius and his disciples were enshrined, the *seowon* was for scholars who had renown for their high virtue and learning,

Figure 31. The spirit gate at Dodong Seowon

Figure 32. Udongsa, the shrine at Piram Seowon

Figure 33. A memorial rite at Sosu Seowon

such as An Hyang, Jeong Mong-ju (1337-1392), and Yi Hwang. Some *seowon* were used to uphold figures known for their loyalty, and toward the late Joseon, figures respected by the family were also venerated at the shrine.

Most shrines have a three-*kan* in length and two-*kan* in width. At the front of the foundation platform of the shrine, two sets of stairs are on the right and left. An additional *kan* of floor space (*toetgan*) outside the building proper is provided for the performance of the ritual, and it usually had a gabled roof. As the shrine houses the spirit tablet, there is only one entrance at the front. The rest of the building is surrounded by thick walls to darken the room, giving it a simple, elegant atmosphere.

4. Auxiliary Buildings

1) Gojiksa

The Gojiksa is where the stewards who look after and manage the *seowon* live and work. In general, it is located to the left or right outside the study compound, and is encircled by its own wall. The stewards usually prepared meals for scholars and students as well as the offerings for the memorial rites. There is a storehouse for food and supplies for this purpose.

The Gojiksa is similar to an ordinary residence in that it consists of a room, a main wood-floored hall, and a kitchen. But it differs in that its inner courtyard is a working area that extends from the kitchen, and there is no *sarangchae*, or men's quarters. The layout of the Gojiksa is usually in the shape of a ㅁ or ㄷ. In Jeolla-do provinces, however, it is shaped like a ㅡ; in Chungcheong-do provinces, like a ㄱ; and in Gyeongsang-do provinces, a ㄷ or ㅁ.

Figure 34. The Gojiksa at Dosan Seowon, which is arranged around a yard

Figure 35. Jeonsacheong at Byeongsan Seowon, which is located in front of and to the left of the shrine

Figure 36. The *saengdan* at Dodong Seowon, which is located to the left of the lecture hall

2) Jeonsacheong and Jegigo

The Jeonsacheong and Jegigo are attached to the ritual compound. Ritual food is prepared at the Jeonsacheong, while ritual vessels and other ritual implements are kept at the Jegigo. Due to their functions, both buildings are located near the shrine.

5. Other Facilities

1) *Saengdan*

The *saengdan* is a small stone altar for inspecting the sacrificial animal. The ritual of inspecting and evaluating the sacrifice, i.e. *saengganpum*, begins with the ritual officiant and related officials taking their places around the altar. The *chukgwan* who reads the prayer, standing to the west of the altar, asks whether the sacrifice is "pure" (by saying the word *dol*), and the officiant affirms by saying "appropriate" (by saying the word *chung*). This would end the ritual, to be followed by the preparation of ritual food.

2) *Gwansewi*

The *gwansewi* is where the officiants can wash their hands before a ritual. The *gwanbun*, or washbasin, is placed on a short stone prop. If the shrine faces south, the *gwansewi* is placed east of the eastern stairs in front of the shrine. The officiants usually stand to the side in the front yard of the shrine and wash their hands before climbing the steps on the eastern side to enter the shrine for the ritual.

Figure 37. *Gwansewi* at Donam Seowon, which is located below the foundation platform of the shrine

Figure 38. Stone lantern and *gwansewi* at the shrine of Namgye Seowon

Figure 39. Stone lantern in front of the lecture hall at Oksan Seowon

3) *Mangnyewi*

The *mangnyewi* is a place for the burning and burial of the ritual prayer after the ritual. It is also called *mangnyowi*. When the sacrificial offering is complete, the *chukgwan* who reads the ritual prayer climbs down the western stairs of the shrine, holding the *chukpan*, the wooden plate on which the ritual prayer is placed, and the *pyebaek*, the offerings to the ritual. Going to the *mangnyewi* to the west of the shrine, he burns and buries the ritual prayer.

4) Stone Lantern

A fire is lit using pine knots in the stone lantern (*seokdeung*), which is placed in front of the shrine and the lecture hall. It is also called *jeongnyodae* or *yogeoseok*.

6. Trees

1)Pine Trees

Considered the best trees in Korea, the strong roots and branches of pine trees serve to block the cold during the heart of winter. They symbolically represent honor, fidelity, loyalty, spirit and humbleness. The symbolic meanings given to pines reflect the values and spirit pursued by Confucian scholars. Therefore, most entrances to *seowon* and the surrounding mountains were thick with pines.

In "Hwamok gudeungpumje" of *Yanghwa sorok* (A Brief Record on the Cultivation of Flowering Plants), written by Kang Hui-an (1417-1464) on flowering plants and gardening, Kang named pines as one of the best plants along with

Figure 40. Pine trees at the entrance of Sosu Seowon

bamboos, lotuses and chrysanthemums. This was because the Confucian scholars of the Joseon era hoped to learn the ideals they aspired to from the beauty and elegance of the pine tree.

Thick pine forests are found at Sosu Seowon at Punggi, Dosan Seowon at Andong, Oksan Seowon at Gyeongju, Namgye Seowon at Hamyang, Byeongsan Seowon at Andong, Donam Seowon at Nonsan, Mukgye Seowon at Andong, Gosan Seowon at Andong, Yerim Seowon at Miryang, Deokbong Seowon at Anseong, Heungam Seowon at Sangju, Cheonggye Seowon at Hamyang, Docheon Seowon at Sancheong, and Naesan Seowon at Yeonggwang.

2) Gingko Trees

A number of large, old trees such as gingko and zelkova are planted at the entrance of many *seowon*, enhancing their dignity. Also called *seowonmok* (tree of *seowon*) or *hakjasu* (scholar's tree), these trees are the symbol and evidence of the history of *seowon*. Gingko trees in particular appear in an old story related to Confucius. Confucius used to preach on a low platform where a gingko tree was planted, and this platform is called *haengdan*. As the *haengdan* came to signify the place where people studied Confucius' teachings, many gingko trees were planted at various educational institutions related to Confucian teachings, such as Seonggyungwan, local schools and private academies.

As gingko trees need a lot of sunlight and moisture, due to their deep roots, they were mostly planted at the entrance of the *seowon*. Many gingko trees are found at Sosu Seowon at Punggi, Dosan Seowon at Andong, Dodong Seowon at Dalseong, Museong Seowon at Jeongeup, Simgok Seowon at Yongin, Deokcheon Seowon at Sancheong, Piram Seowon at Jangseong, and Jukjeong Seowon at Yeongam.

3) Zelkova Trees

Zelkovas were planted at the entrances of traditional villages in Korea and used as pavilion trees or village guardian trees, expressing wishes for the prosperity and well-being of the village. Villagers sat beneath the tree to chat and watch people coming into and leaving the village. Due to their strong growth and dignified appearance, they symbolized scholars or high official ranks and were thus planted at the entrances of *seowon* to express the wish for highly educated scholars.

Zelkova trees are found at Dosan Seowon at Andong, Oksan Seowon at Gyeongju, Simgok Seowon at Yongin, Hoeyeon Seowon at Seongju, Ujeo Seowon at Gimpo, Jaun Seowon at Paju, and Pasan Seowon at Paju.

4) Plum Trees

Because they are strong, elegant and graceful, and flower even in the snow of winter, plum trees symbolize righteous integrity, which Confucian scholars held up as an ideal. Plum trees are compared to a noble scholar who has retired from the world with an empty mind to transcend the secular. Kang Hui-an thus regarded plum trees as the best trees in "Hwamok gudeungpumje" of his book *Yanghwa sorok*. He held the beauty and elegance of the tree in high regard. He wrote: "They are all the more rare for their twisted trunks and sparse, thin, old and strange-looking branches." The physical appearance of plum trees was imbued with Confucian virtues and attracted the hearts of Confucian scholars. Plum trees are found at Dosan Seowon at Andong, Oksan Seowon at Gyeongju, Namgye Seowon at Hamyang, Byeongsan Seowon at Andong, and Hoeyeon Seowon at Seongju.

5) Crape Myrtles

Crape myrtles appear calm yet full of strength. Their red flowers bloom for one hundred days in the middle of summer under the hot sun, and the pure, white branches symbolize sacredness and purity. With such symbolism, crape myrtles taught people about the importance of duty and not losing one's essence. They were thus planted at government offices, local schools, pavilions, temples, ordinary houses, and graves, as well as at *seowon*. Beautiful crape myrtles are found at Namgye Seowon at Hamyang, Byeongsan Seowon

Figure 41. Crape myrtles at the entrance of Byeongsan Seowon

at Andong, Donam Seowon at Nonsan, Dodong Seowon at Dalseong, Deokcheon Seowon at Sancheong, Geumo Seowon at Seonsan, Mukgye Seowon at Andong, and Okdong Seowon at Suncheon.

6) Chinese Juniper Trees

Chinese junipers have a unique fragrance. They are thought to possess the power to cast away evils and are regarded as a medium between the human and divine. For these reasons, junipers were planted at places related to rituals, and their incense was burnt during rituals. Old junipers are found at local schools, temples, and royal palaces, along with such *seowon* as Dosan Seowon at Andong, Oksan Seowon at Gyeongju, Donam Seowon at Nonsan, Simgok Seowon at Yongin, Jaun Seowon at Paju, Sinhang Seowon at Cheongju, Gosan Seowon at Andong, Hoeyeon Seowon at Seongju, Deokbong Seowon at Anseong, and Ganghansa at Yeoju.

References

Primary Sources

Dongguk wonurok 東國院宇錄 (Records of Figures Enshrined in Korean Private Academies and Shrines)

Jeon-go daebang 典故大方 (Records of Important Figures in Korean History)

Jeungbo munheon bigo 增補文補獻備考 (Enlarged and Annotated Collection of Documents)

Jodurok 俎豆錄 (Records of Sacrificial Halls)

Seowon deungnok 書院謄錄 (Records of *Seowon*)

Yeoreup wonu sajeok 列邑院宇事蹟 (Materials on Private Academies and Shrines in All *Eup*)

Books and Articles

Andong Munhwa Yeonguso, Andong National University. 2000. *Seowon, hanguk sasang-ui sumgyeol-eul chajaseo* (*Seowon*: In Search of the Breath of Korean Thought). Ye Moon Su Won.

Choe, Wan-gi. 1991. *Hanguk-ui seowon* (Seowon of Korea). Daewonsa.

Chung, Man-jo. 1997. *Joseon sidae seowon yeongu* (A Study of Joseon Era *Seowon*). Jipmoondang.

Jung, Soon-mok. 1979. *Hanguk seowon gyoyuk jedosa yeongu* (Study of the History of the *Seowon* Educational System in Korea). Yeongnam University Press.

Kim, Bong-ryol. 1998. *Seowon geonchuk* (*Seowon* Architecture). Daewonsa.

Kim, Byeong-gu. 1996 (1993). *Hoeheon An Hyang seonsaeng-ui saengaê-wa sajeok* (The Life and Achievements of Hoeheon An Hyang). Sinji Seowon.

Kim, Eun-jung. 1994. *Hanguk-ui seowon geonchuk* (*Seowon* Architecture in Korea). Mun Un Dang.

Kim, Ji-min. 1996. *Hanguk-ui yugyo geonchuk* (Confucian Architecture in Korea). Bareon.

Kwon, Oh-bong. 1989. *Toegye-ui yeon-geo-wa sasang hyeongseong* (Toegye's Seclusion and Thought Formation). Pohang University of Science and Technology.

__________. 1991. 『退溪家書の總合的研究』. 京都: 中文出版社.

Lee, Hae-jun. 1993. "Joseon hugi munjung seowon yeongu" (A Study of the Lineage *Seowon* in the Late Joseon Period). Ph.D. diss., Kookmin University.

Lee, Sang-hae. 2001. "Toegye-ui seowon geonchukgwan-gwa dosan seodang mit dosan seowon geonchuk-e banyeongdoen joyeong sasang" (Toegye's Views on *Seowon* Architecture and the Construction Ideology Reflected on the Dosan Seodang and Dosan Seowon). *Dosan seowon*, 293-321. Hangilsa.

__________. 2002. *Seowon*. Rev. ed. Youlhwadang.

__________. 2004. *Gunggweol-gwa Yugyo geonchuk* (Royal Palace and Confucian Architecture). Sol.

Lee, Sang-yun. 1993. "Joseon sidae seowon-ui ipji-wa gonggan guseong teukseong mit byeonhwa gwajeong-e gwanhan yeongu" (A Study of the Location, Characteristics of Spatial Structure, and Changing Process of *Seowon* in the Joseon Era). Ph.D. diss., Sungkyunkwan University.

Lee, Song-mu. 1996. "Joseon-ui seonggyungwan-gwa seowon" (The National Confucian Academy and *Seowon* of Joseon). *Hanguksa simin gangjwa* 18: 45-71.

Lee, Soo-hwan. 1996. "Seowon geollip hwaldong" (*Seowon* Building Activities). *Hanguksa* (Korean History) 28: 278-306.

Lee, Tae-jin. 1984. "Sarim-gwa seowon" (The *Sarim* and *Seowon*). *Hanguksa* (Korean History) 12: 115-163.

Lee, Woo-sung. 1982. "Yi Toegye-wa seowon changseol undong" (Yi Toegye and the *Seowon* Founding Movement). In *Hanguk-ui yeoksasang* (Historical Image of Korea), 282-285. Changbi.

Sosung Institute for Advanced Studies, Kyonggi University. 2002. *Hanguk-ui seowon-gwa hangmaek yeongu* (A Study of *Seowon* and Academic Tradition in Korea). Gukhak Jaryowon.

Sung, Dae-kyung. 1985. "Daewongun-ui seowon hwecheol" (The Destruction of *Seowon* by Daewongun). *Cheon Gwan-u seongsaeng hwallyeok ginyeom hanguk sahak nonchong* (Collection of Korean History in Commemoration of the Sixtieth Birthday of Cheon Gwan-u), 745-770.

Author

Lee Sang-hae
(Department of Architecture, Sungkyunkwan University)

Lee Sang-hae is Professor of Architecture at Sungkyunkwan University. He received his Ph.D. in the History of Architecture from the Cornell University. He is currently President of the Korean Committee of ICOMOS and advisory member of the National Committee for the Preservation of Cultural Haritages. He has many books and articles, including *Private Academies* (1998), *The Royal Ancestral Shrine* (1998), and *A Century of Korean Architecture* (2001). E-mail: lsh-skku@hanmail.net

Chapter 10

VILLAGE GROVE CULTURE

I. Introduction

"The forest is man's primordial home. Therefore, the forest attracts humans into the world of fairy tales. The forest is a world of wonder. The forest is the world of home. The sound of trees singing on the hill behind the house on a winter night, a spring mountain full of pink azaleas and cuckoos singing, baby lilies on the hill at the front, a village guardian tree and a slope leading to the Seonangdang, and stone pagodas and *jangseung* are all reminiscent of home.

Life in the forest is quiet, clean and pure. It is a good place with clear water and fresh air. The water running through the valley and the singing of the birds can be heard, the untroubled eyes of a young deer can be seen, the tender passion of raspberries can be felt, and the warmth of the morning sun shining through the trees can be felt. The forest is a poem, a song and a painting. The forest is, therefore, a home."

II. What Is a Village Grove?

In villages where traditional culture is well preserved, a wooded grove can often be found at the entrance of the village or nearby. Surrounded by mostly old-growth trees, a sacred village guardian tree soars high as if to pierce the sky, and various decorative objects such as tutelary posts (*jangseung*), village guardian poles (*sotdae*), stone pagodas, and altars are placed here.

The village grove may center on one or two old pavilion trees. It may be small or large. The term "village grove" refers to many different types of small forested areas, and it is one of the dominant scenes of home that evokes a primal sense of nostalgia in Korean people.

The Chinese character for a village grove is *su* (藪), which means "a marsh or forest with densely grown trees and grass."[1] Therefore, the village grove can be called *dongsu* (洞藪). It is also called *magi, jaengi, jeong, jeongja,* or *jeongja namu*. The terms *magi* and *jaengi* appear in reference to village groves that were created to complement the topography or to provide shade, while *jeong* and *jeongja* referred to places for villagers to rest.

As human culture began in the forest, the origin of the village grove can be traced back to primitive communities. Though the concept of the village grove appears in different cultures throughout the world, the unique culture of indigenous religion is particularly embedded in Korean village groves. Village groves are also called *dangsup, seonghwangnim* and *sillim,* and have long been regarded as sacred religious objects that determined the fortune of the villagers. They have also been known as sacred forests that house the indigenous religion deeply rooted in people's hearts. In brief, village groves were sacred places that ruled the village's destiny, and as such, they were the objects of villagers' religious worship.

Village groves are also closely related to *fengshui* (K.: *pungsu*), or traditional geomancy. When considering the purpose of *fengshui,* which is to select and create a good place and environment for people to live in, the village grove was also used to perfect the *fengshui* landscape by adjusting and complementing excessive or deficient elements in the village topography.

1　漢韓大字典 (Chinese-Korean Dictionary) (1966, Min Joong Seo Kwan), p. 1082. In *Zhouli* (Rites of Zhou Dynasty), it is recorded "牧濱藩鳥獸" where *su* is where a great number of fish, birds and animals gather and a marsh with densely grown trees and grass.

While the village grove, which contains the indigenous, traditional culture of Korea, has been used to conduct the ritual events of a village such as *dongje* or *gut*, various folk games including *jisin bapgi* (stepping on the spirit of the earth), *ssireum* (wrestling), and *geune* (swinging) were also conducted there, as well as modern activities.

Deep, dense, green forests with their cool shade have long been used as communal resting places for villages. As village groves usually stood in the most prominent and beautiful spot in the village, and as the grove itself was beautiful in appearance, pavilions were sometimes built, accompanied by quiet ponds. Therefore, this beautiful village grove was used by the Confucian scholar-officials of the Joseon era as a place of leisure or as an appropriate

Figure 1. Pine trees of Geumdangsil village at Sanggeumgok, Yongmun-myeon, Yecheon-gun, Gyeongsangbuk-do

place for poetry composition and nature appreciation.

The village grove thus had a diverse cultural background. As part of the rural village in which Korea's unique lifestyle, culture and history exist in whole, the village grove bears the traces of the unique lives of Korean people, including their inherited lifestyles, historical essence, and traditional culture.

Most Koreans who were raised in the country or who had even the slightest interest in rural villages have memories of the village grove or know stories related to the grove. This is because of their personal memories, including the games they once played in the grove. The reason that the village grove is remembered by so many is because its significance, function, and usage were not limited to adults but also extended to the children of the village who used the grove as the setting for various games.

Old maps, geographical records and old documents show that most village groves were created when the village was newly built. Though a great number of village groves have already disappeared, many still exist and have maintained their role in rural villages.

Large city parks, used for daily life, culture, leisure and entertainment, are like lungs that breathe for the city. In modern society, the city represents the life of man, and as an archetype, they can be traced back to villages. Therefore, the archetype of urban parks originated from the village grove.

Given the concept of today's public park, the village grove is a park-like, traditional cultural facility that can be defined as "the Korean archetype of a park."

III. Indigenous Beliefs and the Village Grove

Since ancient times, large soaring trees were regarded as religious objects or spiritual beings because they were believed to be passages connected to the sky or sun. As trees in particular live longer and grow taller than any other living beings, and are formed by the interaction between sky and earth, they have been objects of worship since ancient times. Therefore, the village grove and its old-growth trees have been the central objects of indigenous religion in Korean villages. When visiting village groves throughout the country, indigenous religion is found wherever there is a good forest, and when indigenous religion has been in steady existence, one can easily discover that there was once a beautiful village grove that had since disappeared.

Indigenous religion is based on animistic beliefs that have been transmitted by villagers and are expressed as the divine power of the village created within the sacred dimension of the forest. This is a value system that appeared based on animism, the belief that all beings have a divine spirit, thus, the trees of the village grove contain divine power. Therefore, when animistic beliefs ruled in the past, the forest was treated as a sacred place that could never be destroyed; this archetype has been preserved intact.

Zelkova trees were the most popular village guardian trees or pavilion trees in Korean villages. Zelkova trees are called *goe* (槐), which refers to either zelkova or locust trees. The Chinese character consists of the radical 木 (tree) and 鬼 (spirit). In other words, the character for *goe* contains both tree and spirit, making it possible to read the character as "tree spirit" or "tree with a spirit." Therefore, the reason zelkova trees were the first to come to mind when people thought of village guardian trees might be because of the literal meaning of the word *goe*, as well as because of the longevity, beautiful shape and elegance of old zelkovas.

"Sindansu" in Dangun myth is a sacred tree in the City of the God called Sinsi; accordingly, Sindansu must have had symbolic value in indigenous religion. Like the village guardian tree in village groves, the Sindansu was both a place where the heavenly god descended to earth and a sacred religious object that served as a vertical medium connecting heaven and earth.

As reflected in the Dangun myth, ancient Koreans held a shamanic view of the world, which centered on a tree that vertically joins heaven, earth, and the underworld. According to Mircea Eliade, an anthropologist of religion, the vertical cosmology is a general concept that existed in most primitive religions, and it is manifested in all religious structures that pursue the dimension of the sacred. Consequently, a concept of space that was shared in common among

Figure 2. Village grove at Anbo-ri, Sangmo-myeon, Chungcheongbuk-do

ancient people is reflected in these forms. Eliade explains such vertical religious objects with the concept of the cosmic tree. The cosmic tree is said to rule over the earth, exist above all things, and communicate with heaven. It refers to elements of the sacred that rise vertically above the flat and mundane secular world, and is thus synonymous with the Sindansu of Dangun myth. The *gan* (pole) used in the practice of *ipgan* (the raising of a sacred pole) in indigenous Korean religion represents the cosmic tree; *sotdae*, or village guardian pole with a wooden bird, and *sinmok*, or sacred tree, are further examples.

In the story of Gyerim (Rooster Forest), located near Banwolseong, Gyodong, Gyeongju City, it is said that "in the 9th year of King Talhae's reign (65), the king heard a rooster crow in the underbrush of the woods to the west of the walled city, and sent Hogong to see what was happening. They found a small golden box on a branch and a white rooster crowing underneath it. The king opened the box and found a baby boy inside. The king raised the baby and called him Alji and named the forest Gyerim, which later became the name of the country."[2] This is the birth story of Kim Alji, one of the founders of Silla. Along with Gyerim, Najeong at Yangsan where Bak Hyeokgeose was born, and Ajinpo, Seok Talhae's birthplace, make up the three forests related to the founders of Silla, and together they were called "Heorim." Heorim (墟林) literally means "a forest as an old historic spot," but due to their importance as sacred forests where dynastic founders were born, a government office was established for their strict management.

In the West, the shrine gardens of Egypt and the sacred gardens of Greece are similar to the Sindansu and Heorim. By 15 BC, the Egyptians had built a

---

2 Yu Deuk-gong (1991, 338).

Figure 3. Gyerim at Gyeongju, Gyeongsangbuk-do

huge mortuary temple for Queen Hatshepsut at Deir el-Bahiri, based on their religious views, and created a shrine garden by planting a great number of trees around the temple. Similarly, forests planted around temples in Greece were sanctified as sacred gardens. A space 60 to 100 meters in width near the Temple of Apollo in Greece is believed to have been a forest, and a sacred garden decorated with various statues and bronze objects also existed at the Temple of Zeus near Olympia. Such forests originated from the reverence Greek people felt toward trees, and these forests were regarded more highly than the rituals performed at temples, so much so that they later became sacred forests that were worshipped as religious objects.

As such, the indigenous religion embedded in village groves has been motivation for villagers to believe in the divine power and sacredness of groves, leading them to regard these groves as objects of reverence and worship; they were thus maintained and strictly managed.

Also, rituals such as *dongje* and *gut*, which are based on indigenous religion, were held in the forest. *Dongje* and *gut* are included largely in the category of "village rituals," which were mostly held in villages in the past. Village rituals were both calendar-based and seasonal rituals dedicated to the guardian deities of the village to pray for new birth, rebirth, order and prosperity. Each year, the village elected a new ritual officiant and held a ceremony for the guardian deities of the village. Through such village rituals, the old year of the village passed and the new year began full of hope. Therefore, most village rituals were held on the first full moon day (15th day) of the first lunar month, called Sangwon.

Seonghwangnim at Seongnam 1-ri, Sillim-myeon, Wonju-si, Gangwon-do is a well-known village grove related to indigenous religion. It contains various types of trees and is located about four kilometers away from Sangwonsa temple inside the Chiaksan National Park. It stands inside a curve formed by the narrow end of a winding valley. Below, in Seongnam 2-ri, another village grove of pine trees is called the "lower village shrine grove" (*araetdang sup*), while Seonghwangnim is called the "upper village shrine grove" (*utdang sup*). These groves are typical of the style associated with indigenous religion.

For a long time, the beliefs that "the village will perish if the tree is hurt" or "to make the village cozy, the front of the village should be blocked with a forest" have greatly influenced the villagers; the village rituals held in the 4th and 7th lunar months in Seonghwangnim confirm the existence of these beliefs. Furthermore, the village shrine inside Seonghwangnim is located at the highest spot in the grove between a fir tree ("masculine") and a Caster Aralia

Figure 4. A village shrine inside Seonghwangnim, located at Sillim-myeon, Wonju-si, Gangwon-do

("feminine"), symbolizing harmony between *yin* and *yang*.

In the pine forest at Hanbam village, Daeyul-ri, Bugye-myeon, Gunwi-gun, Gyeongsangbuk-do, an altar for a village ritual called Jindongdan stands at the entrance. This pine grove stands on each side of the path leading to the village as if to block the wide valley that lays ahead immediately after one turns the corner of the mountain, located about 12 kilometers on the way to Bugye from Hyoryeong-eup of Gunwi-gun. The villagers called this grove Dongnim or Seongan Grove, after a grove located inside a stone wall. The word Jindongdan is carved on each side of the *sotdae* (village guardian pole), which is also found inside the grove. The Jindongdan was originally a pole with a carved wooden duck, which was newly erected every three years as a wish for peace in the

Figure 5. Jindongdan in Donglim, located at Hanbam village, Bugye-myeon, Gunwi-gun, Gyeongsangbuk-do

village. After 1966, they were made from stone as wood was difficult to use; it has remained unchanged ever since. The village ritual has been held here every year on the 5th day of the first lunar month. As the Jindongdan is both a symbol of the village ritual and a shrine for the guardian deity of the village, the wooded area surrounding the Jindongdan constitutes the village grove where the villagers feel a sense of sacredness and solemnity.

In the village grove, traditional games such as *jisin bapgi*, *ssireum*, and tug-of-war were held, in addition to communal village rituals. Traditional games required a space or location that could accommodate them and the village grove was such an ideal space.

IV. Fengshui and the Village Grove

Fengshui (K.: *pungsu*), literally "wind and water," is a form of traditional geomancy used for choosing appropriate building sites. According to *fengshui*, an auspicious site is an open space surrounded by mountains on three sides with a forest in front to block strong winds, making it easier to farm the land, and with a ready source of clean drinking water. The more abundant the forests, the more auspicious the site is considered to be. Thick forests help to soften and block strong winds as well as provide abundant sources of water.

In *fengshui*, village groves were a form of *sugumagi*. *Sugumagi* is a generic term for pagodas or forests that help to supplement areas of deficiency or weak geographical energy, such as when the entrance of the village is open or there is a flow of water out of the village.

Most *sugumagi* were complemented by forests. In a typical *baesan imsu* (water in front, mountain in back) village, when the ends of the mountain ridges stretching to the left and right of the mountain at the back (*jusan*) do not meet each other, a forest belt was created to connect both ends. This was called "making *sudae*," which seems to have originated from the fact that the *sugumagi* was made from forest belts.

Though the *sugumagi* was a solid forest belt planted to control the flow of water, it was not a rigid structure like a dam. Instead, it was a *fengshui*-style structure in that, by blocking an open space, the aim was to create the psychological effect of a dam. In addition to being a physical outlet, water flowing out of the village was also regarded as a psychological outlet through which the symbolic values of wealth, prosperity, fecundity, and abundance could flow out of the village. By blocking such symbolic energy from leaving

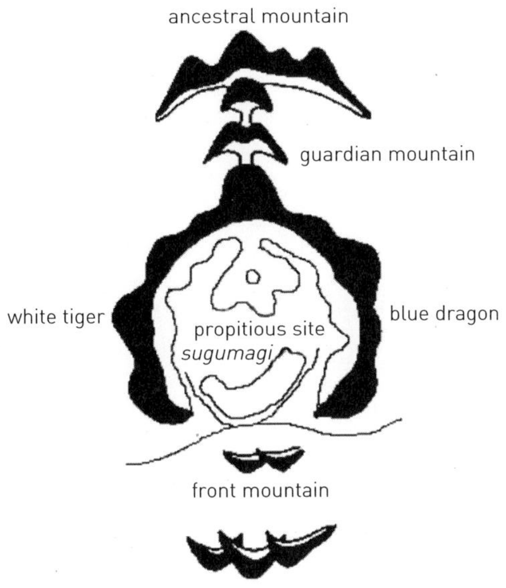

Figure 6. Overall plan of the village grove

the village and storing it instead, the *sugumagi* reflected the desire to maintain the well-being of the village.

The belief that an open space in front of a village should be blocked in order to keep the wealth of the village contained, and thus ensure wealth and prosperity, is deeply rooted in Korean consciousness. This concept originates from the Korean view of nature based on *fengshui*, which has long been transmitted in Korean culture.

More specifically, the village grove was designed based on such *fengshui* principles as *jangpung* (protection from wind) and *deuksu* (access to water). According to this theory, once the water was blocked, the negative influence that wind has on the energy of a place is prevented, and the beneficial storage of water is increased. Subsequently, the energy that flows within and above the earth is also stored, like water, and the good energy that is accumulated by the *sugumagi* ensures the village's good fortune. In other words, the *sugumagi* reflects how the *fengshui* principles of "protection from wind and access to water" were applied to the village grove.

The Gaehosong grove at Naeap village, Cheonjeon-ri, Imha-myeon, Andong-si, Gyeongsangbuk-do is a typical example of a *sugumagi*. According to *fengshui*, the shape is called *wau* type (臥牛形), which refers to the image of a cow, which belonged to the head family of the Uiseong Kim of Naeha village, lying down and eating grass. This grove, located northwest of the village, was created as a *sugumagi* to reflect the desire for abundant food for cows, thus complementing the specific geographical conditions.

Figure 7. Gaehosong grove at Naeap village, Imha-myeon, Andong-si, Gyeongsangbuk-do

Other *fengshui*-style methods for designing village groves were *bibo* and *yeopseung*. *Bibo* meant artificially complementing areas that were lacking or deficient, whether physically or psychologically. Even before the *fengshui* principle was established, this concept was found in primitive Korean society: it originated from the belief in strengthening weaknesses by displaying objects that had spiritual powers. *Bibo* methods included building pagodas, creating artificial mountains, or planting groves; such groves were called *bibosu*.

On the other hand, *yeopseung* referred to the display of symbolic structures such as *haetae*, stone dog and *jangseung* (a tutelary post), or the planting of a grove to block evil energy from entering. In other words, while the *bibo* method was a way of adding to lacking or empty areas, *yeopseung* was used to suppress or control harmful energy or weaken excessively high energy.

A zelkova tree grove found in Naeha village of Songmal-ri stands in line with a ridge of Mt. Wonjeoksan on the right side, about 1.5 kilometers northwest from Hyeonbang-ri where the office of Baeksa-myeon, Icheon-si, Gyeonggi-do is located. With Mt. Wonjeoksan as the guardian mountain, Naeha village is hugged by the two mountain ridges, and a *sugumagi* was built at the front to block the flow of water. Naeha village is shaped like a *yeonhwa busu*, or a lotus flower floating on water. The open space between the ends of the two ridges was closed, using a *sugumagi*, in order to complete the shape of the *yeonhwa busu*. As the land where the base of the mountain ridge meets the river was low, large trees were preferred to other methods, such as filling in the area with mud, so that it would have the same scale as the surrounding topography. Furthermore, trees that have a long life and can grow tall were chosen to create the grove that blocks the open area at the front of the village. Also, the pond that collects water from the valley inside the grove was used as

Figure 8. Pond and grove inside Naeha village at Songmal-ri, Baeksa-myeon, Icheon-si, Gyeonggi-do

Figure 9. *Sugumagi* at Noha-ri, Jangsu-eup, Jangsu-gun, Jeollabuk-do

an outside reservoir and as a cool resting place; it complemented the energy of the village by completing the shape of a lotus. This type of grove helps to adjust the temperature. Cold winds from outside are softened as they pass through the grove, and hot winds are cooled by the shade and pond.

Another *sugumagi* forest is the Noha-ri grove at Jangsu-eup, Jangsu-gun, Jeollabuk-do, located about 0.5 kilometers northwest of Jangsu-eup. The grove actually consists of one large and one small grove, which function as both *bibo* and *sugumagi* forests near the Geumgangcheon stream that flows from south to north to the west of Jangsu-eup. Noha-ri grove is said to date back to when Prime Minister Hwang Hui's father was the county magistrate of Jangsu. At the time, Hwang Hui's mother prayed devotedly at the base of Mt. Danbongsan to give birth to an important son. The entire area is called *danbong hajeon*, i.e. it is in the shape of a softly landing phoenix. Hwang Hui's mother created the present-day Noha-ri grove to protect this land; it was also known as the Bonggang (ascending phoenix) grove. As the mountain at the back is still in the shape of a phoenix and has reddish, protruding rocks, it is also called Mt. Danbongsan. The grove was created to complement the phoenix shape in order to receive positive energy from the phoenix by symbolically providing a place for the phoenix to stay.

Some say that because the village was in the shape of a ship without a sail, causing it to experience various misfortunes, the grove was created at Noha-ri to symbolize the making of a sail. In fact, near the village there is a place named Seonchang, which means a place to anchor a ship, supporting the theory that Noha-ri is in the shape of a ship. Whichever the case may be, the method of creating a grove to supplement the shape of Noha-ri village also seemed to have served the practical function of complementing the northwest side of the village, where it lay open to the strong winter winds and experienced frequent calamities.

The village grove at Ogong-ri, Sanoe-myeon, Jeongeup-si, Jeollabuk-do was created, as if to wrap the village on the right and left centering on a pond at the south end of the village. When looked at from the stream, the western end of the Ogong-ri grove reaches the base of Mt. Jinesan, while the eastern end turns in front of the house of Kim Dong-su (Important Folk Material No. 26), constructed by Kim Myeong-gwan (1755-1822) in 1784, and follows the path that surrounds the village.

In particular, the Ogong-ri grove fulfills both the *bibo* function to complement the shape of Mt. Jinesan and the *yeopseung* function to suppress the "fire" energy of Mt. Hwagyeonsan. The Ogong-ri grove becomes so thick in summer that it covers the entire village. The reason so many trees were

Figure 10. Village grove at Ogong-ri, Sanoe-myeon, Jeongeup-si, Jeollabuk-do

planted was both to beautify the scenery and to complement the topography of Mt. Changhasan in the north, which is also called Mt. Jinesan as it resembles a centipede. Because centipedes live in damp places, the grove was created to provide a suitable home for the centipede.

Kim Myeong-gwan built the house of Kim Dong-su and planted many trees towards Mt. Hwagyeonsan to block it from view. He also dug a pond and created the Ogong-ri grove to symbolically weaken the fire energy of Mt. Hwagyeonsan. He planted 40 zelkova and nettle trees to the left of the main gate and 26 to the right in the shape of a half moon, and the left side in particular was made to reach Mt. Jinesan.

Similarly, the mountain at the back of the village at Sinseong-ri, Dogok-myeon, Hwasun-gun, Jeollanam-do is in the shape of a tiger with a tiger-shaped rock at the east end of the mountain. As people were made nervous by the sight of a tiger, a grove was planted to cover and surround the entire village, starting from the tiger rock, in order to provide a safe hiding place within the grove, thus complementing the tiger shape.

Similar to the Sinseong-ri grove, Dongnim grove and pine forest were built to control the flow of water for Hanbam village in Daeyul-ri, Bugye-myeon, Gunwi-gun, Gyeongsangbuk-do. Located at the central point of village in the shape of a tiger, according to *fengshui,* the Dongnim grove was also a type of *sugumagi* designed to prevent bad energy from entering the village. Two small ponds were made to resemble the two eyes of a tiger, and stacked embankments were built on the right and left at the end of the nose to complement the shape.

Meanwhile, the pine forest was created along the bank of the stream east of the village. This forest was created to screen and suppress the rocky hill in the east field of the village, which was a "white tiger" according to *fengshui.*

Figure 11. Grove at Sinseong-ri, Dogok-myeon, Hwasun-gun, Jeollanam-do

The most typical example of *yeopseung* is the Jangsan-ri grove at Maam-myeon, Goseong-gun, Gyeongsangnam-do. This grove was created by Heo Gi (posthumous name: Jeongjeolgong; pen name: Ho-eun) of the Gimhae Heo family during King Taejo's reign in Joseon era. As it was considered unlucky that the sea was visible from an open space in the southeast, the Jangsan-ri grove was created. This was an example of *yeopseung*. At first, the grove was one kilometer in length, long enough to connect the village and the mountain at the front; today, it is approximately 100 meters in length and 60 meters in width.

The Yeondun-ri grove in Dongbok-myeon, Hwasun-gun, Jeollanam-do was created about 450 years ago by a man with the surname of Kang, who had then settled in the village. He built it as a form of yeopseung to cover a large rock in the mountain behind the village, as it was believed that a great disaster occur if

Figure 12. Dongnim at Hanbam village, Bugye-myeon, Gunwi-gun, Gyeongsangbuk-do

Figure 13. Jangsan-ri grove in Maam-myeon, Goseong-gun, Gyeongsangnam-do

Figure 14. Yeondun-ri grove in Donqbok-myeon, Hwasun-qun, Jeollanam-do

this rock could be seen from Guam-ri, located across Dongbokcheon stream at the front of the village.

In Mukchon village at Jeopjeong-ri, Yongsan-myeon, Jangheung-gun, Jeollanam-do, it was said that because the back of the blue dragon was short, according to *fengshui*, the village would be destroyed if the fire from the potter's kiln at Eodong-ri were reflected on the village. Therefore, a grove of pine, bamboo, and camellia was created from the foot of the back of the blue dragon to the entrance of the village.

Likewise, at Hahoe village, a typical Korean traditional village, in Pungcheon-myeon, Andong-si, Gyeongsangbuk-do, a grove of pine trees called Mansongjeong was planted along the Nakdonggang river. Mungyeonggong Ryu Un-ryong planted this grove in the middle of King Seonjo's

reign in Joseon era. By taking the environment of the village into consideration, he planted 10,000 pine trees, giving it the name Mansongjeong. Mansongjeong was planted to weaken the excessively strong energy of the rock called Buyongdae on a steep cliff across the Nakdonggang river south of the village.

V. Confucianism and the Village Grove

Most village groves that remain today in rural areas throughout the country have trees that were planted during the Joseon era. Therefore, it can be said that village groves are most closely related to Confucian culture.

Figure 16. Gaehosong grove at Naeap village, Cheonjeon-ri, Imha-myeon, Andong-si, Gyeongsangbuk-do

In a petition to the king concerning the protection of the Gaehosong grove at Naeap village in Imha-myeon, Andong-si, Gyeongsangbuk-do, it is written that "Our ancestors planted pine trees where water flowed out of the village in order to protect the family site and the family graves. Therefore, those who respect the ancestor and regard the head family highly should do their best to protect this pine forest, which guards the Naeap village, where the ancestor's shrine and head family are located."[3] This reflects the Confucian ideology embedded in the village grove that is held by the Confucian literati of the Joseon era.

For clan villages of the Joseon era, which were created by people who shared the same surname, respecting the significance of the village grove planted by an

---

3 Kim Duk-Hyun (1986).

ancestor and taking good care of it was an important village affair. As people believed that bad things would happen if the village grove was damaged or collapsed, hence going against the ancestors' will, they took good care of the grove. In turn, a well-cultivated village grove made for a healthier village.

As the village grove was located in the most scenic part of the village, harmonized well with the surrounding environment, and thus formed the most beautiful environment, it was also frequented by people seeking seclusion and retreat. In this regard, the Joseon-era village grove was a place of beauty where the local elites united with nature. The aesthetic significance of the village grove at the time can be seen through the poetry composed by local elites enjoying the grove.

At the pavilion by the water where an aged pine tree with graceful foliage droops,
I, too, am aging like this faithful pine.
The wish I had to build a pavilion in this beautiful place
has finally been fulfilled. Time flows with me, and this place
is comfortable enough to stay in. This beautiful forest has aged with me,
and the famous pavilion has found an owner, which is also
just right. I wish to live here and learn the meaning of the infinite
just as fish and birds enjoy nature.

This poem was extracted from the name plaque at the Sehanjeong pavilion in the Docheon-ri pine grove in Byeonggok-myeon, Hamyang-gun, Gyeongsangnam-do. It depicts a Joseon scholar who has retired into the woods in a rural village and who lives free from worldly cares. In their rural life, local

Figure 17. Hahanjeong in the pine grove at Docheon-ri, Byeonggok-myeon, Hamyang-gun, Gyeongsangnam-do

elites appreciated thick trees and the beauty of nature, and took on a sense of transcendence, like that of immortals. Therefore, the village grove was a concrete place that represented this symbolic meaning.

Likewise, the poem written by Gyeomam Ryu Un-ryong on Mansongjeong, located at the Hahoe village in Pungcheon-myeon, Andong-si, Gyeongsangbuk-do, also depicts the village grove well. The Hwacheon stream that surrounds the Hahoe village is the upper stream of the Nakdonggang river, and it is surrounded by a wide, sandy dune. Mansongjeong is located to its northwest, creating very beautiful scenery. Whereas the village side of the Nakdonggang river is covered in white sand, the opposite side is a precipitous wall of stratified rocks called Buyongdae, where a number of pavilions are

Figure 18. Mansongjeong at Hahoe village, Pungcheon-myeon, Andong-si, Gyeongsangbuk-do

located, both of which contribute to the beautiful surroundings.

Ten thousand pines planted long ago

have grown into a dense forest over time.

The wind through the pines is faint on a quiet night,

and a blue shadow lies over the empty river.

Leisure is naturally plentiful

and a good time can be easily had.

Where the heat is cooled while taking a walk,

warm energy does not dare reach.

Various buildings or facilities for worshipping the ancestors or praising their virtuous deeds, such as family shrines, buildings for rituals, pavilions, altars, structures for monuments, and stone steles, are also found in the village grove. These objects directly show that the village grove is related to the Confucian cultural background.

In the Seonmongdae grove in Baeksong-ri, Homyeong-myeon, Yecheon-gun, Gyeongsangbuk-do, a well-known pavilion named Seonmongdae is built alongside Confucian facilities such as the family shrines, buildings for rituals, altars, structures for monuments and stone steles. The Seonmongdae pavilion was constructed approximately 400 years ago and was named Seonmongdae or Mongdae after its designer saw a fairy in a dream; the grove was called

Figure 19. Seonmongdae grove at Baeksong-ri, Homyeong-myeon, Yecheon-gun, Gyeongsangbuk-do

Seonmongdae grove after the name of the pavilion. The name of the pavilion was written by Toegye Yi Hwang himself, and poems written by Toegye Yi Hwang, Yakpo Jeong Tak, Seoae Ryu Seong-ryong, Kim Sang-heon and Yi Deok-hyeong are displayed inside the Seonmongdae pavilion, showing that various Confucian cultural activities were held there in the past.

VI. The Future of Village Grove

As seen above, Korean traditional culture, from indigenous religion, to *fengshui* and Confucianism, is embedded in village groves. They reveal the philosophical ideas held by people at the time in regards to planting groves. To villagers, the village grove was the substance of their destiny, and the health of the forest was related to their happiness and misfortune. Furthermore, the cultural significance of the grove bears both historical traces of the villagers' past and a means of predicting the future. Historically, healthy woods meant that its significance was still alive, and the declining health of a forest meant a loss of its significance. Thus, village groves could be preserved for hundred of years.

Over the past fifty years, however, village groves have been disappearing dramatically due to sudden changes and trials in Korean society and the decline of the traditional value system. The main reason for the gradual destruction of village groves can be found in the weakening of consciousness of traditional culture. Therefore, in order to preserve the essence of the village grove, reviving the cultural significance and activities embedded in the village grove is more important than taking any physical action.

The village groves that were created to block wind or water around pavilions have performed their roles well and will continue to do so. Even though development in areas surrounding the village grove causes changes to the topography or to waterways, and even though forests are devastated due to excessive number of visitors, the future of village groves is not so dark as long as people still have an interest in them. However, due to recent confusion in the traditional value system and the tendency of villagers to prefer development and quick profit, village groves are being pushed out of people's interest area. Therefore, if the state or local government does not intervene more actively and lead the preservation and restoration of village groves, it may not be long before these groves leave us forever. Furthermore, the preservation and restoration of the village grove should develop further into the creation of a comprehensive cultural and ecological park where such environmental features as natural streams and a biotope are combined with Korean traditional culture. If more than one village grove is to be created in the near future, a comprehensive survey of village grove resources should be done to establish a comprehensive information system and systematic state or local government-led management should be implemented after designating existing village groves as national and local cultural and ecological parks.

References

Chinese-Korean Dictionary (漢韓大字典). 1966. Seoul: Min Joong Seo Kwan.

Jang, Dong-su. 1995. "Jeontong dosi jogyeong-ui jangsojeok teukseong-e gwanhan yeongu" (A Study of the Locationality of Traditional Urban Landscape Architecture). Ph.D. diss., Seoul City University.

__________. 2001. "Suhae bangjirim-ui jogyeong baegyeong-gwa bunpo" (Background of Landscape Architecture and Distribution of Flood Prevention Forests). *Hanguk jeongwon hakhoeji* (Journal of Korean Institute of Traditional Landscape Architecture) 36.

__________. 2002. "Joseon sidae gunsajeok gineung imsu-ui yuhyeong mit ipji-e gwanhan yeongu" (A Study of the Types and Location of the Military Functional Groves in the Joseon Period). *Gukto gyehoek* (Journal of Korea Planners Association) 37.7.

Jang, Dong-su, *et al.* 1999. "Gangwon jiyeok imsu-ui jeontongjeok gineung-e gwanhan yeongu" (A Study of Traditional Functions of Forests in the Gangwon Region). *Hanguk jeongwon hakhoeji* (Journal of Korean Institute of Traditional Landscape Architecture) 28.

Kim, Hak-beom. 1991. "Hanguk-ui maeul wollim-e gwanhan yeongu" (On Village Groves in Korea). Ph.D. diss., Korea University.

Kim, Hak-beom, and Jang Dong-su. 1993a. "Gomunheon-e natanan hanguk maeulsup-ui siwon-e gwanhan yeongu" (A Study of the Origin of Village Groves in Korea as Represented in Old Documents). *Hanguk jeongwon hakhoeji* (Journal of Korean Institute of Traditional Landscape Architecture) 11.

__________. 1993b. "Jimyeong sok-e natanan hanguk maeulsup-ui uimijeok yuhyeong-e gwanhan yeongu" (A Study of Symbolic Types of Korean Village Groves as Represented in Place Names). *Hanguk munhwa yeoksa jiri* (Journal of the Association of Korean Cultural and Historical Geographers) 5.

__________. 1994. *Maeulsup –hanguk jeontong burak-ui dangsupgwa sugumagi* (Village Groves: Village Guardian Groves and *Sugumagi* of Korean traditional Villages). Youlhwadang.

Kim, Duk-hyun. 1986. "Jeontong chollak-ui dongsu-e gwanhan yeongu" (A Study of Village Groves in Traditional Villages). *Jirihak nonchong* (Collection of Thesis on Geography) 13.

Yu, Deuk-gong. 1991. *Donggyeong japgi* (Miscellaneous Records of the Eastern Capital, Gyeongju). Translated by Yi Seok-ho. Dongmoonsun Munye Sinseo 49. Seoul: Dongmoonsun.

Authors

Kim Hak-beom

(Department of Landscape Architecture, Hankyong National University)

Kim Hak-beom is a professor in the Department of Landscape Architecture at Hankyong National University. He received his Ph.D. from Korea University in 1991. He is currently President of Korea Institute of Landscape Architecture and a member of the Cultural Properties Committee. His main publications include *Maeulsup: The Korean Village Grove* (1994), and *History of Landscape Architecture in the West* (2005). E-mail: hbkim@hknu.ac.kr.

Jang Dong-su

(Department of Landscape Architecture, Hankyong National University)

Jang Dong-su is a professor in the Department of Landscape Architecture at Hankyong National University. He received his Ph.D. from the University of Seoul in 1995. He is currently a member of the Gyeonggi-do Construction Advisory Committee. His main publications include *Maeulsup: The Korean Village Grove* (1995), *Korean Traditional Ecology* (2003), and *Maeulsup and Real Life* (2007). E-mail: jds@hknu.ac.kr

Glossary

"Ailianshuo" (애련설 / 愛蓮說): On Loving Lotuses

anchae (안채): women's quarters

ansan (안산 / 案山): front mountain (geomantic term)

Baekdudaegan (백두대간 / 白頭大幹): mountain range that forms the backbone of the Korean peninsula, connecting Mt. Baekdusan in the north to Mt. Jirisan in the south

baesan imsu (배산임수 / 背山臨水): mountain in back and water in front

bibo (비보 / 裨補): method of *fengshui* in which auspicious sites are created by supplementing weak or deficient areas

bigak (비각 / 碑閣): building which the gravestone or the stele is housed

budo (부도 / 浮屠): funerary stupa where the relics of the head monks of the Buddhist temple are enshrined

byeolseo jeongwon (별서정원 / 別墅庭園): Korean retreat garden

chagyeong (차경 / 借景): borrowing the landscape

chamdo (참도 / 參道): ritual path between the Hongsalmun gate and the Jeongjagak

cheonbuin (천부인 / 天符印): Three Heavenly Treasures

cheonin habil (천인합일 / 天人合一): Unity of Heaven and Man

chukgyeong (축경 / 縮景): miniaturizing the landscape

dae (대 / 臺): high platform built piling flat stones

daecheong (대청 / 大廳): the main wood-floored hall

danbong hajeon (단봉하전 / 丹鳳下田): the shape of a softly landing phoenix

danggan jiju (당간지주 / 幢竿支柱): supporting pillars raised on both sides of the *danggan*. A *dang* is a type of flag hung at the gate of the temple, while *jiju* is a pole, usually made of stone or iron, to which the flag is attached.

dongjae (동재 / 東齋): eastern dormitory

doricheon (도리천 / 忉利天): world of the "Thirty-three" devas

dosolcheon (도솔천 / 兜率天): world of the "joyful" devas

eojeong (어정 / 御井): well for the king's drinking water

eupseong (읍성 / 邑城): fortress towns built around the regional boundary of a local administrative unit called *eup*, within which government offices and commoners' residences were built

fengshui (Ch.) (풍수 / 風水): *pungsu* in Korean; the art of choosing an auspicious site; traditional geomancy

gangdang (강당 / 講堂): lecture hall

gi (기 / 氣): life force; energy; material force

goebuldae (괘불대 / 掛佛臺): pole on which a large painting of Buddha is hung

gojiksa (고직사 / 庫直舍): building where the stewards who look after and manage a private academy live and work

gokjang (곡장 / 曲墻): low, semi-circular wall that surrounds the mound on the back and sides except the front

goksugeo (곡수거 / 曲水渠): curved water channel for floating wine cups

goksuyeon (곡수연 / 曲水宴): form of recreation in which the king and other noblemen would float wine cups on water while composing poetry

goseok (고석 / 鼓石): drum-shaped stone that supports the *honyuseok*

gwansewi (관세위 / 盥洗位): stand where the officiants can wash their hands before a ritual

haengju type (행주형 / 行舟型): the land resembling a boat crossing the sea

haengnangchae (행랑채): servants' quarters

hamaseok (하마석 / 下馬石): dismounting stone

hongik ingan (홍익인간 / 弘益人間): widely benefit all of humanity

hongsalmun (홍살문): red arrow gate; symbolic gate, consisting of two poles and a crossbar comprising two horizontal bars supporting a row of vertical red arrows

honyuseok (혼유석 / 魂遊石): wide, flat stone table for the spirit to rest on when it emerges from the grave

hoseok (호석 / 護石): stone slabs around a grave

Hwaeom ilseung beopgyedo (화엄일승법계도 / 華嚴一乘法界圖): Diagram of the Realm of Truth as the One Vehicle of the Avatamska Sutra, a diagram that represents the spirit of *haein sammae,* or the state of mental absorption the Buddha entered immediately following his enlightenment

hwagye (화계 / 花階): terraced flowerbed

hwarakcheon (화락천 / 化樂天): world of devas "delighting in their creations"

hyanggyo (향교 / 鄕校): local schools managed by the state

ihwa segye (이화세계 / 理化世界): righteously govern the world

imcheon jeongwon (임천정원 / 林泉庭園): forest and stream garden

Jaesil (재실 / 齋室): building where the government officials in charge of the tomb reside or where the ritual officiant stay the night before the ritual

janggun daejwa type (장군대좌형 / 將軍大座型): the land with the two generals, i.e. a blue dragon on the left and white tiger on the right, facing each other with small hills representing soldiers scattered around the area

jangpung deuksu (장풍득수 / 藏風得水): protection from wind, access to water

jeong (정 / 亭) or *jeongja* (정자 / 亭子): pavilion; building characterized by openness to nature, usually incorporating a loft which is open on all four sides

Jeongjagak (정자각 / 丁字閣): building where ritual offerings are made

Jeonsacheong (전사청 / 典祀廳): building for preparing offerings

jongga (종가 / 宗家): the head family

jusan (주산 / 主山): the mountain behind houses or graves; the guardian mountain

kan (칸 / 間): bays, the rectangular space delineated by four columns, a traditional unit for measuring the size of houses *mangnyowi* (망료위 / 望燎位): place to bury the ritual paper after a sacrifice

munmyo (문묘 / 文廟): Shrine for Confucius

myeongdangsu (명당수 / 明堂水): river or stream that surrounds the tomb

myo (묘 / 墓): the graves of the prince and princess by the queen, prince and princess by a concubine, and concubines

neung (능 / 陵): the graves of the king and queen

nu (누 / 樓) or *nugak* (누각 / 樓閣): two-story structure with a raised wooden floor beneath which people could pass

numun (누문 / 樓門): pavilion gate

ongnyeo sanbal type (옥녀산발형 / 玉女散髮型): the land resembling a woman who has let her hair down before applying make-up

panwi (판위 / 板位): stone which marks the position of the officiant during rituals

pungbaek (풍백 / 風伯): Earl of Wind

saaek (사액 / 賜額): royal warrant, government approval by conferring an official name

saaek seowon (사액서원 / 賜額書院): academy on which, together with a name plaque, the king bestowed books, land and servants; chartered private academy

sacheonwangcheon (사천왕천 / 四天王天): world of Four Great Kings

sadaebu (사대부 / 士大夫): the ruling elites of Joseon who were obliged, in accordance with Confucian teaching, to perfect themselves morally first before ruling the people through moral persuasion

sadang (사당 / 祠堂): shrine where ancestral tablets are enshrined

saengdan (생단 / 牲壇): stone altar for inspecting the sacrificial animal

sagyeong (사경 / 寫景): copying the landscape

sajeol yutaek (사절유택 / 四節遊宅): another type of detached housing used for seasonal retreats

sajikdan (사직단 / 社稷壇): altar for the god of earth and the god of crops *samsinsan* (삼신산 / 三神山): "three divine mountains" for immortals to live: Mt. *Bangjangsan* (Ch.: Fangzhangshan), Mt. *Bongnaesan* (Ch.: Penglaishan), and Mt. *Yeongjusan* (Ch.: Yingzhoushan)

sangseok (상석 / 床石): stone table on which offerings were placed during rituals

sansinseok (산신석 / 山神石): altar on which the ritual for the mountain spirit is performed

sarangchae (사랑채): men's quarters

sarim (사림 / 士林): scholars; members of the local elite, usually landowners with small- or medium-sized landholdings, steeped in Confucian morality and philosophy, usually without office

"Saryunjeonggi" (사륜정기 / 四輪亭記): writing by Yi Gyu-bo on a mobile pavilion designed to be moved to different locations in the garden so as to take best advantage of the beautiful landscapes

seodang (서당 / 書堂): private school

seojae (서재 / 西齋): dormitory

seokgasan (석가산 / 石假山): artificial mountain; man-made mountain

seogyeonji (석연지 / 石蓮池): stone pond for lotus

seonggyungwan (성균관 / 成均館): National Confucian Academy

seonghwangdan (성황단 / 城隍壇): alter for the village guardian deity

seongyeong (선경 / 選景): selecting the landscape

Shuowen jiezi (설문해자 / 說文解字): the first comprehensive Chinese character dictionary, compiled by Xu Shen in AD 98 during the Han Dynasty

sinmun (신문 / 神門): spirit gate; another name for the *naemun*, the entrance gate to the shrine compound

sinseon (신선 / 神仙): immortals

sinseon sasang (신선사상 / 神仙思想): Taoist ideology of immortality; the idea of sinseon (immortals)

somaetdol (소맷돌): beautiful stones attached to the both sides of stairs on which diverse patterns such as lotus flowers, vines and the Taegeuk are carved

subokbang (수복방 / 守僕房): building where lower officials in charge of the tomb reside

sugumagi (수구막이): a generic term for pagodas or forests that help to supplement areas of deficiency or weak geographical energy, such as when the entrance of the village is open or there is a flow of water out of the village

tahwajajaecheon (타화자재천 / 他化自在天): world of devas "with power over others' creations"

uigyeong (의경 / 意景): imagining the landscape

unsa (운사 / 雲師): Master of Clouds

usa (우사 / 雨師): Master of Rain

waho eumsu type (와호음수형 / 臥虎陰水型): the land representing a tiger crouching down to drink water

won (원 / 園): the graves of the Crown Prince and his wife and their eldest son

wuwei (Ch.) (무위 / 無爲): non-action

yamacheon (야마천 / 夜摩天): world of devas "without fighting"

yeodan (여단 / 厲壇): altar for wandering spirits who had no one to perform rituals for them

yeonhwa busu type (연화부수형 / 蓮花浮水形): the land in the shape of a lotus flower floating on water

yeopseung (엽승 / 厭勝): method of *fengshui* in which auspicious sites are created by suppressing strong areas

yukgamjeong (육감정 / 六感亭): pavilion where the six roots (eye, ear, nose, tongue, body, and heart) are calmed in order to wisely self-reflect

Index